Generations and Collective Memory

Generations and Collective Memory

AMY CORNING AND
HOWARD SCHUMAN

The University of Chicago Press   Chicago and London

AMY CORNING is research investigator at the Institute for Social
Research at the University of Michigan.

HOWARD SCHUMAN is professor of sociology and research
scientist emeritus at the University of Michigan.

The University of Chicago Press, Chicago 60637
The University of Chicago Press, Ltd., London
© 2015 by The University of Chicago
All rights reserved. Published 2015.
Printed in the United States of America

24 23 22 21 20 19 18 17 16 15   1 2 3 4 5

ISBN-13: 978-0-226-28252-7 (cloth)
ISBN-13: 978-0-226-28266-4 (paper)
ISBN-13: 978-0-226-28283-1 (e-book)
DOI: 10.7208/chicago/9780226282831.001.0001

Library of Congress Cataloging-in-Publication Data
Corning, Amy, author.
  Generations and collective memory /Amy Corning and
Howard Schuman.
      pages cm
  Includes bibliographical references and index.
  ISBN 978-0-226-28252-7 (cloth : alk. paper)—
ISBN 978-0-226-28266-4 (pbk. : alk. paper)—ISBN 978-0-226-28283-1
(e-book)   1. Collective memory. 2. Autobiographical memory.
3. Memory—Sociological aspects. 4. Memory—Social aspects—United
States. 5. United States—History—Public opinion.   I. Schuman, Howard,
author. II. Title.
  BF378.S65C68 2015
  153.1'3—dc23

                                        2014046112

♾ This paper meets the requirements of ANSI/NISO Z39.48–1992
(Permanence of Paper).

Time present and time past
Are both perhaps present in time future,
And time future contained in time past.

—T. S. ELIOT, "FOUR QUARTETS"

Contents

Preface ix

Authors' Note xi

Acknowledgments xiii

Introduction: The Meanings of Collective
Memory and Generation — 1

PART ONE Revising Collective Memories — 21

1 Collective Memories and Counter-Memories of
   Christopher Columbus 23
2 Sally Hemings and Thomas Jefferson:
   Sex, Slavery, and Science 46
3 Abraham Lincoln: "Honest Abe" versus
   "the Great Emancipator" 66

PART TWO The Critical Years and Other Sources — 75
of Collective Memory

4 The Critical Years Hypothesis: The Idea and the Evidence 77
5 Exploring Collective Memory in Eight Countries 104

PART THREE Beyond Critical Years Effects — 133

6 Does Emigration Affect Collective Memory? 135
7 Generational Experience of War and the Development of New
   Attitudes 147
8 Autobiographical Memory versus Collective Memory 160

9   Collective Knowledge: Findings and "Losings"   177

10   Commemoration Matters: The Past in the Present   191

Closing Reflections   210

Appendix A: Statistical Testing and Its Limitations   219

Appendix B: Survey Response Rates   221

Appendix C: Formal Tests of Critical Years Effects   223

Appendix D: Robustness of Standard Events Question   225

References 227

Index 245

Preface

The term "collective memory" has many meanings, and that variation helps account for its wide appeal, not only across the social sciences but in much other writing as well. In the most general sense, the term refers to how groups, small or large, recall and think about the past. In our introduction, we consider the range of ways in which the collective memory concept has been employed and connect it to the equally important concept of generation, which includes the idea of location in time. Throughout the rest of the book, we develop and examine the varied ideas and research that grew out of our thinking about generations and collective memory. In part, the book also exemplifies many of the different ways in which social scientists can gather evidence to explore and test ideas.

Authors' Note

Our names are listed alphabetically on the title page in order to indicate equal authorship. Schuman began the research in the early 1980s, and Corning joined it in 1998. We have collaborated closely on this book and share responsibility for the ideas developed, the evidence presented, and the conclusions reached.

Our book draws on previous articles, but in no case do we simply reprint an earlier publication. The book is newly conceptualized and integrated, and it incorporates recently collected as well as previously published and unpublished evidence. In some instances, an earlier publication included more substantive and technical detail than was appropriate for the present book; for example, the findings on Lithuania, Israel, Germany, and Japan are reported in separate articles more fully than we are able to do here. In these and other cases, we include citations of the original articles so that interested readers can refer to them.

Acknowledgments

Barry Schwartz contributed significantly to the research reported in chapters 1 and 3, and we have drawn on his advice in other chapters as well. Beyond his specific contributions to our book, however, Barry's ideas and range of empirical research have been a stimulus to our own work over many years. We dedicate this book to Barry, and also to our families (Jo, Marc, Elisabeth, and David Schuman; and Ben, Maxie, and Alex Broening).

We also wish to acknowledge a number of other individuals who made important contributions to our research and thinking: Willard Rodgers, Jacqueline Scott, Cheryl Rieger, Vladas Gaidys, Hannah d'Arcy, Bärbel Knäuper, Hiroko Akiyama, Amiram Vinokur, Robert Belli, Vered Vinitzky-Seroussi, Tom W. Smith, Eleanor Singer, and Katherine Bischoping. Marc Schuman and Ben Broening have provided essential technical support from the beginning through today—we could not have completed the book without their help. We are grateful as well to Douglas Mitchell, executive editor, and Mary Corrado, manuscript editor, at the University of Chicago Press.

Our research received financial support over the years from the National Science Foundation (SES-8410078; SES-8411371; SES-0853381; SES-0001844; SES-0206472) and the National Institute on Aging (1 RO1 AG08951). The initial NSF grant was in response to a proposal by Philip Converse and Howard Schuman; although Converse could not continue with the research because of his other responsibilities, his 1987 article on the impact of the Vietnam War on public opinion reported certain of the initial results in relation to his now-classic ideas about elite and mass differences in beliefs and attitudes.

Thanks to the generosity of the Survey Research Center (SRC) at the University of Michigan's Institute for Social Research (ISR), we were able to gather a set of supplementary data via the Surveys of Consumers, conducted by SRC, and in many other ways we benefited greatly from our location in SRC and ISR, including highly efficient administrative help by Nancy Tracy and overall advice and support, earlier from Laurie Staples and more recently from Catherine Thibault. We are also indebted to Richard Curtin and Rebecca McBee of the Surveys of Consumers, who made it possible for us to collect a further set of supplementary data. In addition, their assistance with our many data collection efforts on the SRC monthly survey has been very important.

Many people at other institutions provided significant support to our research. We are especially indebted to Ronald C. Kessler, principal investigator of the U.S. National Comorbidity Survey, for allowing us to include questions at the end of his 2001–2003 survey interview. We are grateful to Mark Handelman and the New York Association for New Americans (NYANA) for making their refugee resettlement records available to us for drawing a sample. We also benefited importantly from the opportunity to collect data through Time-Sharing Experiments for the Social Sciences (TESS) twice in 2011 and again in 2014 (NSF Grants 0818839 and 1227179), Jamie Druckman, Jeremy Freese, and Penny Visser, principal investigators. Vladas Gaidys of Vilmorus (earlier the Public Opinion Research Center at the Lithuanian Academy of Sciences) included our questions in three surveys in Lithuania, and M. Kent Jennings provided for our use the data from China he had previously collected. Without the help from these many sources, we would not have the extensive evidence that we report in the following pages. A major strength of this book is the extensive replication—both literal and construct replication—that we carried out, and this was possible only because of the support acknowledged here.

Archived Data

For the benefit of other researchers, we plan to archive the survey data used in this book at the Interuniversity Consortium for Political and Social Research (ICPSR). A keyword search on the term "collective memory" or the names Howard Schuman or Amy Corning will identify datasets used here.

Introduction: The Meanings of Collective Memory and Generation

"Generations" and "collective memory" are the main themes of our book, and we begin with thoughts about each, though more about collective memory because the term is more recent and elusive in meaning. The concept of "generations" may seem more familiar, though we will see that it also is complex, embodying two quite different meanings.

Conceptualizing "Collective Memory"

"Collective memory" is a neologism that has rapidly shifted from specialized usage to broad appeal beyond its appearance in social science writing. This is not because it has a single or unique meaning—just the opposite. It combines two quite different concepts: an essential, valued individual capacity—memory—and at the same time, the group, societal, and cultural settings that are so central to human life. The simplest definition is that of a memory shared by the members of a group, with the memories helping to create and sustain the group, just as the group supports the continued existence of the memories. No specification of the size of the group is given or implied by the term, and it can range in principle from just two individuals to a nation or an even larger collectivity.

Furthermore, the term has been used in ways both congruent with and in opposition to "history": it is sometimes seen as an important form of historical evidence (for example, Schwartz 2013), but sometimes as the opposite of trustworthy historical research (for example, Novick 1999: 3–4). With the meanings of the term so varied, "collective memory" lends itself to whatever reasonable sense fits a writer's preference.

Yet many uses of the term refer to one of two ways in which collective memory can be understood and studied, as exemplified by its appearance in different contexts by the British historian of science Janet Browne, though she may not have been aware of her own variation in usage. (In the quotations below and elsewhere in this chapter, we have added italics to highlight the term "collective memory.")

First:

Darwin's book, and Darwin's theory, became public property, and the event was to etch itself into the *collective memory* as a defining moment in Victorian history.

(BROWNE, *CHARLES DARWIN: THE POWER OF PLACE*, 2002, 115)

Second:

[about visitors to Darwin's home in his last years] The more unusual guests naturally etched themselves into the family's *collective memory*.

(BROWNE, *CHARLES DARWIN: THE POWER OF PLACE*, 2002, 386)

Browne's first passage treats collective memory not only as something of great importance ("a defining moment"), but also as likely to be most accessible to historians or other researchers studying documents from that period—a component of what we might think of as a mixture of "cultural history" and "the history of ideas." Part of the evidence in our book is based on historical accounts, some from writings of several centuries ago, though some from relatively recent newspaper and television archives.

Browne's second passage assumes that collective memory is a property of living family members—something that might have been studied at the time, as it could be today, by a sociologist conducting individual interviews. Collective memory in this sense is of common lived experiences, sometimes of a family event, though often of something much larger than a family, such as the September 11, 2001, attack on the World Trade Center—remembered after it occurred with intensity and emotion not only by those directly involved but also by those in distant cities who watched televised images of planes crashing into the twin towers. Part of our evidence in this book comes from interviewing in the form of sample surveys, in order to find out, for example, how people at present think of remote historical figures like Christopher Columbus, or to learn which events that occurred during their own lifetimes they remember as especially important.

Both approaches to learning about collective memory are valuable, and regardless of method of study or source of evidence, the goal is the same: to learn about the collective memories held and shared by real people, whether in the past or in the present.[1] Furthermore, it is important to recognize that, as time passes, evidence obtained from interviews in the present will become a new type of document to be drawn on in later historical studies of collective memory.

Although the broad distinction between historical and contemporaneous evidence is useful in introducing our later chapters, it fails to capture nuances in usage that come alive when the phrase "collective memory" is employed not only by historians or social scientists (as in the first example below), but also in a much wider range of perfectly acceptable writing by others. The following examples culled from our own reading should be kept in mind when trying to consider the meaning of the term "collective memory."

An important historian used the term to describe how a crucial part of American history was kept alive over the years:

Long after the end of the Civil War, the experience of bondage remained deeply etched in blacks' *collective memory*.

(ERIC FONER, *RECONSTRUCTION: AMERICA'S UNFINISHED REVOLUTION 1863–1877*, 1988, 78)

As suggested by the second Browne quote, memories shared by families can also be described as "collective":

At Thorn Rose [cemetery], records of the dead seemed to exist only in the *collective memory* of the families whose ancestors were buried there.

(HENRY LOUIS GATES, JR., "PERSONAL HISTORY: FAMILY MATTERS," *NEW YORKER*, DECEMBER 1, 2008, 34)

1. We ordinarily use the term "collective memory" without distinguishing between singular and plural forms. At points, however, we refer to "collective memories" in order to emphasize the multiplicity of memories held by individuals or of cultural representations of the past.

The term can be used even when the reality behind the memory is regarded as illusory in a sense:

The man of science in me was content that there was no more of K. Sreenivasan. At this point he was reduced to a construct in a *collective memory*, a set of images to be stored and accessed, a series of anecdotes that triggered emotions, but to think that, much less to say such a thing to some of my relatives was blasphemous.

(HARIHARAN SREENIVASAN, "IN MEMORY OF MY FATHER K. SREENIVASAN," 2011)

Moreover, the group and the memory can be entirely new creations:

It does not take long for nonstandard expressions [emotive punctuation, omission of capitalizations, etc.] to achieve normative status in a chat-room interaction. Each group has a *collective memory* of usage arising out of repeated online contacts, and new members of the group are expected to conform.

(DAVID CRYSTAL, *THE STORIES OF ENGLISH*, 2004, 521)

Informal connections can develop as a result of sharing a collective memory:

"My frustrated neighbors share a *collective memory* of those ubiquitous Asplundh trucks trimming back trees around power lines," he continued.

(ARTICLE HEADLINED "CMP'S [CENTRAL MAINE POWER COMPANY'S] RELIABILITY CALLED INTO QUESTION," *TIMES RECORD*, BRUNSWICK, MAINE, C. 2009, 7)

The "group" may sometimes be quite large—for example, a whole nation:

Fifty years later, his home movie is still known to the world as the Zapruder film, forever linking him and our family name with the *collective memory* of one of America's darkest days.

(ALEXANDRA ZAPRUDER, "THE ZAPRUDER LEGACY," ON HER GRANDFATHER'S INADVERTENT FILM RECORDING OF THE ASSASSINATION OF PRESIDENT KENNEDY, EXCERPTED IN *PARADE*, OCTOBER 19, 2013)

In addition, at the national level, different collective memories can help to distinguish competing subgroups:

By 2001 the Republicans had already controlled the White House for twenty of the previous thirty-two years [and] . . . had opened the way for ambitious Republicans such as the Vulcans to accumulate more years of on-the-job experience in foreign policy than their counterparts in the Democratic party. They had a long history, a *collective memory*.

(JAMES MANN, *RISE OF THE VULCANS: THE HISTORY OF BUSH'S WAR CABINET*, 2004, X–XI)

Although a single collective memory may be mentioned, more than one version of the memory may be implicit for those who know the relevant history:

The fact that a 70-year-old conflict should so quickly come to mind indicates just how deeply ingrained the civil war is in the *collective memory* of the country and how it continues to have a profound influence on the way Spaniards speak about national politics.

(ANTONIO FEROS,"CIVIL WAR STILL HAUNTS SPANISH POLITICS," ON THE EFFECT OF THE MADRID TRAIN BOMBING ON SPANISH ELECTIONS, *NEW YORK TIMES*, MARCH 20, 2004, B9)

The content of a collective memory may also be openly ambiguous:

For 8,000 British soldiers serving in Iraq . . . the banners hanging at their bases are emblems of a *collective memory*—of how to prevail in foreign wars, and, just as surely, British officers say sardonically, of how to lose them.

(JOHN F. BURNS, "DRAWING FROM ITS PAST WARS, BRITAIN TAKES A TEMPERED APPROACH TO IRAQI INSURGENCY," *NEW YORK TIMES*, OCTOBER 17, 2004)

On the other hand, collective memory may obliterate variation:

Although 19th century white and black minstrel shows . . . are reduced in the *collective memory* to grinning blackface clowns performing corny comedy or sentimental songs about the South (or "Mammy") . . . they were showcases for diverse talent. Gifted minstrel-show performers included opera singers like the brilliant Sissieretta Jones, elocutionists . . . magicians, ventriloquists.

(YUVAL TAYLOR AND JAKE AUSTEN, *DARKEST AMERICA*, 2012, 6)

Sometimes the term is used simply to signify a sense of connection to a cultural heritage:

Early Christians believed icons were like portals that allowed the viewer to communicate directly with the sacred figure represented. Modern secular icons like *American Gothic* still retain some vestige of sacredness, in the sense that they connect with something larger—not with the divine, but with the *collective memory* of our image-loving culture.

(MIA FINEMAN, "THE MOST FAMOUS FARM COUPLE IN THE WORLD: WHY AMERICAN GOTHIC STILL FASCINATES," *SLATE*, JUNE 8, 2005)

Finally, participants in a collective memory need not be human:

When a group of villagers from Katwe went out to reclaim the man's body . . . the elephants refused to budge. . . . In the end, the villagers resorted to a tactic that has long been etched in the elephants' *collective memory*, firing volleys of constrained gunfire into the air at close range, finally scaring the mourning herd away.

(CHARLES SIEBERT, "AN ELEPHANT CRACKUP?" *NEW YORK TIMES MAGAZINE*, OCTOBER 8, 2006, 72)

In sum, the term "collective memory" appears in many different contexts, used by writers of all kinds; the common conceptual element is simply remembrance of the past in some form by or for a collectivity, large or small. Within those broad boundaries, there are many variations, and we need to allow for such diversity when the term is used.

Four Theoretical Perspectives on Collective Memory

The progenitor

Our sense of the breadth of the collective memory concept can be strengthened further by considering examples mentioned by Maurice Halbwachs at one point or another in his writing from 1925 into the 1940s. Halbwachs is rightly credited with having used the term in ways that led to its widespread adoption within the social sciences. However, he did not offer a single formal definition, was not systematic in his treatment of the concept, and wrote in a different time and intellectual setting that make his ideas somewhat difficult to follow today. But his three books dealing with collective memory provide examples that show his interpretation of the term to have been more flexible than is sometimes assumed.[2]

2. The three books are *The Social Frameworks of Memory*, first published in French in 1925, but not available in English until much later when a large part was translated by Lewis Coser (Halbwachs 1992a); *The Legendary Topography of the Gospels in the Holy Land*, originally published in 1941, but also translated in part by Coser (Halbwachs 1992b); and *The Collective Memory*, a collection of essays brought together and published in France in 1950, then translated and published in English in 1980.

In a 1950 book of essays, *The Collective Memory*, published after his death as a prisoner at Buchenwald in 1945, Halbwachs wrote mainly in terms of concrete groups such as families or sets of friends. He saw the collective memory of such a group as "not exceeding, and most often much shorter than, the average duration of a human life" (Halbwachs 1980: 84): "Every collective memory requires the support of a group delimited in space and time," and with the group's dissolution, the memory disappears. He also viewed individuals as immersed successively or simultaneously in several different groups, each with its own collective memory. Thus the main impression one takes from the book is of small groups, each of which has memories that its members share, but memories that do not extend beyond those in the group. This fits well the account by Halbwachs's later translator and editor, Lewis Coser, of himself having immigrated to the United States as a teenager, and finding his relations with new friends hampered because he did not share their memories of famous baseball players, girls, and other topics that made up the conversation of adolescent American boys (Coser 1992, "Introduction," 21). Such examples locate collective memory at the level of individuals in real groups who might be observed or studied directly in some way.

In his earliest book, *The Social Frameworks of Memory*, Halbwachs writes as well about the importance of collective memory for a family, but he also speaks of the concept in a way that goes beyond such a primary group. He tells of "two nobles who meet each other for the first time . . . and recognize themselves as two members of the same extended family that established their kinship link or alliance. This presupposes that, in the nobility, through the generations there continues a totality of well-linked traditions and remembrances" (1992a: 128). Further, "it must be said that the noble class has for a long time been the chief upholder of collective memory" (1992: 128). Here Halbwachs indicates that a collective memory is not limited to a small primary group, but can continue to exist for later generations, across both space and time, as part of a larger culture.

In *The Legendary Topography of the Gospels in the Holy Land*, Halbwachs characterizes the Gospel writers as recording "what remained in the collective memory of the Christian group" (1992b: 196)—apparently the disciples who formed around Jesus. His writing suggests that any set

---

Since the 1950 book was posthumous, we cannot know how Halbwachs would have developed his ideas further had he lived beyond World War II. Each of the three books suggests a somewhat different conception of collective memory, and the various examples that Halbwachs gives in each book are important for indicating the breadth of his thinking at different points and in different contexts. (Our citations of pages are to the English translations of the French books.)

of people who come together for some important purpose can be said to develop a collective memory. He also notes that as the group of followers became more distant from the events, it would have "burnished, remodeled, and completed" the collective memory, changing it over time. In addition, he shows how supposed "sacred places" in Jerusalem became the object of Christian memories, and that the collective representation of Christian ideas survived for later members of the "Christian group" in part because that representation was able to "attach itself to some points in the terrain" (202).

Halbwachs thus indicates that collective memory has a "double focus," in part centered on a "material reality," such as a place, and in part on a meaningful symbol (1992b: 204). In this way, commemoration grounded in objects and places becomes important to the collective memory of later generations. As new groups are formed, they absorb, transform, and make their own the memories of earlier groups; in the case of the Gospels, this included adopting with new meaning a number of locations that had been significant to Jews from the years before the time of Jesus. Thus collective memory can define objects and places anew, and can do so over great lengths of time: "It is not actual events that are 'legendary,' i.e., invented; rather it is the place of their commemoration" (Barry Schwartz, personal communication, June 2014).

Although Halbwachs appears not to have focused on collective memory at the national level, his use of the term varied with the time and purpose of his writing. We cannot be certain of how he would view our concern in later chapters with national collective memories in terms of both rememberers and remembered events, but we believe that if he could be transported to the present, he would accept our approach as valid, even if different from his own examples from an earlier time. Halbwachs was a wide-ranging theorist and methodologist himself (Vromen 1975), and there is reason to think that he would have welcomed the research drawn on in this book, as well as our inclusive understanding of what constitutes "collective memory."

This is just the catholic view taken by Aleida Assmann (2007) when she writes that:

personal interaction is not the only way in which a collective memory is created. If we replace face-to-face interaction with symbolic communication via media such as newspapers, television, history textbooks, museums, monuments, and commemoration rites, the range of participation in a collective memory widens considerably. If there is a leap of analogy involved in the thinking about "collective memory," it is not from individual memory to a mysterious collective mind, but from unmediated (face-to-face) interaction to mediated symbolic communication and from informal practices to more formal channels, occasions, and institutions of communication. (34)

Moreover, we assume there can be significant effects on collective memory when many individuals separately but simultaneously—each in his or her own home—see or hear of the same dramatic event by means of radio, television, or social media, though later interaction with family members, neighbors, friends, media commentators, and others may well change the memory in important ways.

Some writers do seem to require "discussion, negotiation" or "contestation" for memory to be considered truly "collective" (e.g., Zelizer 1995: 214, though Zelizer 1992 indicates a wider conceptualization). Furthermore, some scholars (e.g., Olick 2007) attempt to distinguish between "collected" and "collective" memory, where the former refers to memories of ordinary individuals, raising doubts about whether they should be regarded as a legitimate part of "collective memory." We ourselves treat the term "collective memory" as ranging in meaning from the cultural history transmitted by texts, objects, and practices, to individual beliefs about the past that can be investigated more directly. We do not see a compelling reason to restrict the term to fit the personal preferences of particular writers.

A major successor

Barry Schwartz, one of the most important successors to Halbwachs, has used the collective memory concept in wide-ranging empirical research over a number of years. He provides a definition of collective memory that recognizes the centrality of individuals, but also extends beyond them to groups and to memory conveyed by cultural representations:

Collective memory refers to the distribution throughout society of what individuals believe, feel, and know about the past. Only individuals possess the capacity to contemplate the past, but this does not mean that beliefs originate in the individual alone or can be explained on the basis of unique experience. Individuals do not know the past singly; they know it with and against other individuals situated in different groups and through the knowledge and symbols that predecessors and contemporaries transmit to them. (Schwartz 2008: 11)

Thus Schwartz identifies individuals as the primary carriers of memories, yet he also stresses the social and cultural character of what and how individuals remember.

Schwartz is unique in the range of evidence he draws on in his many studies of collective memory: photographs, poems, cartoons, statues, newspapers, records of visitors to shrines, and whatever else can be taken to reflect the memory of a period. Nothing is excluded that throws light on how important a person or object was to people at the time or on how a representation evolved. No evidence from any source is deemed irrelevant to "what individuals believe, feel, and know about the past." Schwartz's two books on Lincoln (2000, 2008) include a graph that illustrates the increasing number of visitors between 1971 and 2001 to Ford's Theatre, where Lincoln was shot, and also a table showing the percentage of Americans in a national sample survey who designated Lincoln as one of America's three greatest presidents, with the table further divided by race, region, political party, and several other social-background variables.

Even when examining portraits or written accounts about George Washington from the early nineteenth century, it is clear that Schwartz is not merely concerned with iconography or other symbols for their own sake; he assumes that the work of artists and writers tells us something about general beliefs and feelings at the time:

No one can be certain what most people who lived between 1865 and 1920 actually believed and felt about George Washington. We can only study the impressions of Washington that a small number of people wrote down for others to read, or painted or chiseled for others to see. . . . Yet, many portrayals of Washington during this period reflected the public taste. . . . Thus the producers of Washington's image did their best to make it appealing, or to get it right, while those who financed their efforts, such as publishers and art patrons, were confident of the public's readiness to recognize writers' and artists' achievements. (Schwartz 1991: 221–236.)

This may or may not be correct, but it indicates Schwartz's assumption that collective memory embodied by representations is not divorced from what ordinary individuals believe.

Of course, the feelings that lead to a monument or other representation often fade in later years, and the representation may cease to retain for later generations the meaning intended by the original writer, painter, sculptor, or planner—or indeed to retain much meaning at all. According to Nora (1989: 7), such symbols become "*lieux de mémoire*, sites of memory, because there are no longer *milieux de mémoire*, real environments of memory." Lincoln's Gettysburg Address keeps alive for us today a collective memory of the Civil War (Wills 2006), though not every scholar accepts Wills's interpretation of the address as attempting to reshape American collective memory. In addition, although Lincoln wrote: "The world will little note, nor long remember what we say here, but it can never forget what they did here," ironically it is his words more than the deeds of fallen soldiers that have been carried on in collective memory—perhaps because the larger sentiments they express still resonate for Americans alive today, while details of Civil War battles and deaths are remote from our present lives and concerns. Thus it is crucial to consider the meaning and resonance of cultural representations for individuals.

Schwartz is often directly concerned with connecting cultural representations to beliefs at the individual level, a focus that emerges clearly in his book *Abraham Lincoln in the Post-Heroic Era* (2008). He uses as one starting point the cultural representations of Lincoln outlined by Peterson in *Abraham Lincoln in American Memory* (1994). He then analyzes survey responses of Americans to determine how Peterson's representations of Lincoln are distributed within the population, and how ordinary Americans' images of Lincoln have changed over time. (We consider further variations in collective memory of Lincoln in chapter 3.)

Because he employs such a wide range of documentary evidence from the past, Schwartz's work has been drawn on by a number of historians, as well as by many sociologists and others across the social sciences. His assumption that individuals are crucial as creators and carriers of collective memory is one we accept; at the same time, his emphasis on the cultural resources that represent, communicate, and shape what is remembered is equally important.

A useful variant

James E. Young is another writer whose ideas have been helpful to us, though his own research is very different from ours in both subject and method. In his book on Holocaust memorials, Young prefers to examine "collected memory"—the same term used by Olick (1999) to contrast "aggregated memories" to those forms he considers genuinely collective. But Young's emphasis is different: he wishes to examine

the many discrete memories that are gathered into common memorial spaces and assigned common meaning. A society's memory, in this context, might be regarded as an aggregate collection of its members' many, often competing memories. If societies remember, it is only insofar as their institutions and rituals organize, shape, even inspire their constituents' memories. For a society's memory cannot exist outside of those people who do the remembering—even if memory happens to be at the society's bidding, in its name.

For even though groups share socially constructed assumptions and values that organize memory into roughly similar patterns, individuals cannot share another's memory any more than they can share another's cortex. They share instead the forms of memory, even the meanings in memory generated by these forms, but an individual's memory remains hers alone. By maintaining a sense of collected memories, we remain aware of their disparate sources, of every individual's unique relation to a lived life, and of the ways our traditions and cultural forms continuously assign common meaning to disparate memories. . . . We will not speak of the collective memory in these memorials, but of the collective meaning passed down from one generation to the next in our national traditions, rituals and institutions. (Young 1993: xi–xii)

A prominent practitioner

Some historians have made collective memory the focus of major empirical work, without considering its conceptual meaning explicitly. In *Race and Reunion: The Civil War in American Memory* (2001), David Blight never defines the term "collective memory," nor discusses its interpretation in a theoretical way, but either the phrase itself or a closely related term—sometimes simply the word "memory"—appears on virtually every one of the book's 485 pages. We must infer its meaning from the way it is used by a serious historian interested in how the past has been construed by those who lived through and beyond it.

Thus Blight writes on pages 1–2 that he is "primarily concerned with the ways that contending memories clashed or intermingled in public memory," and he proceeds on the next page to say that his main interest is "in how Americans made choices to remember and forget their Civil War." That there is not a unitary Civil War memory becomes clear as he considers what he calls "the reconciliationist vision," "the white supremacist vision," and the "emancipationist vision"—each evidently a form of memory held and promulgated primarily in particular parts of the country and each struggling in the years after the war for supremacy in what Blight calls "the politics of memory" (9). (The phrase refers to "memory as a contested object of differently empowered communities" [Schwartz 2005], and the politics of memory has been the subject of work by many scholars, including, for example, Hobsbawm [1983], Bodnar [1992], Schudson [1992], and authors included in Gillis's [1994] edited volume).

The "emancipationist" vision concerned black freedom and justice arising out of the Civil War. It was held most strongly by many blacks and by those white abolitionists who regarded former slaves and blacks more generally as full citizens, consistent with what became the Fourteenth and Fifteenth Amendments to the Constitution. The "white supremacist" belief can be thought of as part of the Lost Cause memory of the Civil War favored by many Southerners, who held a highly positive view of their pre–Civil War society and saw it as overwhelmed by Northern numbers and industrial resources. The "reconciliationist" vision emerged strongly in the decades after the war as a means of emphasizing the heroism and suffering of both North and South, and the desirability of putting aside differences in beliefs about the causes of the war, stressing instead the coming together of both regions in a single strengthened Union. The triumph of the combined reconciliationist and white-supremacist memories in both political and Supreme Court decisions permitted and promoted racial discrimination in the form of forced segregation and barriers to black voting. Thus the politics of memory led to the decline of the emancipationist vision at the national level until it was restored in the second half of the twentieth century. Blight is concerned not only with the politics of memory at the level of elites, but also with the ways in which ordinary individuals and the communities to which they belonged responded to, resonated with, and supported or rejected the different visions that made up the collective memory of the Civil War.

Situating our own orientation

Our own work throughout this book attempts to understand how ordinary individuals recall, interpret, respond to, enact, or disregard representations of the past—that is, how ordinary people participate in collective memory. In this effort, we have drawn on and been inspired by each of the four theoretical perspectives outlined above: Halbwachs's stress on the role of groups in memory; Schwartz's emphasis on individuals who remember and his notion of collective memory as a distribution of beliefs within society; Young's concern with the multiple meanings encompassed and communicated by a collective representation; and Blight's assumption that ordinary people and their communities can adopt, adapt, or reject representations of the past developed by elites.

We agree with Confino (1997) and later Kansteiner (2002), who emphasize the importance of "reception" and the role of memory "consumers" in the production, maintenance, and transformation of collective memory. We note, however, that the passivity implied by the "reception" and "consumption" metaphors does not adequately portray the degree to which individuals make, in Blight's words, "choices to remember and forget." De Certeau's consideration of consumption is helpful here (Wertsch 1998); he emphasizes that although people may be constrained by the cultural resources available, they are far from passive. In the course of employing tools provided by the culture in which they are situated, ordinary people sometimes use those resources "for ends and references foreign to the system they [have] no choice but to accept" (de Certeau 1984: xiii). Although de Certeau does not explicitly consider collective memory, his theoretical understanding of the process by which individuals use and reshape cultural resources in general seems applicable to how they might use and reshape representations of the past as well.

Kansteiner's concern about the relative neglect by scholars of the ways in which individuals "use, ignore, or transform" (2002: 180) representations of the past leads him to a later (2004) empirical study of German television audiences' response to programs on Nazism. Yet inexplicably, he seems to accept Olick's (1999) exclusion of individuals' "collected memory" from the general concept of collective memory (2002: 186). Historians—whose evidence ordinarily consists of documents of some kind—may seldom consider the possibility of gathering new data. Thus Kansteiner points to the possible use of archived poll or ratings data, but views the collection of survey data as a "laborious project" (p. 194).

Our own goal is to employ methods of all kinds to learn how ordinary people make sense of cultural representations of the past, how they are affected by them, and how they themselves in turn influence those representations.[3]

Conceptualizing "Generations"

The term "generations" will be familiar to most readers, but it turns out to be more complex than often realized. One dictionary defines "generation" as a "group of generally contemporaneous individuals regarded as

---

3. We have not attempted to provide here a systematic review of the literature on collective memory. Readers who are interested in further background can consult Hutton (1993) on earlier literature, Olick and Robbins' review (1998), Misztal's textbook (2003), and the many references given by Schwartz and others we do discuss.

having common cultural or social characteristics and attitudes" (*American Heritage Dictionary* 1992, third edition). Other editions, including Internet editions, offer similar definitions.

There are two parts to the definition that are important to distinguish. First, a generation locates a set of people in a particular time period, often with respect to an event or set of events. For example, we can refer to the "Revolutionary generation" of Washington, Jefferson, and other figures associated with independence from England and the successful effort to create a new nation. All those alive at the time can to some extent be identified as part of the "Revolutionary generation," though of course their roles varied from major leaders like George Washington to ordinary individuals who may have been part-time militiamen, supporters of independence in other ways, or simply onlookers or even opponents.

If we date the Revolutionary period as extending from roughly the early 1770s to about 1790, we can then use the birth years of those who were old enough to be a part of or witness to the Revolution to define the "Revolutionary generation." Birth cohorts—that is, individuals born during a particular year or set of years—provide a useful way of locating people in time because, unlike ages, birth years do not change for individuals. A person's birth date in relation to the date of an event immediately gives the person's age at the time of that event—a simple subtraction that is important to our research.

The second part of the dictionary definition of generation—"having common cultural or social characteristics and attitudes"—turns out on reflection to be close to what is meant by the term "collective memory," at least when studying individuals. As we noted earlier, collective memory can refer to a "distribution . . . of what individuals believe, feel, and know about the past" (Schwartz 2008: 11)—in other words, to shared forms or meanings of memory (Young 1993). When this distribution of beliefs, feelings, knowledge, and forms is anchored in time, it reflects the second part of the meaning of "generation."

Defining generations in terms of the first meaning is fairly straightforward, requiring that individuals be identified by their birth cohort, usually in relation to the date of an event of interest. Investigating generations in terms of the second meaning, which we have tentatively identified with collective memory, is more complex, and that part of the concept itself is more recent. Thus, it is useful to keep in mind that much of our book can be regarded as exploring the relation between these two senses of the term "generation"—one designating a location in time by means of birth cohorts, and the other referring to what we can think of as collective memory, resulting from the experiences of particular cohorts.

Subjective generational identification

We note here one other avenue of research on generational memory that we have largely ignored: subjective identification with one's generation. We agree with Mannheim ([1928] 1952) when he writes that a generation is not a "concrete group" with recognized bonds and ideology. Our limited data suggest that at least for the United States, such personal identification is not an important feature of social life. In one of our surveys (the Detroit Area Study 1991, discussed in chapter 9, p. 178), we posed the following question to the total sample of more than one thousand adults eighteen and older:

By a "generation" we mean people who grew up in the same time period. Do you think of yourself as belonging to a particular generation?

Of those who responded, 56 percent said yes, they did think of themselves in such terms, but nearly half (44 percent) said they did not. Moreover, when "don't know" answers and vague replies to a follow-up question ("What generation is that?") are taken into account (including examples such as mentions of belonging to the "older generation," or simply "senior"), more than half of the sample appeared to be lacking any clear generational identity. For the most part, respondents who did see themselves as belonging to a generation simply cited a decade (1940s, 1950s, 1970s), perhaps because of the original question wording "grew up in the same time period."

There were two partial exceptions. One was the 10 percent who used the words "baby boomer," adopting the term that refers to the large number of births that occurred in the years following World War II. The birth dates of three-quarters of this small proportion of self-described baby boomers did fall within that nineteen-year period, and most of the remainder were from 1944 and 1945, the two years prior to the census-defined dividing line. The one other meaningful identification was "the sixties," but only seven percent used such a term or a related one ("Hippies").

Generational labels are typically imposed by external observers, rather than reflecting any important sense of identity by individuals themselves.[4] We will continue to treat "generation" primarily as an objective characterization of individuals, specified in terms of their birth cohort and then studied mainly through the events that individuals experience and later remember.

Organization of the Book

In the chapters that follow, we use two different levels of analysis—cultural and individual—to study "collective memory" as well as the two senses of "generation." In part I (chapters 1–3), we consider three important figures from the American past: Christopher Columbus, Thomas Jefferson, and Abraham Lincoln. The names themselves evoke collective memories, as does the name of Sally Hemings in connection to that of Jefferson. We investigate what was known earlier and believed about each of the individuals, the attempts to shape or reshape the memories by revisionist writers and activists, and the outcome in beliefs by Americans as assessed at present. We draw primarily on historical and other texts for accounts of the past, and on interviews with national samples of Americans for beliefs in the present. In the case of Lincoln, we are concerned less with deliberate "revisionism," and more with the evolution of different perspectives over time, as well as with change due both to how questions are framed and to the occurrence of unexpected political events in the short term. As we show, each of these factors affects beliefs about Lincoln as a person and as a president.

In Part II we develop and investigate a middle-range hypothesis regarding collective memory at the level of individuals: that people are most affected by the national and world events they experience during late childhood, adolescence, and early adulthood, and that these effects show up as enduring memories of the past. We call this the *critical years* hypothesis, and in chapter 4, we test it in eight national surveys

4. For example, such labels are used in Taylor's (2014) *The Next America: Boomers, Millennials, and the Looming Generational Showdown*. The two categories in the title and others (the Greatest Generation, Generation X, and the Silent Generation) become the author's way of organizing evidence on recent changes in race and ethnicity, income, marriage, and other basic divisions in the United States. No discussion of the origin or justification for the labels is provided, and the author simply ignores the fact that birth dates constitute a continuous variable rather than a set of obvious or fixed categories. As a rough way of presenting a great deal of data from the past century, the book is useful. However, the author might well have included a warning to readers that each of the generational designations includes internal variation along the dimension of time, and that the end point of one category and the beginning point of the next may not be distinguishable. Examples would have made the issue clear.

conducted over some twenty-five years in the United States. We consider not only results that are positive, but also negative findings and in some cases ambiguous results that allow competing interpretations. Exceptions turn out to broaden and support the hypothesis, but also shift the theoretical emphasis from demarcating specific ages to understanding the forces that make particular ages important. (Robert Merton wrote that a middle-range theory does not attempt to deal with broad, abstract entities such as society as a whole, but "involves abstractions . . . close enough to observed data to be incorporated in propositions that permit empirical testing" [(1949) 1968: 39]. The distinction between a "theory" and a "hypothesis" is not always clear-cut, and we prefer the more modest term "hypothesis" for what we have done thus far, though perhaps it may develop eventually into a full theory. In any case, it is certainly, in Merton's terms, "middle-range.")

Next, chapter 5 presents a series of additional replications in other countries that provide further evidence on the hypothesis, as well as somewhat more in the way of exceptions. Furthermore, the additional countries—China, Germany, Japan, Israel, Lithuania, Pakistan, Russia, Ukraine—also offer opportunities for studying collective memory from new angles, and they add ideas and evidence valuable beyond testing the critical years hypothesis itself.

Part III explores extensions, limits, and applications of the critical years hypothesis, and examines the separate role of commemoration as a force contributing to collective memory. In chapter 6, we consider the journey from childhood through adolescence to adulthood as one form of transitional experience and investigate whether a very different kind of transition—emigration from one country to another—has a similar impact on memory. We also examine, in chapter 7, whether critical years effects are useful in predicting attitudes toward new issues that arise suddenly, and we discover a limitation in our broader hypothesis that can be interpreted in a larger way that is meaningful. In addition, we branch out in chapter 8 to investigate whether an extension of the critical years to a younger age range helps to account for memories of events that are personal in nature, rather than having to do with national or world events. Chapter 9 discusses intriguing findings and "losings" from research on what can be called "collective knowledge." The final substantive chapter, chapter 10, reports our investigation into the effects of commemorative activity on the preservation and revitalization of collective memories. Our conclusion reviews the main approaches and findings of our research, and we briefly consider implications for future research.

Our Methods

When assessing collective memory from the past (for example, how Christopher Columbus was viewed in earlier years), we draw on and refer to qualitative historical accounts, being careful to sample texts widely. For contemporary evidence about current beliefs and attitudes, much of our data consist of responses obtained from cross-section survey samples in the United States and other countries. Evidence based on changes in media content is also valuable at different points, and we make use of other archives whenever possible. We are catholic in the evidence we use.

In survey interviews, we often use relatively simple open-ended questions that respondents can answer in their own words, and that we are able to code later into categories having conceptual meaning. Quotations from interviews are frequently added to more quantitative analysis to illustrate a result, or to provide a sense of the meaning of a finding, or to help explain an unexpected outcome.

Many of our hypotheses concern the relation between dates of important events and the responses that people give, which in turn are connected to their birth cohort. We display such relationships visually for readers to evaluate in terms of the hypothesis being tested. Wherever possible, our major criterion for judging the reliability of results is to obtain a replication, often a literal replication, except as time may create inevitable variation. We also use construct replication, where question wording is changed or some other variation is introduced in order to focus more closely on a point at issue.

Throughout our book, we rely on graphical plots of our data, for as John Tukey (1977: vi) wrote, "The greatest value of a picture is when it *forces* us to notice what we never expected to see." Our interpretations of the graphical evidence are aided by statistical testing at a number of points, but we keep such tests in the background and are careful to bear in mind their limitations (e.g., Ioannidis 2005; Cumming 2012). We *never* employ the term "significant" in reporting results of statistical tests because of its misleading suggestion of importance. Instead we use the terms "reliable" or "highly reliable" as ways of indicating that we think the result can be trusted. (Where we do use the term "significant" it is as part of ordinary language, not to refer to a statistical result. For interested readers, appendix A briefly describes our use of statistical tests.) Again, though, some skepticism is always in order, and any claim about reliability is best combined with independent replication—which we carry out to the extent possible and practical.

In the course of our research, we consider all results, whether positive or negative. For example, in chapter 9, hypotheses about the relation of collective knowledge to birth cohort were initially confirmed exceptionally well, then subsequently disconfirmed in a replication, so we report both sets of results equally. (It should also be recognized that a single non-replication may in the long run turn out itself not to be replicated.) No result—no matter how seemingly reliable—should be accepted as valid without replication, including, where possible, testing steps in the reasoning that led to the result.

———

In the pages that follow, we consider many of the significant events of American history between 1930 and 2010, and also events regarded as important in the other eight countries we studied. The word "event," as we will see, is much wider in meaning than its modest number of syllables suggests.

PART ONE

Revising Collective Memories

"Those of us who grew up in the fifties believed in the permanence of our American-history textbooks. To us as children, those texts were the truth of things, they were American history," wrote Frances FitzGerald (1979: 7) in her study, *America Revised: History Schoolbooks in the Twentieth Century*. Included in such texts were highly favorable characterizations of important figures from the American past, such as Christopher Columbus, Thomas Jefferson, and Abraham Lincoln. There may have been dissent by some, but little reason to doubt the acceptance of the traditional positive representations by much of the educated general public.

By the end of the twentieth century, however, these collective memories were being seriously questioned. Our first three chapters provide an account of earlier representations of these three figures, the challenges or changes the representations faced, and the present outcomes. We consider collective memories *both* as part of cultural history and as held by representative samples of Americans. The challenge to Columbus has been the greatest of all.

ONE

Collective Memories and Counter-Memories of Christopher Columbus

The first significant commemorations of Columbus's landfall in 1492 occurred on its three hundredth anniversary in 1792, with the discovery of America called "the greatest event in the history of mankind since the death of our Savior" (de Lancey 1893). Columbus was seen as "the solitary individual who challenged the unknown sea . . . [and] was ultimately betrayed by royal perfidy [but] as a consequence of his vision and audacity, there was now a land free of kings, a vast continent for new beginnings" (Wilford 1991: 252). Although he had never reached the North American continent, nor indeed understood what it was he had come upon, the phrase "Columbus discovered America" increasingly merged the landing in the Bahamas in 1492 with the birth of the United States itself (Koch 1996).

Columbus continued to be idealized through the nineteenth and early twentieth centuries, as indicated by the installation in 1847 of the great John Vanderlyn painting, *The Landing of Columbus on San Salvador*, in the Rotunda of the U.S. Capitol, and the placement of other commemorative symbols in towns and cities across the nation (Groseclose 1992). A multivolume biography by the celebrated author Washington Irving ([1828] 1981) characterized Columbus in terms of "the grandeur of his views and the magnanimity of his spirit. . . . Instead of ravaging the new found countries . . . he sought . . . to civilize the natives" (565). The eminent historian William Prescott wrote that it would be "difficult to point to a single blemish in his moral character" (1874: 254), and the 1492 voyage resonated with divine purpose in Walt Whitman's (1874) "Prayer of Columbus": "a message from the Heavens . . . sped me on."

The four hundredth anniversary of the landfall in October 1892 was celebrated over a yearlong period, starting with "a grand civic parade of more than eighty thousand participants led by the president of the United States and including the entire cabinet, the Supreme Court, and most of the Congress" (West and Kling 1989: 56–57)—a national commemoration almost inconceivable at present. The celebrations culminated in the spectacular World's Columbian Exposition in Chicago, which drew over twenty-seven million visitors and "produced an unparalleled surge of creative energy that had an important influence . . . on the cultural values of the nation" (*Columbia Encyclopedia* 2000c: 3108). The inaugural oration spoke of "the crowning gift to humanity from Columbus . . . in search of a great land"—identified with the United States—and the official history of the Exposition declared Columbus "the greatest human benefactor of the human race" (Johnson 1897, vol. 1, p. 2). Such celebration and commemoration of Columbus illustrate Olick's conception of collective memory as "public discourses about the past as wholes or . . . narratives and images of the past that speak in the name of collectivities" (2007: 33).

Having started as a symbol of American individualism and progress, Columbus then became an ethnic hero as well, with Italian Americans playing a major role in turning Columbus Day into a full federal holiday in 1968. But ironically, his enshrinement in the federal calendar occurred just as his reputation was caught "in a riptide of conflicting views of his life and his responsibility for almost everything" wrong that could be linked to 1492 (Wilford 1991: 247). The revolution in minority rights over the second half of the twentieth century not only changed the attitudes of the American public regarding race, gender, and other social divisions (Pinker 2011), but also led to revisions in beliefs about individuals and events from the past.

During the 1980s and 1990s, according to revised editions of the *Columbia Encyclopedia*, "the image of [Columbus] as a hero was tarnished by criticism from Native Americans and revisionist historians. . . . His voyages [came to] symbolize the more brutal aspects of European colonization and represent the beginning of the destruction of Native American people and culture" (1993: 605; 2000a: 629). The contestation of the

"Sorry, Ed, but the revisionist historians finally caught up with you."

1.1   New Yorker cartoon

meaning of Columbus's landfall in 1492, especially as its five hundredth anniversary approached in 1992, was the starting point for our research on the relation between revisionist efforts, on the one hand, and the collective memories held by the wider public, on the other.

Christopher Columbus: Hero or Villain?

Countermemories (Foucault 1977) came from different sides. In 1973 the geographer and historian Alfred Crosby wrote of the havoc produced by diseases that Europeans brought to Native Americans. A broader critical book in 1975 by historian Francis Jennings bore its thesis in its title: *The Invasion of America*. Probably the most widely read early attack appeared in the opening chapter of Howard Zinn's (1980) *A People's History of the United States*, which spoke of 1492 from the standpoint of Indians and emphasized their oppression by Columbus and his successors. Zinn's book sold more than a million copies (personal report by the author), is owned by more than four thousand libraries (Worldcat database), and has been translated into Spanish and at least eleven other languages. Also important in terms of popular impact was James Loewen's *The Truth about Columbus*, a detailed summary of revisionist thinking for students, published in the Quincentenary year of 1992. Much of that short book then appeared three years later as a chapter in Loewen's *Lies My Teacher Told Me* (1995), which has had sales of well over a million copies (author's report). Moreover, in addition to the major focus on injustice toward Indians, Columbus was connected to the despoiling of the natural environment, "now threatening . . . the existence of the earth as we have known it and the greater proportion of the species, including the human" (Sale 1990: 4). There were counterattacks against revisionist critiques as well (e.g., Snow 1991; Royal 1992), but even such defenses of Columbus's reputation showed that he was no longer an undisputed hero. He was now a divisive figure (Fine 2001: 8–9).

It is important to recognize that revisionist views of Columbus did not result mainly from the discovery of new facts, but from attention to and reappraisal of information already available. A hundred years earlier at the time of the four hundredth anniversary, Justin Winsor published a book that characterized Columbus quite negatively: for example, Columbus "had no pity for the misery of others . . . [consigning Indians] to the slave market" (Winsor 1891: 505–506). Moreover, much of Winsor's information came from a manuscript written in the early sixteenth century by a close observer of the Spanish colonization of the Americas, Bartolomé de las Casas ([1965] 1974, 1992), who admired Columbus as a navigator but was highly critical of his and other Spaniards' treatment of the Indians. Even Samuel Eliot Morison's (1942) widely acclaimed biography includes such negative information, though the criticisms are overshadowed by the book's focus on Columbus as a great mariner.

Even earlier than the main revisionist writings and at least as important was the influence of the civil rights movement during the 1960s. With the growing emphasis on Black Power and black identity, other minorities with long-held grievances against the white majority came to the fore (Rhea 1997). In particular, the rise of Red Power ideology at the end of the 1960s (Nagel 1995) challenged white views broadly, and one effect was to question the assumption that Columbus Day is an occasion for celebration. Instead, Columbus's destruction of native peoples and culture was said to call for condemnation. Then, as Indian and scholarly critiques came together, reinforced by the anticolonial sentiments that had developed in the wake of World War II, major white organizations with a much wider reach began to express guilt over what Columbus represented. For example, the National Council of Churches, which includes thirty-six denominations with more than fifty million members, passed a lengthy resolution in 1990 that included among other similar statements: "For the indigenous people of the Caribbean islands, Christopher Columbus's invasion marked the beginning of slavery and their eventual genocide. . . . For the Church this is not a time for celebration" (National Council of the Churches of Christ in the USA 1990). Criticism of Columbus also made its way into the mainstream media, for example, appearing prominently in an episode in 2003 of the popular television drama *The Sopranos*.

College campuses were major sites for protests against positive commemoration of Columbus. We located six college newspapers from October 1992: those at Bowdoin College, the University of Georgia, the University of Illinois in Chicago, the University of Michigan, the University of Oregon, and San Francisco State College. Each contained at least one article damning Columbus or reporting a local protest. Although not a random or large sample, the six were diverse enough to suggest that something similar probably occurred on many nationally known campuses at the time of the Quincentenary. In the years since 1992, occasional campus demonstrations against Columbus Day have continued, some led by American Indians and others by interested non-Indian students. It is difficult for us today even to imagine the glorification of Columbus that occurred in 1892, as in the nineteenth century generally.

The fact that the *Columbia Encyclopedia* included in its final paragraph the words quoted above about "tarnishing" indicates that revisionist ideas made an impact well beyond a limited set of writers and Indian activists. Indeed, revisionist beliefs about Columbus began to appear in writing for children of all ages, such as *Encounter* (Yolen 1992); *Discovering Christopher Columbus: How History Is Invented* (Pelta 1991); and *Who Really Discovered America?* (both Krensky 1987 and Hart 2001). It is also clear that attempts in 1992 on the five hundredth anniversary to reinvigorate the traditional heroic view of Columbus were almost entirely unsuccessful, as recounted in detail in the book *Sinking Columbus* by two knowledgeable historians (Summerhill and Williams 2000). Thus it seemed possible that the picture of America's founding event, which developed over some two hundred years of commemorating Columbus's voyage and landing in 1492, had been turned upside down for a large part of the public that had previously been taught to think of both the man and the date in triumphal terms.

Yet we know from a number of past studies that intense debates at the level of elites and political activists do not always stir the larger public. For example, Stouffer (1955) found that relatively few Americans in the early 1950s appeared greatly worried about either an internal communist menace or a McCarthy-inspired threat to civil liberties, even though Stouffer's research itself had been funded by a major elite foundation because of just such concerns. More generally, in 1964 Converse delineated sharp differences between elite and mass political beliefs in levels of knowledge, sophistication, and organization across a wide range of political ideas and issues. In another twist, during the Vietnam War the growing opposition to American military involvement had a quite different basis in the general public than it did for activists on college campuses (Schuman 1972). Thus one cannot simply assume that revisionist efforts and Indian protests had much effect on public thinking about the meaning of 1492.

The five hundredth anniversary in 1992 offered an opportunity for reviving a positive image of Columbus. He could have been portrayed as the embodiment of individualistic and adventurous enterprise, as he had been in the nineteenth century (Phillips and Phillips 1992), perhaps stressing a connection to the then recent triumph of American capitalism over Soviet communism. But it was exactly in 1992 that revisionist criticism and the active protests by Native Americans peaked. Within elite groups that attempted to mount celebrations, there were conflicts, doubts, and trepidation over controversy, and few if any commemorations were successful (Summerhill and Williams 2000). A Smithsonian exhibit for the Quincentenary leaned over backward to present negative as well as positive views of Columbus, and to focus less on the man than on diseases, foods, and other indirect effects of 1492—informative but unlikely to inspire commemorative enthusiasm similar to that of 1892. "The most striking difference between the fourth and fifth Columbian centenaries [was] that native Americans a century ago were relegated to the footnotes while today they not only dominate the text but have begun to rewrite it" (Axtell 1992: 337).

Beliefs of the general public

To explore beliefs about Columbus in 1998, we asked a basic open-ended question to a national cross-section sample of 1,511 Americans, six years after the peak of criticism and protest during the five hundredth anniversary of the 1492 landfall. In keeping with the assumption that collective memories are ordinarily passed from one generation to another, our question was:

Suppose a nephew or niece about fourteen years old had just heard some mention of Christopher Columbus and asked you to explain what Christopher Columbus had done. What would you say in just a few words?

The indirect phrasing avoided having the question appear to be a threatening test of personal knowledge, and interviewers were instructed to reassure hesitant respondents that there were no right or wrong answers, "just whatever you would say to a young person to explain what Christopher Columbus had done." They were to record responses verbatim, and to probe non-directively where clarification was needed.[1]

After reviewing a sample of responses and taking into account our theoretical goals, we developed five major categories:

1. *Heroic Traditional.* Responses stating or implying that Columbus discovered America and also including something especially admirable about Columbus, for example:

    "[He] had the courage and enterprising spirit to go on uncharted territories."

2. *Simple Traditional.* Most of these responses consisted essentially of the words "He discovered America," and others were variants such as references to Columbus's three ships. The responses differ from those coded "Heroic Traditional" in that they do not explicitly mention admirable personal qualities of Columbus, though they are not at all negative.

3. *Other Europeans.* The remaining three categories challenge the traditional view of Columbus as "the discoverer of America" in increasingly critical terms. The mildest and least novel, "Other Europeans," refers to others thought to have reached the Western Hemisphere prior to Columbus. For example: "Actually the Vikings were here first." Since high school texts going back at least to the 1930s noted evidence of pre-Columbian landings by Vikings, such responses do not reflect recent revisionist criticism of Columbus. For that reason, along with their small number, we do not focus on this category, though we continue to include it when reporting results.

4. *Indians Already Here.* A clear critique of the traditional view of Columbus is the assertion that he could not have "discovered" America because the people he named

---

1. The question was included toward the end of the University of Michigan Survey Research Center's (SRC) monthly telephone Surveys of Consumers. (Throughout the book, we refer to these simply as the SRC monthly surveys.) The question was asked in three successive months (September to November) to provide a total *N* of 1,511. For details on sample design and response rates, see Schuman, Schwartz, and d'Arcy 2005: 9. Fuller results are also in the same article.

Indians were already here. For example: "They say he discovered America but he didn't, the Native Americans did." Such responses reject the Simple Traditional view of Columbus as "the discoverer of America," but they offer no explicit criticism of him or of his treatment of Indians, which has been the main emphasis of the revisionist position.

5. *Villainous Columbus*. Finally, there were responses that not only recognize the priority of the American Indians, but also portray Columbus in ways consistent with attacks by revisionist historians and Indian activists. This was the most important category in terms of our theoretical focus on the effects of revisionist criticisms. For example: "He met up with Native Americans and he slaughtered them." (Occasional answers noted that Columbus was brave but criticized him severely in ways that clearly fit the Villainous category. With such mixed responses, we coded in the more negative direction in order to obtain a maximum estimate of revisionist influence.)

Our first major finding is that 85 percent of the overall sample of 1,305 Americans (omitting don't know and other non-substantive responses) gave only Simple Traditional answers that basically describe Columbus as the "discoverer of America." Only 6 percent gave more laudatory Heroic responses, while at the other extreme fewer than 4 percent characterized Columbus in the Villainous terms advanced by revisionist writers and protestors, and another 2 percent simply acknowledged the priority of the Indians, for a total of just under 6 percent holding revisionist beliefs broadly defined. (Three percent referred to prior discovery by the Vikings or other Europeans.)

Because so few respondents were either clearly positive or clearly negative, we wondered if our question had failed to capture fuller sentiments about Columbus. It was possible that our inquiry was deficient by not encouraging respondents to go beyond an initial remembered cliché from childhood about the "discovery of America." Hence, we repeated our initial question once more in October 2000 (N=130), but omitted the "few words" phrase and pressed respondents harder with a follow-up inquiry: "Can you add anything else important about Columbus or about what he did?" To this additional question, almost half the respondents replied that they could add nothing more, but enough did respond further to change the distribution somewhat. It now had fewer Simple Traditional responses, though they still constituted two-thirds of the total. The largest increase was in the direction of Heroic responses (now increased to 12 percent of the total). The main revisionist category of Villainous Columbus increased to 8 percent, but the Indians Already Here category scarcely moved (now 3 percent). Thus, by pushing respondents hard to go beyond their initial response, we raised slightly the several non-Traditional answers, but clearly positive (Heroic) or negative (Villainous) responses remained a very small minority.

Perhaps our open-ended inquiries still missed the full extent of revisionist influence on ordinary Americans, so next we tried a more direct approach to clarifying the Simple Traditional responses that constitute by far the largest category of answers—responses that seem on their face positive about Columbus as the "discoverer of America." We repeated our standard open inquiry in February 2002, then followed it with a blunt closed question to all those classified as Simple Traditional responders: "Do you think young Americans should admire Christopher Columbus?" But this emphasis on the key word "admire" failed to reduce positive views of Columbus appreciably: of the 478 respondents who gave Simple Traditional responses to the initial question in this new sample, the great majority, 81 percent, said yes, young Americans should admire Columbus. (If we restrict our focus to white respondents, the figure is 87 percent.) In addition, the small proportion who said no to the admiration question were asked: "Why not?" Of the 13 percent of white respondents who had said either "No, should not admire" or simply "I don't know," more than half gave reasons that did *not* reflect primary revisionist criticisms, for example: "If he hadn't done it, someone else would have." Thus despite a leading question inviting respondents to indicate whatever reservations they might have about Columbus, only a handful showed signs of revisionist influence.

In sum, beliefs of Americans about Columbus, assessed after the height of revisionist writing and protests, pointed to continued regard for him as "the discoverer of America," which in turn was seen in positive terms. At the same time, since only a small percentage of Americans spontaneously attributed Heroic qualities to Columbus in response to our basic open question, this also calls for explanation, the more so since revisionist criticism evidently had little impact on most people. Thus we had two distinct issues to investigate further:

First, why is there so little evidence of effects on the American public of the many revisionist attacks on Columbus?

Second, why is the continued positive belief in Columbus as discoverer of America not accompanied by more explicit characterizations of him in Heroic terms?

In the analysis that follows, we work with our original large national sample of 1,305 Americans and look separately at white Americans and minorities.

White Americans

If there has been a decline in Heroic characterizations of Columbus within American culture, the oldest respondents in our sample should continue to express a more heroic view of Columbus that they had absorbed when growing up in an earlier era. Likewise, younger respondents should be more influenced by the recent revisionist attacks on Columbus, especially if we take seriously Mannheim's ([1928] 1952) emphasis on adolescence and early adulthood as critical ages for political learning, as amended and developed further in our chapter 4. In addition, greater education should also be associated with more critical views of Columbus, because awareness of revisionist ideas depends at least partly on reading or attending to serious media. We examined the results for white Americans in an analysis that held constant either age or education, depending on which factor was the main focus.

The most reliable finding is that older white Americans are indeed more likely than those younger to hold a Heroic rather than a Simple Traditional view of Columbus. This provides evidence of a decline over time in honorific characterizations of Columbus. (An alternative interpretation in terms of "aging" lacks plausibility here.) There is no relation of Heroic responses to education, nor any evidence that education affects the age relation, so only having grown up in more recent years is involved in the decreased glorification of Columbus.

However, given the paucity of Villainous responses, the decline in Heroic answers seemed unlikely to be due to revisionist efforts, and a different explanation is called for. Schwartz (2008) has documented an erosion of historic reputations that affects collective memories of past U.S. leaders generally. In addition to loss of trust in government growing out of failures in the earlier Vietnam and Watergate periods, there appears to have been a continuing decrease in historic reputations, perhaps promoted by the pervasiveness of television and now the Internet, which expose America's historical narrative to more widely held skepticism than in earlier days. The waning of spontaneous heroic characterizations of Columbus—despite his continuing image as the discoverer of America—fits well a general diminution of past heroic reputations in the eyes of the larger public.

Responses critical of Columbus

Since revisionist attacks on Columbus date from the 1970s and especially from the years leading up to the five hundredth anniversary, it should be younger white respondents who show the two more critical answers (Indians Already Here and Villainous Columbus). Both types of response do reveal a tendency to be given more by younger cohorts, but contrary to our expectation the relation appears slightly weaker rather than stronger for the most critical type, the Villainous category. Younger cohorts thus appear more likely to emphasize Indians as the First Americans (the element common to both categories), but youth does *not* account for the additional negative emphasis of the Villainous responses. Similarly, greater education is related to giving both types of nontraditional responses, but slightly more so for "Indians Already Here" than for the more extreme Villainous answer.

Thus we still have the problem of accounting for the highly negative nature of what we label Villainous responses. Because of their extremely critical content, their tiny proportion in the total population, and their lack of a distinctive connection to age, education, and other demographic features, we came to believe that such answers draw on a more general negative attitude toward conventional American verities. We tested this possibility by using a standard question asking respondents their religious preference: Protestant, Catholic, Jewish, Other, or None. Those who said "None" were individuals who rejected the widely accepted norm in the United States of claiming an attachment to *some* religious faith. (See Lipka 2013, Pew Research Center's "5 Facts about Atheists.") Dwight Eisenhower famously stated the norm a month before his inauguration as the thirty-fourth U.S. president: "Our form of government has no sense unless it is founded in a deeply religious faith, and I don't care what it is!"

The hypothesis is clearly supported when we add self-reported religious preference to an analysis that holds age and education constant. Answers classified as portraying a Villainous Columbus show a very large and reliable association in the predicted direction for the dichotomy of no religious preference versus all others (Protestant, Catholic, Jewish, Other combined): those who view Columbus most negatively are those who claim to have *no* religious preference whatever. Moreover, there is no relation of that dichotomy (no religious preference versus some religious preference) to any of the other Columbus categories, so the impact of rejecting a religious preference is solely on the Villainous category. These findings provide evidence that among white respondents, the characterization of Columbus as Villainous draws not so much on specifically revisionist attacks as on a larger receptivity to nonnormative beliefs generally, presumably in a liberal or radical direction.

Views of American minorities

Indians should be the single racial or ethnic group most likely to perceive Columbus in Villainous terms (e.g., Deloria 1969), and despite their very small number in a national sample, that is clearly the case, as shown in table 1.1: 42 percent give Villainous responses, as compared to 4 percent or less of whites, blacks, or Hispanics. Yet it is important to note that half the Indian sample and some 84 percent of the black sample fall into the first two traditional positive categories. Thus the impact of revisionist ideas has been far from complete even on the two groups most likely to be receptive to them.

Consideration of Hispanic responses leads, however, in a different direction, for there was considerable Hispanic involvement in planning the Quincentenary celebrations because of its connection to Spain. Furthermore, both de la Garza, Falcon, and Garcia (1996) and Rosenzweig and Thelen (1998) report Mexican Americans (the only Hispanic group they studied) to be at least as conventionally patriotic as whites, and quite different in this respect from both African Americans and American Indians. Indeed, 78 percent of Hispanic respondents in table 1.1 hold traditional views of Columbus as the man who discovered America. Hispanics also show a small trend toward a higher percentage (11 percent) of Heroic responses than whites (6 percent).

Textbooks

If we take seriously Yerushalmi's (1982: xxxiv) thesis that "collective memory is not a metaphor but a social reality transmitted and sustained through the conscious efforts and institutions of the group," then history textbooks are probably the single most important medium by which a society transmits and legitimizes what to believe about its past. Therefore, we collected fifty-five American high school history textbooks dating from the mid-1940s through the 1990s in order to study what has been taught about Columbus in schools. We used the index in each book to find all pages dealing with Columbus, and then identified two kinds of statements: evaluations of Columbus or his actions, and evaluations of the American Indians he met. Next we categorized the statements as follows:

Positive: Columbus/Indians are characterized in terms that would be viewed positively today (e.g., Columbus described as brave or as the source of positive American

Table 1.1 Beliefs about Columbus by Respondent's Race/Ethnicity[a]

	White (%)	Hispanic (%)	Black (%)	Indian (%)
1. Heroic Traditional Columbus	6	11	2	0
2. Simple Traditional View	86	78	82	50
3. Other Europeans	3	4	4	8
4. Indians Already Here	1	4	9	0
5. Villainous Columbus	3	3	4	42
Total	99	100	101	100
(N)	(1,069)	(73)	(110)	(12)

[a]Due to rounding, totals may not add to 100 percent. Don't know and other non-substantive categories are omitted from the table.

development; Indian culture is described positively or Indians seen as the "first Americans").

Negative: Columbus/Indians are characterized in terms that would be viewed negatively today (e.g., Columbus takes captured Indians to Spain; Indians called childlike or savage).

Unclear: No clear characterization of Columbus/Indians is provided.

The percentages of positive and negative codes for Columbus by decade are shown in table 1.2A. For example, of the eleven books from the late 1940s and 1950s combined, ten or 91 percent were coded as having a positive statement about Columbus, three or 27 percent a negative statement, and one or 9 percent had no characterization. (Each book could be coded for more than one type of statement.) The overall pattern for Columbus in table 1.2A starts off as predominantly positive, moves in the 1970s to much more negative characterizations, and then recovers a more positive view in the 1980s and 1990s, though the latter two decades continue to include negative statements as well. Despite the small number of decades and limited number of books per decade, statistical testing supports the observed pattern: Columbus's reputation suffered considerably in the texts published in the 1970s, but then moved to a more "balanced" portrayal that included both positive and negative characterizations during the last decades of the twentieth century.

The pattern for American Indians is simpler, and since there are no books coded both positively and negatively, the percentages in table 1.2B add to 100. Positive characterizations increased from zero before 1960 to above 50 percent in the 1970s, and they remained close to that level in subsequent decades. Negative characterizations began at a middling level—no higher because Indians were rarely mentioned at all in the earlier decades—then negative characterizations of Indians disappeared

Table 1.2 Results of Content Analysis of High School Textbooks[a]

A. Evaluations of Columbus by decade

	1944–1959 (%)	1960s (%)	1970s (%)	1980s (%)	1990s (%)
Positive	91	83	17	40	80
Negative	27	17	42	50	50
Unclear	9	17	58	30	0
(N of books)	(11)	(12)	(12)	(10)	(10)

B. Evaluations of American Indians by decade

	1944–1959 (%)	1960s (%)	1970s (%)	1980s (%)	1990s (%)
Positive	0	25	58	40	50
Negative	36	42	8	0	0
Unclear	64	33	33	60	50
(N of books)	(11)	(12)	(12)	(10)	(10)

[a]Since a book could be coded for both positive and negative evaluations, the percentages in a column may not add to 100 percent.

completely in the 1980s and 1990s. The trend is clearly reliable when tested statistically.

Qualitative review of the textbook statements supports the quantitative results. Passages appearing in the 1940s and 1950s, for example, speak of Columbus in terms of his vision and sacrifice, describe him as a hero, and refer to his "great service to civilization." In those early decades, when Indians appear at all, it is as "half naked savages" or as "childlike." By the 1970s, different Indian tribes began to be discussed in geo-cultural terms rather than as merely a welcoming party for Columbus. Increasingly, the texts state that the Indians were really the "first Americans." The 1970s also saw more negative pictures of Columbus, as in one book's characterization of European explorers (including Columbus) as "shameful," and another book's tongue-in-cheek account of an American Indian who steps off an airplane and "discovers" Columbus's birthplace of Italy. In the more recent years Columbus himself continues to be seen as courageous and skillful and thus deserving of praise, but there is also recognition of the destruction that he and his successors (not always clearly distinguished) perpetrated on Indians and their cultures.

Stimulated by Frisch's (1989) observation that beliefs about the past may be laid down at early ages, we also examined a set of eighteen "social studies" texts intended for elementary schools. Within the limits posed by their miscellaneous character and smaller sample size, they present much the same trends as the high school texts and indeed there were two books from the midsixties that already showed signs of change. Like the history textbooks, the social studies texts present an increasingly positive picture of Indians and a mixed, positive/negative picture of Columbus.

We cannot connect our interview respondents directly to the textbooks, but in the aggregate we expect the part of the American population that went through middle and high schools from the 1970s onward to have somewhat different views of both Indians and Columbus than older cohorts. In an approximate way this fits well the findings in the survey data that indicate among younger cohorts some erosion of heroic coloring to Columbus and some increased belief in Indians as "the first Americans."

Mass media

We also looked for evidence in the mass media of both traditional and revisionist views of Columbus, with virtually all of it prompted by the five hundredth anniversary in 1992. The *Readers' Guide to Periodical Literature* yielded sixty-two relevant articles in 1992, far more than in the previous ten years. Fourteen of the articles were positive with regard to Columbus's reputation, nine were negative, nine mixed positive/negative, and the rest simply used the Quincentenary as a peg for writing having little or nothing to do with the controversy, for example, astronomy (*Scientific American*), food (*Gourmet*), and travel (*National Geographic*).

We also searched the nation's leading newspaper, the *New York Times*, and found that it published fifty stories in the 1980s and 1990s that referred to the Quincentenary: eighteen dealt with or at least mentioned revisionist or Indian critiques, but the rest were entirely positive (e.g., described replicas of Columbus's ships due to arrive in the New York harbor). The *Washington Post* had some twenty-four stories, half entirely positive, half with at least some mention of negative concerns, while somewhat surprisingly twelve of the fourteen stories in the *Chicago Tribune* (1985–1996) at least mentioned criticisms of Columbus. Drawing on the LexisNexis archive of newspapers from some twenty other American cities (e.g., *Houston Chronicle*, *Denver Post*), we searched ten of these using the keywords "Quincentennial" and "Quincentenary." Overall, sixty-six articles touched on Columbus, the largest number simply noting a local plan for a "Columbus Day Celebration" but without further comment. Some local protests were reported, though seldom given major play.

The Vanderbilt Television News Archive yielded eleven brief stories from the three national news networks in 1992. Four were positive accounts of replicas of Columbus's ships arriving in New York harbor. The others concerned the controversy over Quincentenary celebrations, though most of these included replies to criticisms of Columbus. A set of seven one-hour public-television documentaries, entitled *Columbus and the Age of Discovery*, was carefully balanced to present both exciting positive aspects of Columbus's voyages and negative consequences for Indians. The programs were widely promoted and had four to five million households watching on average over the series, according to the WGBH research office. Two films about Columbus were released for the five hundredth anniversary: *Christopher Columbus—The Discovery* and *1492: Conquest of Paradise*. Both were primarily action films that presented Columbus in a generally favorable light; only the former showed cruel treatment of Indians, but attributed it mainly to Spaniards working to undermine Columbus. In sum, the mass media gave the public some exposure to revisionist ideas during the Quincentenary period, but the exposure was not great and of course would have reached only that fraction of the public that attends to such accounts.

It is also useful to learn what government officials believe the public expects to hear about Columbus. All presidents from FDR to Barack Obama issued glorifying proclamations for Columbus Day (e.g., "Today, we recall the courage and the innovative spirit that carried Christopher Columbus and his crew from a Spanish port to North America, and we celebrate our heritage as a people born of many histories and traditions," proclaimed President Obama on October 5, 2012, though he noted also "the tragic burdens tribal communities bore in the years that followed" [Obama 2012]). The 1992 Congressional Record had 144 entries for "Quincentenary" or "Quincentennial": 128 entirely favorable, just four presenting revisionist ideas, two defenses against revisionist ideas, and ten positive about Indians but with no criticism of Columbus. The U.S. Postal Service (2001) issued four stamps in 1992 in honor of the five hundredth anniversary: one showed Columbus seeking Queen Isabella's support, two pictured his first voyage, and one depicted his 1492 landing but with no sign of Indians present. It was left to the more elite Smithsonian Institution to take account of revisionist ideas, but to do so along with positive views of 1492, thus presenting a "balanced" picture to those interested enough to visit the museums, or to read a related special issue of *Newsweek* (1991).

The Inertia of Memory

Revisionist ideas that may have reached the public through textbooks and occasional treatment in the mass media have had to face the "inertia" of Columbus's long established reputation as the intrepid discoverer of America. One force supporting that tradition is the reappearance each year of Columbus Day, especially its institutionalized recognition by schools (see Schudson 1989a on cultural calendars). Informal conversations with primary school teachers indicate that they often continue to use the day to speak of Columbus, his three ships, and the obstacles he overcame to reach American shores, even while they provide a much more positive view of Indians than might have been expressed in earlier years. The Columbus story also remained in elementary schoolbooks, including a widely used series to teach first to third graders how to read, so that children absorb both reading lessons and stories about Columbus simultaneously (Krensky 1991). The text of the series was careful to speak of Columbus not as "discovering America" but as finding "a new world that no one in Europe knew" (48); yet most of the words and the colorful pictures conveyed a traditional image of Columbus's perilous first voyage and its successful outcome.

In addition to the forces that shape historical consciousness in early childhood, there continues to be later reinforcement as well: the many paintings, statues, and other commemorative symbols that maintain Columbus's visibility, along with more than a thousand schools, natural sites, and other places named after him. "Once commemoration gets under way," observes Schudson (1989b: 108), "it picks up steam; it operates by a logic . . . of its own. Not only are records kept, diaries saved, and news accounts written, but statues are built, museums are endowed, brass plaques are engraved." The importance of this symbolism is evident in the intensity with which critics attack it. "Beginning with Columbus," declared an Indian activist, "we are insisting on the removal of statues, street names, public parks, and any other public object that seeks to celebrate or honor devastators of Indian peoples" (*News from Indian Country*, October 15, 1992, 2). Indian activists would feel no need to remove these symbols if they were not seen as a legitimation of Columbus. The concern has extended to any reference to Indians that is not seen as respectful. For example, the name of the Washington Redskins professional football team has provoked national controversy since 1988, with renewed protests in 2013 and 2014 (Wikipedia 2014).

Language underscores the inertia of reputation. Not only the familiar rhymes that many children still learn ("In fourteen hundred and ninety-two . . ."), but Columbus's name itself has remained a symbol of individual boldness in exploring new ideas. One recent book referred to Albert Einstein as "an intellectual Columbus" who sailed beyond "the safe anchorage of established doctrines" (Cropper 2001: 203). A *New York Times* book reviewer called Gorbachev "a sort of political Columbus—setting out with high ideals to find one thing and achieving something better by discarding them. He is a hero of our times" (Figes 2002). Columbus's name is also perpetuated with a favorable connotation by a myriad of magazine articles and websites that connect it to food, travel, navigation, and much else unrelated to controversy.

Of course, the inertia of Columbus's positive reputation ignores revisionist attacks that define his arrival as the beginning of a European invasion that brought slavery, disease, and death to indigenous peoples. But we should not assume that the public absorbs new ideas without emphatic and repeated use of school instruction and the mass media to spread new beliefs. Careful studies of the factual knowledge of Americans indicate that a good deal of the information most social scientists take for granted is known by less than half—sometimes much less than half—of the general public (Delli Carpini and Keeter 1996). Although revisionist ideas were available to ordinary individuals who were interested, they were not so frequently or forcefully communicated as to offset the traditional image of Columbus as the courageous discoverer of America. "Inertia is a crucially important historical force," Le Goff observed, and "mentalities change slower than anything else" (1985: 170).

Once we recognize that examining different expressions of collective memory may reveal differences in content, our results become more complex than might appear in studies that draw on only a single type of evidence. Had we focused our research entirely on collective memory communicated by cultural tools, such as revisionist writings and protests, we would have concluded with Summerhill and Williams (2000: 1) that by the time of the Quincentenary, the "reputation of Christopher Columbus [was] turned upside down as fully as if the Admiral had indeed found monsters swimming in the Ocean Sea." However, our surveys of the American public, using several different question forms and wordings, produced little evidence of an impact from revisionist ideas: the predominant public belief remained the traditional one that Columbus merits admiration as "the discoverer of America." At the same time, we also found little evidence among Americans, especially younger cohorts, of the heroic image of Columbus that may have been widespread at the four hundredth anniversary in 1892 and in the early twentieth century. This absence of glorification can best be explained, however, not as a result of revisionist attacks and Indian protests, but as part of a broader erosion of idealizations of past American leaders (Schwartz 2008). Furthermore, among the small number of Americans who reject the traditional belief that Columbus discovered America, it proved illuminating to distinguish between two different positions: simple recognition that Indians had "discovered America" long before Columbus, and additional characterizations of Columbus in Villainous terms. The latter characterizations turned out to be linked to, and perhaps a result of, a critical attitude toward conventional American beliefs much more broadly.

When we turned from individual beliefs to what is transmitted through cultural resources, we found that the content of history textbooks showed a clear trend in positive treatment of Indians and a more complex negative/positive trajectory for Columbus. Both were consistent with some effect of revisionist beliefs on younger Americans. It is interesting to note, however, that changes in textbooks appear to have begun by the late 1960s, and thus prior to the main revisionist writings and even prior to what Nagel (1995: 957–958) called "the resurgence of American Indian ethnic identity in the 1970s and 1980s." Quite likely the shift was a consequence of the still earlier post–World War II increase in sensitivity to minorities and their viewpoints, initially with regard to Jews because of the discovery of the Nazi death camps (Stember 1966; Fredrickson 2002) and at about the same point in time affecting attitudes toward African Americans as well (Hyman and Sheatsley 1956; Schuman et al. 1997). Similar sensitivity spread to other groups that had been relegated to the margins of the society, especially as the groups themselves protested their disadvantaged status. Postwar decolonization of large parts of the world previously under European rule also won support in the United States, with implications for reappraising the treatment of Native Americans by early European explorers and colonists. Thus it seems likely that revisionist writings on Columbus were more an effect than a cause of the transformation of attitudes toward Indians and other minorities.

New Evidence of Change in Memory of Columbus

Three conclusions now seem worth entertaining. First, criticisms of Columbus usually reached the larger public in an attenuated form, without the full negative force found in revisionist writings and Indian protests.

41

Second, strong countervailing forces of inertia sustained Columbus's reputation even in the face of revisionist attacks. A third, more positive factor explains why the 1492 landfall inspired commemoration in the first place and continues to do so: the significance of "firstness" or "priority." Frisch (1989) reported that when students in his history courses were asked to write ten names in response to the prompt "American history from its beginning through the end of the Civil War, excluding presidents and generals," the list invariably included the name of Betsy Ross, the apocryphal creator of the American flag, and Columbus's name as well. Their free associations tap memories absorbed at an early stage of life, Frisch believes, and they "stick" because of the lasting importance of "creation stories." Columbus is still believed to have performed the key role in America's founding moment.

It is true that we may be living in a transitional era in which revisions of Columbus's story have begun to appear in many textbooks and in other accounts of the American past, including books for small children. It seemed possible that Columbus's prestige would diminish further as schools adapted to recent characterizations of Columbus. Yet some public commentators have attempted to counter revisionism at the elite level (Himmelfarb 1987; Schlesinger 1991; Fox-Genovese and Lasch-Quinn 1999), and reservations also appeared in the online edition of the *Encyclopaedia Britannica* (2004), which attempted to strike a "balanced" portrayal of Columbus:

The word "encounter" is now preferred to "discovery" when describing the contacts between Europe and the Americas, and more attention has been paid to the fate of indigenous Americans and to the perspectives of non-Christians. . . . The pendulum may, however, have swung too far. Columbus has been blamed for events far beyond his own reach or knowledge, and too little attention has been paid to the historical circumstances that conditioned him. . . . Columbus's towering stature as a seaman and navigator, the sheer power of his religious convictions (self-delusory as they sometimes were), his personal magnetism, his courage, his endurance, his determination, and, above all, his achievements as an explorer, should continue to be recognized.

References to revisionist criticism by the *Britannica* suggest possible longer-term effects not captured by our surveys in the late 1990s and early 2000s, but the article includes praise for Columbus as well, as is the case with *Wikipedia* at present, though the balance there is more negative (2013a). As the controversy sparked by the Quincentenary died

Table 1.3 Beliefs about Columbus by Year of Survey[a]

	1998 (%)	2014 (%)
Heroic Traditional Columbus	6	2
Simple Traditional View	85	80
Other Europeans	3	7
Indians Already Here	2	3
Villainous Columbus	4	8
Total	100	100
(N)	(1,305)	(435)

[a]Don't know and other non-substantive categories are omitted from the table.

down, it was hard to predict what might happen in the future. Rather than attempting such prediction, we gathered additional evidence.

In July 2014, sixteen years after our main survey evidence was collected in 1998, we repeated our original question, asking a new cross-section sample of Americans how they would explain to a young person what Columbus had done (see page 29 for the exact question wording). Table 1.3 compares the percentages giving various responses about Columbus in the two survey years (again omitting respondents who gave non-substantive responses or said "don't know"). The modal response in 2014 was still overwhelmingly that Columbus discovered America (80 percent of respondents). But at the same time, there is evidence that the more critical view of Columbus first apparent among political liberals and Indian activists at the time of the Quincentenary in 1992 has begun to have an important effect within the general public. The overall difference in the distribution of responses between the two years is highly reliable, as is the rise in Villainous responses relative to both types of Traditional response (Heroic and Simple). In addition, within the two Traditional types of response, the over-time decrease of four percentage points in Heroic responses is small but highly reliable with this large sample. In sum, the glorification of Columbus has faded and vilification of him has increased, even though he is still seen by most respondents as the discoverer of America in the general (though often imprecisely stated) sense of that term.[2]

2. The replication was carried out as part of the same national survey (the SRC monthly) as in 1998. As with virtually all surveys, the response rate has dropped substantially in recent years, but such decreases do not appear to have much effect on results unrelated to willingness to take part in a survey itself. One further change in the SRC monthly has been the inclusion of a substantial cell phone component. (For more on both issues, see appendix B, page 221 below.) We assume that

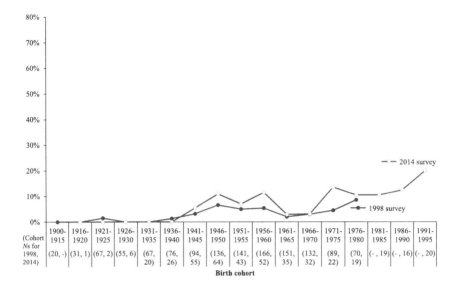

1.2   Percentages of each birth cohort describing Columbus in Villainous terms. (SRC 1998 and
       2014)

More data from future time points will be needed to confirm and extend the present trend, but at this stage is it useful to determine where
in the population the change is located, with age and education the two
prime candidates. Using the recent 2014 data, figure 1.2 plots the percentage of each birth cohort giving Villainous responses, showing that
younger age is a clear source of negative views. (The irregularities in the
curve may well be due to small subsamples for individual cohorts. We
also include the earlier 1998 results, but focus on those from 2014.) At
the older end of the cohort span, no respondent born before the 1940s
expresses serious criticism of Columbus, and at the other end the greatest criticism occurs among those in their midforties or much younger.
Educational attainment shows a smaller but also reliable relation to negative characterizations of Columbus, with those having a college education more likely to see him as Villainous, though no less likely to see
him as Heroic.[3] If the percentage for the very youngest cohort can be

---

the change in beliefs about Columbus and relationships reported here are trustworthy as to general
magnitude.

3. If both cohort and education are included as predictors in a logistic regression, both these
results are confirmed. There is no sign of an interaction between the two predictors.

trusted despite the small number of cases (just twenty), it is respondents recently of school age who are most likely to have been influenced by the decline in Columbus's reputation, as Yerushalmi—with his (1982) emphasis on deliberate transmission of collective memory—might have expected.

Despite this evidence of present and probable future change, the great majority of the public still believes that

in fourteen hundred and ninety two
Columbus sailed the ocean blue

and discovered America. Only further replications will tell whether the change shown in 2014 will be maintained or even accelerate in future years.

TWO

Sally Hemings and Thomas Jefferson: Sex, Slavery, and Science

During Jefferson's two terms as the president of the United States (1801–1809), there were many allusions to his having a slave named Sally Hemings as his concubine, with Jefferson said to be the father of one or all of her children. A newspaper column by James Callender in 1802 ([1802] 1999) is most often cited as the starting point for public notice of such a relationship, but there was much else circulating informally during Jefferson's presidency, including humorous verse by both the poet William Cullen Bryant and the young John Quincy Adams, the latter to become the sixth U.S. president. The ballad by Adams published in a Philadelphia newspaper in 1802 began:

Of all the damsels on the green
On mountain, or in valley,
A lass so luscious ne'er was seen,
As Monticellian Sally

with eight more verses of similar content and tone, one of which is probably a reference to Jefferson and another to "Sally" being a slave (Brodie 1974: 354–355).

Rumors of the relationship subsided after Jefferson's retirement to Monticello, and then his death nearly two decades later. Until recently the claim of a Jefferson-Hemings liaison was treated as uncertain, of little importance, and not likely to be resolved in any definitive way (Ellis 1996). Moreover, by the middle of the twentieth century, Jefferson's reputation seemed firmly established for the general public: he was widely known as the author of the sacralized Declaration of Independence, as one of the greatest of American presidents, and as a personage of remarkable and wide-ranging talents. The imposing Jefferson Memorial in Washington, D.C., was initiated by Franklin Roosevelt in 1938 and officially dedicated by him in 1943, in recognition of Jefferson's role as a principal founder of the republic. Jefferson's eminence as a thinker was enhanced still further when President John F. Kennedy remarked at a dinner honoring forty-nine Nobel laureates: "I think this is the most extraordinary collection of talent and of human knowledge that has ever been gathered together at the White House—with the possible exception of when Thomas Jefferson dined alone" (Kennedy 1962).

One example of the collective memory of Jefferson during the later years of the twentieth century was the entry in the 1975 edition of the *Columbia Encyclopedia*. It offered an outline of milestones in Jefferson's career and noted how "from boyhood he absorbed the democratic views of his Western countrymen," pointed to his actions "to prevent the continuance of an aristocracy of wealth and birth," and reminded readers of the "individual liberty that he cherished" (1457). *Nothing* in the entry of some sixteen hundred words referred to Jefferson's role as a major slaveholder from his birth until his death, nor to his attitudes and beliefs with regard to either slavery or African Americans, nor to his relations with individual slaves. (At about the same time, Edmund Morgan [1975] developed the striking thesis that it was the very existence of race-based slavery that supported and promoted the democratic views of Jefferson and his white countrymen toward one another across social-class lines.)

At the level of the general public, prior to the 1980s it is likely that very few Americans would have read or heard anything about a long-term sexual relationship between Jefferson and one of his slaves, or his alleged paternity of her children, or indeed even much about Jefferson's personal dependence on slave labor. The name of Sally Hemings and her likely relationship to Jefferson only began to reemerge for present-day Americans as a result of Fawn Brodie's biography, *Thomas Jefferson: An Intimate History* (1974), and then five years later the publication of *Sally Hemings: A Novel*, by Barbara Chase-Riboud (1979). Brodie's biography was stimulated in part by Jordan's (1968) discussion of Jefferson's belief in black sensuality, as well as Jefferson's own ambivalence when referring to sex. The biography spent thirteen weeks on the *New York Times* best-seller list, and Chase-Riboud's novel was a Book-of-the-Month-Club selection. According to the cover of the 1994 Crown Press edition of the novel, it had sold 1.6 million copies by then, and subsequent paperback editions have doubtless continued to sell well. The novel is also in many U.S. public libraries: twenty-nine of ninety-two public libraries in Virginia own a copy of the book, but even in the state of Maine, far from Monticello, fourteen public libraries out of approximately fifty possess a copy, though only four of these libraries own at least one volume of Dumas Malone's Pulitzer Prize–winning six-volume biography, *Jefferson and His Time*, each volume having been published separately with its own title as a self-contained book between 1948 and 1982.

These treatments of a Jefferson-Hemings relationship led to considerable controversy among historian-biographers most directly concerned with Jefferson's reputation. Such a liaison was rejected as entirely untenable by Malone (1970, 1981), and also by Merrill Peterson (1960), author of an important study of Jefferson's image in American memory and of other books about the third president. Within a few years, however, attention shifted to Annette Gordon-Reed's (1997) detailed analysis of the evidence for and against a Jefferson-Hemings relationship. A legal scholar, Gordon-Reed took seriously accounts published in the nineteenth century by Sally Hemings's youngest son, Madison Hemings ([1873] 1997), and by another former slave from Monticello, Israel Jefferson ([1873] 1997). Their memoirs in Ohio newspapers stated that Sally Hemings had agreed to be Jefferson's concubine and that he was the father of all of her children. Such assertions had been dismissed earlier by Merrill Peterson as merely "the memories of a few Negroes" (1960: 187; see also Gordon-Reed 1999). The serious consideration of the Jefferson-Hemings relation was quite likely aided by the substantial changes in race relations and greater prominence of racial issues in the 1960s, by the greater openness about and interest in sex beginning around the same time, and perhaps especially by the incisive work of Gordon-Reed, herself an African American at a time when white historians could no longer dominate scholarship on Jefferson.

Popular representations

The possibility—indeed, presumed certainty—of a Jefferson-Hemings liaison was conveyed to the larger public by a fictional film portrayal that treated the relationship as not only real but romantic, and presented it in the form of imagined dramatic scenes and dialogue. The film, *Jefferson in Paris* (Ivory 1995), included Sally Hemings as one of several key characters, and it dramatized a scene in Paris (described in her son's memoir)

2.1 Images used to market Barbara Chase-Riboud's *Sally Hemings: A Novel*, the film *Jefferson in Paris*, and the TV miniseries *Sally Hemings: An American Scandal*

during which Jefferson is said to have promised to free her future children if she returned with him to Monticello.

The film was followed by a made-for-television drama, *Sally Hemings: An American Scandal* (Haid 2000), which portrayed a Jefferson-Hemings liaison as both long-term and highly romantic, along with vivid scenes of slave families at Monticello. The book, film, and television ads shown in figure 2.1 give some sense of how the new claims about Jefferson were presented to the American public. Audiences that saw these portrayals were unlikely to realize that there is virtually no documentation of the actual nature of a Jefferson-Hemings relationship, and nothing whatever in writing about it by either Jefferson or Sally Hemings. (It is not known whether Hemings herself was literate [Gordon-Reed 2008]). Malone and some other biographers of Jefferson had been distraught upon realizing that Chase-Riboud's novel might be brought to the screen, fearing that the public would accept a film or televised version as true history (French and Ayers 1993: 436–438; Gordon-Reed 1997: 182–183 especially).

As it turned out, despite a star-studded cast and the screenwriter-director-producer team of Ruth Prawer Jhabvala, James Ivory, and Ismail Merchant, *Jefferson in Paris* was not a great success, grossing just under $2.5 million (Klady 1996: 38). On the other hand, the opening episode of CBS's *Sally Hemings: An American Scandal* was reported to have been watched by 19.3 million television viewers, making it the second-most-seen miniseries of the season, surpassed only by the 24.1 million viewers who watched *Jesus* (Kissell 2000: 44). One other television account was a documentary on Jefferson by Ken Burns (1996), though it was not regarded as adequately reflecting recent historical scholarship (Lewis and Onuf 1998).

Scientific evidence

An important further development occurred in the form of a widely pub-licized article in the leading scientific journal *Nature* (Foster et al. 1998). The article reported DNA evidence that connected male descendants of Sally Hemings to Jefferson's own lineage. Equally important, the DNA evidence contradicted the main alternative explanations that had been offered by Jefferson's white descendants (Coolidge [1858] 1997) and by earlier biographers (e.g., Miller 1977; Randall [1868] 1997) for the apparent physical resemblance of Hemings's children to Jefferson himself.

An account of the DNA findings appeared on the front page of the *New York Times* on November 1, 1998, and was reported on public television. How widely it circulated in ways reaching the public more broadly is difficult to determine, but the subjects of race, sex, DNA testing, and Jefferson probably made for much greater interest than most scientific articles. The national newspaper *USA Today* printed at least thirteen re-lated articles over the next seven months. Moreover, the impact of the *Nature* report on relevant scholars appears to have been considerable, as captured by Lucia Stanton, a historian at Monticello: "In November 1998, an assortment of historians hopped off the fence on to solid ground, joining a lonely band already there and joined by a few who had seemed firmly rooted on the other side" (2000: 139). For example, the Jefferson biographer Joseph Ellis immediately moved from uncertainty to belief in the relationship (Lander and Ellis 1998). Unfortunately, the *Nature* article itself went too far, carrying a headline asserting that "Jefferson fathered slave's last child"—misleading because the research had only identified Jefferson's lineage, not Thomas Jefferson himself.

Although the evidence in *Nature* could not pinpoint Thomas Jefferson as the progenitor of Sally Hemings's children, it was joined to other supportive data about Jefferson and Hemings, especially the presumed dates of her conceptions in relation to his presence at Monticello. These were noted by Jordan (1968) and then analyzed more fully by Neiman (2000). Today it is likely that most American historians accept the Jefferson-Hemings liaison and Jefferson's parentage of her children as having been real (e.g., Wood 2009: 514), though the exact nature of the relationship is unlikely ever to be known. A recent much-praised biography of Jefferson by Jon Meacham takes for granted Jefferson's "decades-long liaison with Sally Hemings, his late wife's enslaved half-sister who tended to his personal quarters at Monticello" (2012: xxvi). However, Meacham has little to say about Jefferson's role as a slave owner, and almost nothing about his strange views regarding race and sex (e.g., "the preference of the Oranootan for the black woman over those of his own species" [Jefferson 1787, excerpt reprinted by Lewis and Onuf 1999: 265]).

Another recent book, Wiencek (2012), focused almost entirely and quite negatively on Jefferson's life as a slave owner and his beliefs about African Americans, but was less successful in the eyes of historians working on the Jefferson-Hemings relationship (Gordon-Reed 2012). At a more official level, the Thomas Jefferson Foundation includes in a recent *Guidebook to Monticello* the following statement: "Because of genetic testing in 1998 and an ensuing review of other types of evidence, most historians today accept the truth of Madison Hemings's statement and believe that he and his siblings were Thomas Jefferson's children" (2011: 105).

The 2000 edition of the *Columbia Encyclopedia* (2000b) repeated the 1975 entry about Jefferson almost exactly, though with the addition of a single sentence at the end stating: "In the 1990s long-repeated rumors that he had fathered a child or children by the slave Sally Hemings, his wife's half-sister, appeared to be supported by DNA testing, but the matter remained controversial" (1457). The 2009 Internet version of the *Encyclopedia* noted that the Thomas Jefferson Foundation, which administers Monticello, has accepted the DNA results as almost certain, but adds a further qualification: "Some admirers of Jefferson hold that his younger brother, Randolph, is the more likely father of Hemings's descendants." As in the earlier editions, nothing is said about slavery at Monticello, or about Jefferson's views on slavery or race.

Treatment of Jefferson and Hemings in the *Encyclopaedia Britannica* underwent a similar evolution. The 1985 edition included in its five-page biography of Jefferson several sentences concerning his beliefs about black inferiority, as recorded in his book *Notes on the State of Virginia* (1787), but nothing about slavery or about individual slaves at Monticello. However, the 2009 Internet version of the *Encyclopaedia Britannica* offers more detail about Jefferson's likely liaison with Sally Hemings, and it includes a lengthy sidebar on "'Tom and Sally': The Jefferson-Hemings Paternity Debate." Thus the *Britannica*, as well as the *Columbia Encyclopedia*, provides a record of important changes in cultural representations of Jefferson.

Some individuals with kinship or other connections to Jefferson have continued, however, to dispute the existence of a Jefferson-Hemings liaison (see, for example, Coates 2001; Hyland 2009; Yoder 2013: 63). Moreover, a separate organization, the Monticello Association, owns the burial ground at Monticello that holds Jefferson's remains and those of his immediate white relatives. It continues today to allow burial there of Jefferson's "lineal" descendants, but as of this writing the descendants of Sally Hemings have not been permitted to be full members of the association, nor do they have the right to be buried in the Monticello Burial Ground. Thus a controversy that dates from at least 1802 continues at present among the living and extends also to the burial of the dead (*Wikipedia* 2013b).

The impact of information about Sally Hemings and Jefferson, including the DNA results, has undoubtedly spread beyond historians and Jefferson's descendants. Even members of the general public who did not read the historical or fictional accounts or watch the film or TV miniseries would nevertheless have had opportunities to learn about Sally Hemings. Our search in 2009 of the LexisNexis database for mention of her name in the five top-circulation U.S. newspapers (*USA Today*, the *Wall Street Journal*, the *New York Times*, the *Washington Post*, and the *Los Angeles Times*) showed that articles, reviews, and other references to Hemings followed the appearance of each new work or other development about her. Both the *New York Times* and the *Washington Post* ran front-page articles reporting on the 1998 DNA tests; *USA Today* and the *Wall Street Journal* ran reports within their first few pages. The number of articles or other items mentioning Sally Hemings in the five newspapers increased dramatically between 1970 and 2009, with a mean of one to two items per year appearing during the 1970s and 1980s, jumping to a mean of twenty-six items per year during the 1990s and twenty-seven per year during the 2000s. In addition to the major newspapers, popular American magazines reported on the Jefferson-Hemings relationship as well, with articles appearing in *People*, *Time*, *TV Guide*, *Newsweek*, *US News and World Report*, *Ebony*, and *Essence*. (*People*, *Time*, and *TV Guide* each have over three million readers; circulation for the other publications ranges from 1 to over 2.5 million.)

We should note also that the trajectory from Brodie's 1974 revisionist biography of Jefferson through the DNA testing and subsequent writings can be seen as parallel to, or even as part of, a rapidly increasing interest in the history and nature of slavery in the United States, as reflected in a content analysis of newspapers and magazines (personal communication from Barry Schwartz, 2009). Furthermore, although much of the nonblack public may think of slavery as a remote episode in the past, vivid reminders of it continue to occur—for example, news stories and accounts about the mixed racial ancestry of Michelle Obama, the wife of the American president (Swarns and Kantor 2009; Swarns 2012).

Collective Knowledge about Hemings and Jefferson

Of most relevance to our exploration in this chapter, historians Lewis and Onuf wrote that there is now "a widespread belief among the public that Jefferson was the father of the children of his slave, Sally Hemings" (1999: 2). In the introduction to their useful collection of articles by a number of well-known historians, there are other statements and implications at several points about the considerable extent of "public opinion" about the Jefferson-Hemings relationship, though no direct evidence is provided or indeed was likely available at that time regarding the views of the general public. Disbelievers in a Jefferson-Hemings liaison were even more concerned about public acceptance of a relationship they considered to be both false and damaging to Jefferson's reputation. A website created by Herbert Barger, one of the most vigorous critics of those asserting a Jefferson-Hemings liaison, opened one Internet posting with this question and answer: "Did Thomas Jefferson have children with a slave? Almost everyone in America thinks so, and has probably heard of the DNA testing" (Barger 2009). The assumptions by writers on both sides of the issue can benefit from empirical evidence on what the public does and does not know about Sally Hemings and her relation to Thomas Jefferson.

For collective memories to exist at the level of actual individuals requires some amount of what can be called "collective knowledge." The knowledge may be of doubtful accuracy (for example, important parts of the public may believe that John F. Kennedy was assassinated by Somali pirates) and the event itself may or may not have taken place as indicated by other evidence (for example, that God parted the Red Sea to

Table 2.1 Percentage of Americans Able to Identify
Each of Eleven Terms from the Past[a]

Term	Correct or partially correct (%)
Rosa Parks	79
Woodstock	86
The Tet Offensive	36
Joe McCarthy	46
Christa McAuliffe	40
Norman Schwarzkopf	62
Mohammed Atta	31
Battle of the Bulge	48
Village of My Lai	39
WPA	41
Sally Hemings	11
(N)	(992)

[a] The order of names and terms shown here is the order
presented to respondents. For each item, percentages
show answers judged to be correct or partially correct,
divided by all responses.

allow the Israelites to escape from their Egyptian pursuers). However, if individuals do not profess *any* knowledge of a past event, they cannot be said to participate in a collective memory of it: "Collective memory is the outcome of processes affecting the information to which individuals have access, the schemata by which people understand the past, and the external symbols or messages that prime these schemata" (DiMaggio 1997: 275). We therefore considered the extent and nature of the knowledge of Sally Hemings possessed by the American public in 2009.

We included the name Sally Hemings in a list of eleven terms from the past that were presented to a national sample of 992 Americans in 2009.[1] Respondents in this part of the survey were asked first, "Have you heard of _____?" and then those who said yes were asked, "Who is _____?" or "What does _____ refer to?" Each identification was scored for correctness, and all eleven terms and the percentage for each judged to be correct or partly correct are shown in table 2.1.

The list had been constructed to represent different time points over the past eighty years, with the earliest term (the "WPA") probably encountered by the oldest Americans in our sample during their own

1. These questions were included near the beginning of the University of Michigan Survey Research Center's monthly telephone survey (the SRC monthly) in August and September 2009. For details on sample design and response rates, see Schuman and Corning (2011).

lifetime, and the latest term ("Mohammed Atta") within the experience of even the youngest members of the sample during the years immediately following 2001. Of course, Sally Hemings and Thomas Jefferson both lived long before the past century (Jefferson died in 1826 and Hemings in 1835), but the renewed interest in their relationship dates from the late 1970s and especially from the 1990s, and in this sense it could also have been within the life experience of most American adults.

It was entirely acceptable for respondents to qualify their answer with words like "supposedly" or "allegedly," as some 40 percent did. Our coding for correctness proceeded without regard to such qualifications, so that a response stating that Jefferson "allegedly" fathered the children of Sally Hemings was coded as correct. (A check of agreement about correctness between two independent coders yielded 90 percent or better for all terms.) Thus we had no need to make a judgment ourselves about the relationship between Jefferson and Sally Hemings. Indeed, had a respondent indicated total disagreement with claims about Jefferson's paternity or his liaison with Sally Hemings, we still would have scored the response as correct, though we did not discover any respondent who did this. Later, however, we will distinguish between answers that were qualified and answers stated as though factual.

Sally Hemings's name turned out to be much less well known to the American public than the other ten terms from the past that we asked about, as shown in table 2.1. Knowledge of the other names on the list ranged from a low of 31 percent for "Mohammed Atta" to a high of 86 percent for "Woodstock," but the name of Sally Hemings registered as considerably lower at 11 percent. We should not regard the relatively low percentage for Hemings as very surprising, since the other ten names had received more media attention than hers and also in most cases directly affected many more individual Americans. Knowledge of the name Sally Hemings has depended to a considerable extent on reading, and even "best-selling" novels reach only a small minority of the general population. Films, television, and newspaper reports have extended that reach a good deal further, but even the relatively successful television production dealing with Jefferson and Hemings could have been seen by only a minority of Americans, and it had been broadcast almost a decade prior to our survey. The extent of knowledge of Hemings is not trivial considering that her alleged liaison with Jefferson dates from two hundred years ago, and that it is not connected to any major or recent event in American history, as are the names of Mohammad Atta and Rosa Parks.

One might even argue that for roughly one out of ten Americans to know something about a relationship between a president and his slave that was some two hundred years in the past is remarkable. Moreover, we will also see later that the name of Sally Hemings is considerably better known today than that of another woman whose identity was probably once much more familiar because of her connection to an even more famous president, Abraham Lincoln. At the same time, it is clear that belief by the public in a Jefferson-Hemings liaison should probably not be considered "widespread" without some attempt to indicate what that adjective is assumed to mean.

A more differentiated classification of responses

After reading a sample of answers about Sally Hemings, we broke the 113 responses that indicated some knowledge of her name into three broad categories, plus a residual category for all those remaining respondents who said they had not heard of her at all, could not recall who she was, or provided a clearly incorrect answer. Responses in the first two categories were considered "correct," though different in emphasis: the first category referred to Jefferson as the father of Hemings's children, which also implied a sexual relationship of some type between the two, and therefore provided the fullest identification of the name as viewed by most historians today. The second slightly smaller category referred to Hemings as Jefferson's concubine, or used some similar characterization, but made no mention of children; we treat this category as correct also, but not quite as complete as answers mentioning children fathered by Jefferson, since the existence of children is not implied by a sexual relationship per se. Having children connects Jefferson to later Americans and has been of substantial interest over the years, especially though not only to African Americans.

The smallest and most heterogeneous category (partially correct) included responses that mentioned Hemings simply as a slave or were otherwise correct but incomplete, and also included a few answers that were at least partly incorrect (for example, a response indicating that she was Alexander Hamilton's mistress). We did not separate these two types of partly inaccurate answers because neither subset was large enough to allow detailed analysis. Relative to the large number of "don't know" and completely incorrect answers, they indicated that a respondent had absorbed some information about Sally Hemings, so we treat them as partially correct, and for most purposes include them under "correct" when we dichotomize the sample into correct versus incorrect.

Of the large number of answers categorized as incorrect (89 percent of the total of 992 responses), 95 percent were from respondents who simply said "no" or "don't know" when asked if they recognized the name of Sally Hemings. The rest (5 percent) gave an answer that we considered completely wrong. For the majority of these, thirty-four of forty-three (e.g., "early suffrage movement," "writer or actress"), we could not find any particular explanation. However, in nine cases Sally Hemings was identified as an astronaut, and respondents may have had in mind Sally Ride, the physicist who in 1983 was the first American woman to travel into space. (A further analysis, however, did not point to any correlate of the mention of Sally Ride, such as the respondent being a woman or her birth cohort being similar to Ride's.)

Education

The most obvious source of knowledge about Sally Hemings is the education of respondents, which we take to represent not only formal schooling, but also greater exposure to books, serious newspaper and magazine reporting, and perhaps quasi-historical presentations such as the film and miniseries. (Quasi-historical because the film and miniseries, like the Chase-Riboud novel, build on factual information where available, e.g., Jefferson's service as minister to France between 1785 and 1789, and they also draw on Madison Hemings's memoir for other information. Of course, all of the conversation and much else is entirely imagined.) As anticipated and as table 2.2 shows, there is a reliable relation between the Hemings knowledge score and respondent's education,

Table 2.2 Correct Identifications of Sally Hemings by Education of Respondents[a]

	Educational level					
	0–8 years school (%)	9–11 years school (%)	High school graduate (%)	13–15 years school (%)	College graduate (%)	Some graduate school or more (%)
Correct responses only	0	0	3	8	10	19
Correct plus partially correct responses	0	3	4	12	11	23
(N)	(9)	(35)	(253)	(213)	(284)	(196)

[a]Percentages show answers judged to be correct, or correct and partially correct, divided by all responses for a given level of education.

with most of the variation occurring between the two correct categories and between partially correct and the residual category ("don't know" and incorrect answers).

Race

Earlier we stated that few Americans prior to the 1980s would have had any knowledge of claims about a Jefferson-Hemings liaison resulting in children. But this statement is too extreme for African Americans. Some of the descendants of Sally Hemings passed on an oral tradition of what they believed to be a lineal connection to Jefferson (Stanton and Swann-Wright 1999), and in addition and probably as a result of these traditions, there have been occasional stories about supposed descendants of Jefferson in popular publications directed at African Americans. For example, "Thomas Jefferson's Negro Grandchildren" appeared in *Ebony* in November 1954 (Bennett 1954: 78–79), well before any of the recent revisionist books or films (see also the three-page entry for "Sally Hemings" in Appiah and Gates [2005]). Thus we had reason to expect self-identified African Americans to be more likely than white Americans to recognize the name of Sally Hemings. We found that 16 percent of blacks, compared to 11 percent of whites, were able to give at least a partially correct identification of Hemings—a difference that is reliable when education is held constant.

The seemingly small difference by race takes on greater meaning when compared with the effects due to race for the other ten names we asked about in our survey. On nine of the other items, whites show greater knowledge than do blacks; for example, 23 percent of whites were scored as correct or partially correct on Mohammed Atta, as against 9 percent of African Americans. Some of this difference can be attributed to black-white differences in educational levels, though reliable variation remains after education is controlled. More important is the one clear exception among the other ten terms: African Americans are more knowledgeable about Rosa Parks than are whites, reliably so. Thus when a term is one that has more meaning for black respondents, they show greater awareness, as indicated more generally by their flashbulb memories (Brown and Kulik 1977).

As to the size of the difference by race, the overall advantage in knowledge for blacks as against whites is not as great for Sally Hemings as for Rosa Parks: 5 percentage points in the former case and 15 percentage points in the latter. The relative knowledge of Sally Hemings falls between that of Rosa Parks and that of the nine non-race-related terms where whites show greater knowledge, indicating that it draws on the black/white racial distinction with regard to what is personally meaningful, but not as clearly as does Rosa Parks. We believe that the greater knowledge by African Americans in the Hemings case is real, though in some cases the responses are less precise in terms of identifying Jefferson's role. Furthermore, when blacks give what we consider a correct response, they are more likely to mention children than to mention only a sexual relationship. Of those giving one of the first two types of correct responses, 75 percent of black respondents mention children as against 47 percent of whites. This fits the emphasis of media directed toward African Americans, and of the family traditions of lineage connections to Jefferson.

Gender

Women are reliably more knowledgeable about Sally Hemings than are men, when age, race, and education are held constant. This gender difference corresponds to other evidence that women are more likely than men to read romantic novels like Chase-Riboud's: marketing of romance fiction heavily targets women, and representatives at several of the major romance publishing houses have indicated that their readership is mostly female (Radway 1991). We surmise, though we do not have direct evidence, that women are more interested than men in romantic films like *Jefferson in Paris*. As the images shown earlier suggest, advertising for the film and for the CBS miniseries clearly targeted the part of the public interested in the romance genre.

Generation

The first popular treatment of a Jefferson-Hemings liaison was the novel by Chase-Riboud published in 1979, while the most recent attention beyond scholarly writing was in the 1998 *Nature* article on the DNA evidence. It makes sense that we found younger Americans to be less knowledgeable than older Americans, largely due to much less knowledge by the youngest cohorts that reached adulthood after some of the media attention had subsided in the 1990s. At the same time, the oldest cohorts, born before World War II, were also low in knowledge of Hemings. Older respondents probably "missed" the flurry of attention to a Jefferson-Hemings relationship, having been in early adulthood when Jefferson's fame as a statesman and intellectual figure was predominant in shaping collective memory of him. These results are also consistent with findings reported in chapters 4 and 5 about the *critical years* of adolescence and early adulthood during which events are likely to have their greatest impact and therefore to be recalled most easily.

Qualifying answers

Many of the responses were stated in a way that suggested some qualification, whether deliberate or not, by the respondent. Of the forty responses that could be classified as "qualified," eighteen included the term "supposed" or "supposedly," as in "She was a slave of Jefferson and supposedly bore him children." Other forms of qualification were also employed: "apparently" (three cases); "allegedly" (three cases); "rumored" (three cases); "some think" (two cases); "reportedly" (two cases); plus one case each for: "possibly," "speculated," "suspected," "so they say," "they figured," "thought to be," "probably, "may also," and "controversy over."

Two contrasts that bring out the importance of these verbal qualifications are the answers about the names Christa McAuliffe and Mohammad Atta in table 2.1 The identity of Christa McAuliffe was never an issue in the 1986 *Challenger* disaster, and it is not surprising that there is not a single qualification in the 306 responses coded correct for her name. For Mohammad Atta the case is not quite so clear, for if he had survived the crash of the plane he piloted, he might have faced a trial in the United States, just as Khalid Shaikh Mohammed has been slated to do for his alleged role in the 9/11 attacks and other terrorist plots. However, Americans have been given little if any reason to doubt Atta's role as a terrorist in the World Trade Center destruction, and of the 228 answers coded as correct for his name, only five indicated any qualification at all (four used the word "alleged" and one the word "perhaps"). Thus the qualifications introduced for "Sally Hemings" are quite different from the stance taken toward either of these two comparison names and allow for the possibility of some uncertainty about the Hemings-Jefferson relationship.

Conclusions

What can we learn about an alleged relationship two hundred years ago between a famous American leader and his slave? Using the modern science of genetics, the relationship itself has now been documented through a direct tie to that leader's lineage, and then with the use of modern statistical analysis of dates of conception and birth, a closer connection to the leader himself has been further supported. A different but also relatively modern approach to assessing public knowledge—the sample survey—allows us to go from undefined statements about "public opinion" to a much more delimited estimate of collective knowledge and therefore of the roots of collective memory about this same relationship. In order to speak of the memory shared by members of a collectivity—whether explicitly or in the vague terms that are frequently employed—we need first to discover whether there is some degree of "collective knowledge."

Precision need not be claimed for our estimates in this study, but we can state with some confidence that roughly one out of ten Americans knew something about the alleged Jefferson-Hemings relationship at the time of our inquiry, with many but not all such people believing it to be factual. Complete precision is theoretically impossible because our estimate of knowledge—and indeed of memory as well—depends on exactly how inquiries are phrased and what cues are provided. For example, if we had started from general questions about Jefferson's attitudes or even about his children, we might have obtained little or no evidence concerning Sally Hemings. But if we had mentioned to respondents a Jefferson-Hemings relationship and asked if they remembered hearing about it at all, our estimate of knowledge would almost certainly have been higher, even discounting false affirmative replies. Our assessment of knowledge is anchored to the questions we asked, which provided respondents with a full name and asked them to identify it in some way. Fortunately, we are able to compare the identification of the name Sally Hemings with the identification of each of ten other names, so in an important sense we were able to control for the nature of the task respondents faced, and our conclusion is based on this comparison more than on the absolute percentage of answers scored as correct.

When the Brodie biography was published in 1974, it was widely considered a scandalous attack on Jefferson's reputation, especially by those who had invested their own reputations in stressing both his genius and his integrity. Yet the recent biography by Meacham (2012) suggests that Jefferson's reputation has been affected little if at all by the evidence of a secret sexual relationship with his slave. In fact, it may even have served to humanize the third president for readers today, especially as writings and films portray (whether correctly or not) the relationship as romantic in nature. Cross-racial sexual relationships, in or out of marriage, are increasingly widely accepted, and in that sense—though of course only if the context of slavery can be ignored—the third president can be seen as a fuller and more interesting human being because of his relationship with Sally Hemings.

We can also be confident that knowledge about Sally Hemings is a function of educational level, broadly conceived, and we have persuasive evidence that in this particular case African Americans are more knowledgeable than white Americans, and that the same is true of women as compared with men. As these relations suggest, the Americans most likely to be able to identify Sally Hemings are more educated women who are themselves African Americans.[2] Finally, we have some evidence that knowledge of Sally Hemings is greatest among Americans who were reaching early adulthood when the Jefferson-Hemings relationship was being publicized in the form of revisionist biographies, novels, and films, and then further bolstered by one of the major achievements of contemporary science, evidence based on DNA analysis.

Of course, as the evidence enters American history textbooks and other resources like websites, it may become better known to young people who are encouraged as part of their schooling to read about Jefferson—or about a related topic such as slavery in America. One of the indirect but important consequences of the Jefferson-Hemings collective memory is the interest it has stimulated in slavery at Monticello and in slavery in the United States more generally, including the manifold results of "sex across the color line" (Rothman 2003). At the same time, a careful review of the words respondents used in their replies about Sally Hemings suggests that for nearly half of those who gave answers that we considered to be correct, there was at least some sense that there is not complete certainty that Thomas Jefferson was the father of her children.

Collective memories can certainly be studied in contexts other than individual memories and verbalizations. Some of the books cited in references here and others not cited can be thought of as cultural vehicles carrying and promoting collective memories. Discussions back and forth by scholars interested in Jefferson, Hemings, Monticello, slavery, and related matters also contribute to collective memories of Thomas Jefferson and Sally Hemings and their probable relationship. As described earlier, encyclopedias and websites are important vehicles for transmitting collective memories to many readers, and they are no doubt drawn on by those writing textbooks and popular books and articles that in turn

---

2. The relations appear to be additive, rather than reflecting interactions.

become further vehicles for communicating such memories to other readers young and old. Jefferson's visage at Mount Rushmore offers a still different kind of vivid stimulus to collective memory for those who travel to that remote national memorial in South Dakota, whether or not they know much about him as president. Regular tours to Monticello expose bus loads of visitors to mentions of Sally Hemings by guides who to a greater or lesser extent are interested in discussing her.

There is also more and more writing about Jefferson and slavery, much of it focusing on Jefferson's racial attitudes and beliefs. For example, Finkelman (1996) emphasizes statements and actions by Jefferson that reflect a crude form of racism, as well as his reluctance later in life to take any serious action that would lead toward substantial emancipation either at Monticello or nationally. Finkelman also argues against Wilson's (1992) attempt to characterize criticism of Jefferson's behavior as an example of "presentism"—the application of present-day ideas and values anachronistically to the time and place in which Jefferson was born and lived. Jefferson's thinking about both race and slavery is compared unfavorably by Finkelman to that of George Washington and even more pointedly to that of Edward Coles, a younger neighbor and friend of Jefferson's—both living in approximately the same time and place. An equally critical reading of Jefferson's equivocations on slavery was provided earlier by Davis (1975) in the context of his broad treatment of slavery during the age of the American Revolution.

We should keep in mind that none of this addresses Jefferson's other major achievements as president and his role in setting forth fundamental values of freedom of conscience and the separation of church and state. Collective memory of Jefferson includes more than is dealt with in this chapter. In addition, even if Jefferson was not capable of applying his equalitarian ideas to his black slaves, or to blacks generally, those ideas and his commitment to government by consent of the governed (as he defined them) have been seen as providing the basis for crucial later developments in American thought and law by others (Rakove 1999). For example, Maier (1997) describes how the Declaration of Independence contributed to ending slave systems in Northern states in the first decades after independence, and even prompted some moves toward a form of emancipation in the South, though on the assumption that freed slaves would be colonized outside the country. In drafting the Declaration of Independence, Jefferson helped to weaken the institution of slavery in many parts of the world—though paradoxically, not at Monticello.

Another Woman from American History: Ann Rutledge

Spurred by our study of Sally Hemings, we included in a later survey in February and March 2010 a similar question about knowledge of Ann Rutledge, often regarded as Abraham Lincoln's first and truest love. In addition to the fact that her name had nothing to do with race or slavery, an important difference from the Jefferson-Hemings relationship is that the Rutledge-Lincoln story flourished in the 1920s and 1930s as a result of biographies of Lincoln by Carl Sandburg (1926) and others, as well as being prominent in early films, notably *Young Mr. Lincoln* in 1939 and *Abe Lincoln in Illinois* in 1940. Therefore, we expected those who could identify Ann Rutledge to be from older cohorts, in contrast to the younger or middle-aged cohorts who could identify Sally Hemings.

Despite the importance of Rutledge's name in many earlier popular treatments of Lincoln's life, far fewer Americans in 2009 could identify her name than that of Sally Hemings. Only five respondents out of 585 in our February/March national sample were able to provide a reasonably correct identification of Rutledge. Another two responses could be coded as partially correct, and if the two numbers are added together we get a total of just 1 percent of Americans who had anything at all relevant to say about Ann Rutledge. Hence the name of the woman believed by some to have been Abraham Lincoln's deepest love is recognized by many fewer Americans today than the name of Thomas Jefferson's slave whose identity returned to public knowledge only in recent years.

Moreover, while Hemings is best known to younger, though not the very youngest, cohorts, Rutledge is best known to the oldest people in our sample, all of whom were born during or before the 1940s. Thus the two names reflect entirely different pictures in terms of generational knowledge, consistent with evidence provided by Schwartz (2005) about the decline of references to Rutledge in periodicals and newspapers through the 1940s and 1950s.

Standing back from the particular issue of the Jefferson-Hemings relationship, and of that involving Lincoln and Ann Rutledge, we see that the goal of assessing collective knowledge is important to virtually all studies of collective memory. Whether one's focus is directly on the memories of groups of ordinary individuals, or primarily on elite claims made in the form of speeches, texts, or other symbols, it is difficult to study collective memory without making assumptions, explicit or implicit, about what a public or some part of a public knows. In their discussion of the new sociology of knowledge, Swidler and Arditi (1994: 307) regard collective memory as a process in which "knowledge is transmitted through time." Such transmission must allow for the possibility that ordinary individuals can influence the content or emphasis of that knowledge by ignoring, resisting, or using it for some unintended purpose. Even individuals who are not in positions of power can put to use knowledge and narratives about the past in ways that belie the notion of passive "consumers."

THREE

Abraham Lincoln: "Honest Abe" versus "the Great Emancipator"

Lincoln's name is so familiar that the complexity of the real person is difficult to bear in mind. The son of an unlettered farmer in the upper South, he regarded his early life as nothing more than "the short and simple annals of the poor" (Gray [1750] 1944: 42–46). "That's my life, and that's all you or anyone else can make of it," he once said (Donald 1995: 19). Lincoln had almost no formal education, but he read widely from childhood through his adult life, not only history and politics but literature, science, and mathematics as well. Thus he represents in the most literal sense a "self-made man." This trait, together with his life-long reputation for personal honesty and compassion, contributes to the image of Lincoln as a "folk hero" (Schwartz 2000).

At the same time, by the year of his assassination Lincoln had also become, in Schwartz's words, an "epic hero," as both the "Savior of the Union" and "the Great Emancipator," though these two sides were emphasized at different points in his presidency and by different groups over later years. According to Foner (2010: 335),

At the time of his death and for years thereafter, Lincoln was remembered primarily as the Great Emancipator. Not until the turn of the century, when the process of (white) reconciliation was far advanced, would Americans forget or suppress the centrality of slavery and emancipation to the war experience. Lincoln would then be transformed into a symbol of national unity, and the Gettysburg Address, which did not explicitly mention slavery, would, in popular memory, supplant the Emancipation Proclamation as the greatest embodiment of his ideas. More recently, we have returned to the insight Lincoln offered in the second inaugural: slavery was the war's cause and emancipation its most profound outcome.

The use of the Lincoln Memorial as a setting for important civil rights gatherings in the twentieth century—from Marian Anderson's concert in 1939 to Martin Luther King's "I Have a Dream" speech in 1963—has helped to keep Lincoln still relevant in terms of present-day racial issues; indeed, he is widely regarded as a forerunner of the civil rights movement of the second half of the twentieth century.

All these sides of Lincoln are represented at the level of cultural history by a multitude of different books (for example, Carl Sandburg's six volumes [1926] and Michael Burlingame's massive two volumes [2008]); by many films, such as Steven Spielberg's *Lincoln* (2012), with a number of others that purport to cover Lincoln's early life—for example, John Ford's *Young Mr. Lincoln* (1939) and *Abe Lincoln in Illinois* (1940) based on Robert Sherwood's Pulitzer Prize–winning play of the same name (1938); by memorial sites that include not only the most famous one in Washington, but also others at his presumed birthplace and still others marking his later adult years in Illinois (Schwartz 2008, appendix G, pp. 291–294); and by musical tributes such as Aaron Copland's *Lincoln Portrait* (1942), written as part of a World War II patriotic effort.

Valuable as these cultural representations are, we wished to understand as well what the American public remembers at present about Lincoln as a person and as a president, and whether the memories vary depending on how we inquire about them. For this purpose, we designed an experiment that asked what Americans can learn from thinking about Lincoln, with the inquiry posed in two somewhat different ways.

A Question Framing Experiment on Beliefs about Lincoln

The experiment called for obtaining collective memories of Lincoln, but with versions of the question framed differently (Goffman 1974). One frame focused on what Lincoln *did* as president, while the other frame emphasized his personal *life*:

Did question: Abraham Lincoln is one of the past Presidents we sometimes hear about. Is there any lesson you think we can draw from what Lincoln did or said during his lifetime?

Life question: Abraham Lincoln is one of the past Presidents we sometimes hear about. Is there any lesson you think we can draw from Lincoln's life?

The two questions were administered to a national cross-section sample of 398 Americans in February/March 2010. The "Did" question was asked to a random half of the sample, and the "Life" question asked to the other half. Such a randomized "split sample" design can tell us whether the two questions produce a difference in memories of Lincoln beyond what might occur due to chance ("sampling error").[1]

The experiment produced a highly reliable difference between the two versions, indicating that how we remember Lincoln depends on how we frame the question. The Did question yielded many more responses about Lincoln's presidential achievements, primarily "Emancipation" and secondarily "Saving the Union," while the Life question led to many more answers characterizing Lincoln in terms of folk attributes such as "Honest Abe" or "Self-made Man." We treat the two questions as distinguishing between two types of belief that reflect fundamentally different aspects of identity: observable presidential accomplishments such as Emancipation (the Did question), and essential personal characteristics such as honesty (the Life question).[2]

Since the original sample was small and the difference in framing had been based on what might best be considered a theoretical hunch, we decided to repeat the comparison with a fresh national sample in October 2010 in order to have greater confidence in the results. Using an entirely new cross-section sample of 509 Americans, we again obtained a highly reliable difference between the two question frames in the same direction as earlier, a difference that in the new survey could have occurred by chance much less than once in one thousand such experimental tests. Given this very successful replication, we treat the Did versus Life distinction as real and of some importance.

1. The vehicle for our questions was the SRC monthly survey, which included the questions in February, March, and October 2010. For more details on sampling and response rates, see Schuman, Corning, and Schwartz (2012).

2. In an earlier report of this analysis we used concepts developed by Garfinkel (1956) and then further by Katz (1975), with the theoretical distinction discussed here phrased as being between "essence" and "action" (Readers interested in this conceptualization, mainly developed by Barry Schwartz, should see Schuman, Corning, and Schwartz 2012).

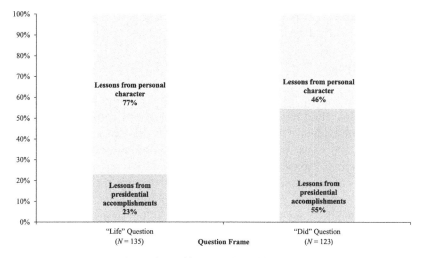

3.1   Percentages naming lessons learned from Lincoln by different question frames
(SRC October 2010)

Omitting minor responses that do not differ due to the framing of
the question, the basic distinction in results is shown in figure 3.1 and
is clear-cut and striking: a more than 30-percentage-point difference in
the images of Lincoln elicited by the two frames. The experiment indicates that how Lincoln is remembered today by individuals is by no
means fixed, but depends on how the inquiry about him is phrased.
The research shows that variation in framing—whether the question focuses on Lincoln's personal characteristics such as honesty, or on his
accomplishments as president such as ending slavery—changes collective memory of him substantially. Both types of memories are real, but
which is brought to mind differs importantly when we ask individuals
what they remember, and indeed the same may be true in terms of cultural representations as writers and artists approach Lincoln with different frames or emphases in mind.

Historical Context as Framing Memory of Lincoln

Question wording is only one source of framing that can influence collective memories of a historical figure. The shifting social context is another source of framing, with the effects reflected in change over time in
the way an important figure is remembered. We have evidence of *both*

long-term and short-term change in memories of Lincoln as a result of what can be thought of as historical framing or historical context.

Long-term change

As part of an earlier investigation, we drew on a Gallup question first asked in 1945, then repeated by Gallup in 2001. The comparison over time yielded evidence that folk responses had decreased substantially over the fifty-six-year period (Schwartz and Schuman 2005; Schwartz 2008). Although the wording of the Gallup question stressed Lincoln's greatness as a president, it asked respondents to explain their belief in Lincoln's greatness, and the comparison over time held that wording constant. The decrease over half a century in folk responses, especially "self-made man," was both appreciable and reliable.

We do not have results over the same lengthy time period for our new questions about "lessons learned" from Lincoln, but birth cohort can be used as an indirect indicator of effects due to learning about Lincoln at different points in time: older cohorts had learned about Lincoln in earlier years, younger cohorts in more recent years. When we hold constant education, gender, and race (white/black), a comparison of results for different birth cohorts shows that older respondents gave more answers about personal character than did younger respondents, and the opposite was true for presidential accomplishments. This indirect replication of the Gallup results indicates that responses of older Americans in 2010 tended to include a greater proportion of folk images of Lincoln than did responses of younger Americans, and to include a smaller proportion of images of an epic nature ("savior of the nation," "great emancipator.") For younger Americans the trends were in the opposite direction. The two ways of examining long-term historical change—the Gallup over-time results and the comparison of birth cohorts at a single point in time—lead to the same conclusion.

Media images over time

In order to consider further evidence of historical change in collective memory of Lincoln, we counted the frequency with which two major images of Lincoln—"Honest Abe" and the "Great Emancipator"—appeared in *New York Times* articles published between 1941 and 2005. Both images of Lincoln have persisted over time, though the Great Emancipator predominates. The largest divergence in attention to the two images occurred at the height of the civil rights movement, when representations of the Great Emancipator symbolized the ideal of racial equality, and far outstripped characterizations of Lincoln as Honest Abe.

The timing of this civil rights era divergence corresponds well to the cohort differences found in our data: individuals born between 1915 and 1952, whose youth and socialization occurred mainly prior to the height of the civil rights movement, tended to think in terms of Lincoln's personal character, but for those who came of age during or after the civil rights movement, his presidential accomplishments were most salient. Thus the findings using content analysis of the *New York Times* are consistent with the survey results.

Short-term change

Separately, we also found evidence of change in characterizations of Lincoln over a much shorter time period because of an immediate political context. Earlier we reported that our main results were similar in February/March and then later in October of the same year, but in the course of further analysis we also noted a change during that eight-month period in the relative proportions of two distinct "folk" characterizations of Lincoln. The Honest response nearly doubled in size over that relatively brief period (from 20 percent to 37 percent), and the Self-made Man response decreased by a little more than half (from 14 percent to 6 percent)—all without altering the basic differences by question framing that we have already reported and discussed. This additional difference over time *within* 2010 is quite large and highly reliable. A major event that occurred during this eight-month period was the midterm national election campaign that reached its peak during the time our October data were gathered. The increase in attributions of Honest to Lincoln seemed to be connected to the heavily negative nature of the national political campaign in October 2010, just before the congressional election when the Tea Party movement first showed its strength.

We classified all mentions of Lincoln's Honesty in terms of whether they also alluded to the honesty or dishonesty of politics in 2010. Of the twenty-four responses that referred in any way to contemporary politics, every single one carried a clear negative emphasis on the election campaign (e.g., "At least he [Lincoln] was honest in his opinions unlike the ones [politicians] we have now—they just tell you what they think you want to hear.") Crucially, the difference in negative mentions of present-day politics between the February/March and October time points is highly reliable, evidence for a relation to the 2010 election campaign.

This therefore appears to be an instance where events in the immediate present serve as a further frame for memories of the distant past. As public trust erodes, people seem to place a premium on honesty (Hetherington 1998; see also Sztompka 2000). The immediate political context can thus evoke contrasting images of "Honest Abe." As Eric Foner has noted: "History, it has been said, is what the present chooses to remember about the past" (2010: 71).

Conclusions about Framing Effects on Memories of Lincoln

Collective memory of Lincoln is not fixed but varies along three different dimensions. First, the content of collective memories of Lincoln has evolved over a period of years, probably in response to changing social contexts and values, even while remaining positive in implication and tone over that same period. Lincoln was seen more as a folk hero in earlier decades of the twentieth century, but his status as the Great Emancipator was reinforced as he became connected to the civil rights movement during the century's second half.

Second, collective memory also changed in terms of content that was emphasized, at least temporarily, when a political campaign spotlighted a particular personal trait, as seems to have occurred with Lincoln's reputation for honesty during the 2010 U.S. national midterm election. Although the effect may not be lasting, it points to the importance of timing relative to specific political contexts when assessing collective memory. From a methodological standpoint, such a temporary spike or dip is also important in showing why replication is needed: not simply to avoid having taken seriously a result due to chance, but to distinguish a longer-term trend from an unusual substantive happenstance.

Finally, and perhaps most important of all, how we frame our inquiry can produce the large difference we show in figure 3.1 between what Lincoln achieved in his official role—Lincoln as president—and what he was like as an individual—Lincoln as a person (folk hero). Both of the frames we used in our questions were perfectly reasonable ways of inquiring about Lincoln, but they elicit fundamentally different collective memories of the sixteenth president.

These individual-level variations in collective memories of Americans probably affect the cultural resources that sustain collective memory as well. The connection of Lincoln to civil rights in the 1960s enhanced the importance of the Lincoln Memorial, which in turn quite likely further increased public interest in Lincoln. At the same time, the various centennial celebrations devoted to Lincoln prompted more reading and learning about him. Although it is useful to distinguish between cultural and individual levels of analysis with a figure like Lincoln, or indeed with any other symbol, we need to recognize that cultural resources and individuals' beliefs are interdependent and that *both* contribute to collective memory. To omit either element as a focus of study is to truncate our understanding.

The pivotal figures from American history considered in chapters 1, 2, and 3—Christopher Columbus, Thomas Jefferson and Sally Hemings, and Abraham Lincoln—are represented in innumerable books, monuments, commemorations, and other reflections of collective memory. We have drawn on these cultural representations, but in addition we have introduced a different and at least equally important perspective: that of the people who receive, are influenced by, and further shape and transmit collective memories.

Public memory is affected not only by historical time and the different sociopolitical contexts and other influences it reflects, but also by such basic social structural factors as education, gender, and race. And in the case of Lincoln, we found that seemingly small variations in the framing of questions can illuminate important differences in memories. Each of these factors or conditions can be seen as influencing the repertoire of cultural images and knowledge available to individuals. We have seen evidence of shifts in memories of Sally Hemings, Ann Rutledge, and Lincoln himself in response to changes in the information available to or resonant with the public.

Often, though, we found collective memories to be relatively stable. Especially for Jefferson, we saw that historians and others concerned with cultural representations and the reputations of historical figures may greatly overestimate the extent to which the general public is familiar with information and is aware of controversy vital to specialists. Our initial 1998 research on memory of Columbus indicated that revisionist controversies so vigorous among activists and historians were hardly visible among much of the public. Moreover, in the case of Columbus different ways of framing questions did not greatly change Americans' picture of his actions—he continued to be seen primarily as the "discoverer of America."

In this sense, collective memories created over a number of earlier years can survive for a considerable time what seem to be highly publicized assaults by committed opponents of the past views. The images of historical figures that are absorbed in childhood, adolescence, and early adulthood (and further reinforced through commemorations and other "rehearsals") appear to persist throughout later life, and it thus can take a generation or more before change in a central and widespread collective memory is discernible. Indeed, another important discovery was that more recently, the collective memory of Columbus did appear to move in a less heroic and more villainous direction, probably due to shifts in school textbooks and teaching, and perhaps in the mass media as well. This finding indicates that cohort replacement—rather than new learning by those brought up in an earlier era—is the major way in which change in collective memory occurs. Only with systematic empirical research that varies time, social and political settings, how questions are framed, and other factors important in shaping memories can we discover what varies reliably and what remains little changed.

The Critical Years and Other Sources of Collective Memory

That each generation receives an imprint from the social and political events of its youth is an old idea, most often associated today with the name of Karl Mannheim ([1928] 1952). We draw on Mannheim's cogent ideas, first, because they link objective and subjective worlds in a way valuable for the description of collective memories of past events. Second, his ideas encourage systematic investigation of what we call the *critical years* hypothesis.

The underlying notion is expressed well by Robert Wohl (1979: 210), author of *The Generation of 1914*:

What is essential to the formation of generational consciousness is some common frame of reference that provides a sense of rupture with the past and that will later distinguish the members of the generation from those who follow them in time. This frame of reference is always derived from great historical events like wars, revolutions, plagues, famines, and economic crises, because it is great historical events like these that supply the markers and signposts with which people impose order on their past and link their individual fates with those of the communities in which they live.

We would modify Wohl's statement to include unexpected traumatic events such as the assassination of John F. Kennedy that have a strong impact on many individuals at the time, even though their long-term consequences may be less visible than those of wars or revolutions. There are also events that may not have appeared "great" initially—for example, the post–World War II change in the U.S. birth rate implied by the term "baby boomers"—but that at a later point are recognized as important. Furthermore, Wohl writes in terms of "generational consciousness," but our approach makes no assumptions about subjective awareness of belonging to a generation, since we identify generations using birth cohorts and define generational membership through the events that individuals remember as especially important.

FOUR

The Critical Years Hypothesis: The Idea and the Evidence

Mannheim stressed that generations do not result simply from the biological rhythm of human existence, but rather from "the historical dimension of the social process" ([1928] 1952: 290)—what Alwin and McCammon refer to as "the unique intersection of biography and history" (2007: 226). Were it not for historical change, there would only be, in T. S. Eliot's (1952) blunt words, "birth, copulation, and death." Belonging to a generation endows each of us with a place in the historical process, and this in turn exposes us (and limits us) to a particular range of experience, thought, and action. However, where novel events are rare and change is slow, as in traditional peasant societies, distinct generations may not appear. Only where events occur in such a manner as to demarcate a birth cohort—"persons born in the same time interval and aging together" (Ryder 1965: 844)—in terms of its "historical-social" consciousness, should we speak of a true generation. We will ordinarily use the term "cohort," implying "birth cohort," to specify what Mannheim called a generation, though we occasionally employ that term also.[1]

1. The meaning of "generation" is sometimes limited by demographers to lineage relationships, but here we accept the wider social and cultural meaning assumed by Mannheim. Although the word "generation" has varied meanings, the term "cohort" indicates an exact year or span of years.

To explain the importance of generations, Mannheim carried out a useful "thought experiment" (Cohen 2005). First, distinctive patterns are produced by the nature of generational transition and could not occur if a cohort lived forever without replacement. Since in real life, cohort replacement does occur regularly, new cultural developments are accomplished by new cohorts that have "fresh contact" with the past cultural accumulation. This leads to some loss of older cultural content, in addition to new assessments of novel events. Moreover, crucial to what we call the *critical years* concept is what Mannheim refers to as "the stratification of experience." Although older and younger cohorts may experience the same new event (for example, the beginning of a major war), they do so differently because "first experiences" are not the same as those superimposed upon other impressions. For example, the weeks leading up to the 1991 Gulf War probably seemed different to those Americans who had lived through the Vietnam War than to younger Americans who had not experienced Vietnam when it occurred. Hence the importance of what Wohl (1979: 75) called "the noncontemporaneity of contemporaries."

According to Mannheim ([1928] 1952: 300), "at the point where personal experimentation with life begins—round about the age of 17, sometimes a little earlier and sometimes a little later"—a distinctive new generation is formed. The active questioning and reflection that occur at this point take the form of experiencing "life's problems" as located in the present, and it is this sense of participation in the present that contributes to the development of a new generation. Using language learning as his model, Mannheim saw generational formation as ending at the age of twenty-five because, according to one linguist (Meillet 1911), "the spoken language and dialect does not change in an individual after the age of 25 years" (Mannheim ([1928] 1952: 300). Thus the ages of seventeen to twenty-five represented for Mannheim the critical age range when "present problems" become the focus for young people, while "the older generation cling to the re-orientation that had been the drama of *their* youth" (301).

The seventeen-to-twenty-five age range that Mannheim delineated for Germany in the 1920s should not be reified, but it points in an approximate way to an important developmental period that includes adolescence and early adulthood in many societies. That sense of participation in the present may be particularly characteristic of adolescence and early adulthood because individuals at that point in the life course are "old enough to participate directly in the movements impelled by change, but not old enough to have become committed to an occupation, a residence, a family of procreation, or a way of life" (Ryder 1965: 848). However, an expansion of Mannheim's upper boundary seems appropriate because many of the social indicators of the transition to adulthood—completion of education, marriage, the birth of children—occur later now than they did a century ago (Furstenberg 2000), pointing to a possible extension of adolescence and young adulthood as a developmental period. At the same time, the exposure of young children to events through the Internet and television suggests a younger age than seventeen as a lower boundary. With these changes in mind, we extended the range that defines the critical years to ages ten to thirty, though the temporal boundaries are necessarily somewhat arbitrary. We will see later that there is sometimes a compelling reason to extend a boundary still further in one direction or the other for a particular event.[2]

We treat "event" as the main unit of historical experience for individuals when they consider the past. An event may be either quite specific (the September 11, 2001, terrorist attack on the United States), or a "compound event" that lasts over a period of time and is made up of a number of distinguishable sub-events, but is regarded later for most purposes by most people as a singularity—for example, "World War II," which included "Pearl Harbor, "the Battle of the Bulge," "Hiroshima," and other sub-events that may be recalled separately by some respondents.

Sewell (2005: 228) restricts the term "historical event" to "(1) a ramified sequence of occurrences that (2) is recognized as notable by contemporaries, and that (3) results in a durable transformation of structures." This definition fits some of what we call events, at least in the eyes of most people. Yet some events that many commentators might characterize as "transformative" at the time—for example, the 9/11 attack on the United States in 2001—leave the lives of much of the public little changed once their immediate involvement as observers has ended after a few days or weeks. Such events do not bring immediate change to society, even though they can change the course of history profoundly; for

2. Mannheim also assumed that youth in two very different societies (e.g., Germany and China) are not part of the same generation. However, the great increase in the speed with which information (and misinformation) can be transmitted around the globe means that a mass event in one society can have repercussions for or stimulate a related event in another distant society. At the same time, groups that differ in ethnicity, gender, or social class within a single society can experience the same event very differently. Mannheim's qualification about the distinctive nature of generations in different societies no longer holds in the way he had assumed.

example, the Kennedy assassination may have affected both American involvement in the Vietnam War and domestic civil rights legislation and actions. Events like 9/11 and the Kennedy assassination are surely transformative in many respects, but not in the sense of quickly transforming the social institutions within which most individuals in the United States live their daily lives. We prefer to think of events as on a continuum of importance, and to use the additional word "transformative" when the everyday lives of a large part of the general public within or across national boundaries are changed in long-lasting ways, as may well have been the case in Lithuania during World War II and its immediate aftermath, and again when the country regained independence in 1990–1991, as we discuss at a later point.

Ordinarily in our research we do not face the problem of how to define and delimit remembered historical events, because we accept the concepts reported by respondents as "especially important," for example, "World War II" or "Vietnam" or the "moon landing." We can also consider sub-events presented to us by some respondents as distinct—for example, Pearl Harbor or Hiroshima. An "event" for us is ultimately what is perceived and defined by the public, not by historians (Le Goff 1992), though of course the two may well coincide.

The Logic of the Critical Years Hypothesis

Our hypothesis states that individuals who were in their critical years when an event occurred are more likely to remember the event as important than are those from earlier or later birth cohorts. For example, Americans who were between the ages of ten and thirty during the Vietnam War (1965–1973) are expected to recall it as especially important at a later time in their lives—more so than those who were alive but at different ages at the time. Our goal in later pages of this chapter is to consider evidence that bears on the critical years hypothesis for understanding the creation of generational memories, while also taking into account competing interpretations of the same evidence.

The basis of the critical years hypothesis is straightforward. First, most people will tend *not* to know well or keep readily in mind events that *preceded* their own lifetime or occurred during very early childhood. As Mannheim ([1928] 1952: 296) stated, only knowledge "personally gained in real situations . . . sticks," and thus even important events (such as World War II) that occurred in the years before birth or during infancy or early childhood will not have registered as clearly as events directly experienced. They therefore should be less often recalled.[3]

Second, only as children approach adolescence do they usually begin to appreciate events beyond their own family and immediate neighborhood. At exactly what age this occurs is likely to depend on both the nature of the event and the aptitude and interests of the child. An example of the combination of a profound event and a young but precocious mind was historian David McCullough's recollection (in an interview on the *Charlie Rose* show, March 21, 2008):

My brother had taken me to the theater. . . . I was eight. And we came out of the theater and there was a crowd gathered and they were all excited because the word had come that Pearl Harbor had been attacked. And it was my first, the first experience that I remember of a world outside my own life, of something happening beyond the realm of our neighborhood and my family.

Many children might not at such an early age and in a less excited setting have been so aware of the dramatic start of U.S. involvement in World War II, no matter its objective significance. However, we will see later that some events can indeed have an impact on children's memories well before the age of seventeen suggested by Mannheim.

Third, we expect there to be a primacy effect for most people, so that the *first* large event experienced as very significant will tend to remain important throughout life. The tendency for what was learned first to carry disproportionate weight is captured in extreme form by David Hume (1795–1796, vol. 5, p. 397), writing long ago:

It was remarked, that no physician in Europe, who has reached forty years of age, ever . . . adopted [William] Harvey's doctrine of the circulation of the blood, and that Harvey's practice in London diminished extremely from the reproach drawn upon by that final discovery.

---

3. It is difficult to specify the earliest age at which children are likely to be affected by national and world events, but we will ordinarily not expect a national or world event to be recalled later in life by those who were much below the age of ten when it occurred. At a still earlier age, what is called childhood or infantile amnesia is thought to leave even personal events from around four years of age or earlier rarely remembered in later years (Hayne and Jack 2011). There is no exact agreement on the age or nature of "childhood amnesia," probably because of variation in both individuals and events. In addition, it is important to recognize that both event and cohort dates are necessarily approximate (for example, World War II only began for Americans near the end of 1941), but this imprecision does not seriously affect our main conclusions.

Hume's example is certainly unusual, but evidence of the general importance of primacy effects dates from the earliest years of experimental psychology on learning (Bower 2000), and order effects within the question-answer process have long been important to survey methodology (e.g., Cantril 1944). Tulving (2008) goes so far as to speak in broad terms of a Law of Primacy, which we draw on at a later point.

The quotations from McCullough and Hume frame our hypothesis about generations and memories: national and world events that occur *between* early adolescence (or even earlier, as in the case of McCullough at age eight) and the later twenties (or even into the thirties in the case of Harvey's discovery) are most likely to have a lasting impact on individual memories. Moreover, if we put together the thrust of the preceding propositions, we are led to a crucial prediction. For *intermediate events* that are neither early nor late with respect to the full range of birth cohorts in a population, we anticipate a curvilinear shape to the distribution of memories. Such an event from the middle of the cohort range will appear relatively less important to those who are oldest because of the primacy for them of still earlier events. An intermediate event will also seem less important to those who are youngest because they did not directly experience the event, but learned about it later and in other ways. The apex of the curve should help in defining the critical years, with the decline from the peak gradual on both sides of the distribution.[4]

Contemporaneous versus later experience

We recognize that for most Americans, personal experience even of contemporaneous national and world events is not direct in any strict sense, but occurs mainly through media reports. However, there is a fundamental difference between contemporaneous and later media experience: the outcome is uncertain in the former case but not in the latter. When President Kennedy was shot in 1963 there were immediate anxious questions about both the cause of his assassination and its ramifications. Learning about that same event some years later—even from watching the identical images of the shooting—does not raise the same urgent questions, and therefore is not likely to have as deep and lasting an emotional impact. Moreover, an unfolding event like the assassination or 9/11 stimulates "rehearsals"—intense thinking and conversations with others (Pennebaker and Gonzales 2009) that should also enhance

---

4. Our interpretations of the graphical evidence are supported by statistical testing of the critical years effect (see appendix C, p. 223, for a description of the tests).

memory (Baddeley 1990). Thus for events that capture immediate public attention, most of those alive at the time should have acquired, and should retain, stronger memories than those who came afterward, no matter how much the latter are exposed to the same events in school or films or in other ways. An event learned about some time after it occurred is *not* the same event as it was immediately after it happened.

The Standard Events Question

It is impractical to study in detail the formation of a generation in the distant past—for example, through the collective memories of the American Revolution by Americans in the eighteenth century—although historians attempt to do so by using whatever documents are available (for example, Young [1999], about the Boston Tea Party in 1773). Here we choose to consider collective memories of events from the past eighty years in order to discover their pervasiveness in an accessible population and their relations to basic divisions like birth cohort. The assumption behind this part of our investigation is that the national and world events that come to mind as especially important in response to a very general question about the past are those that had a large impact on respondents.

We have used an open-ended question to define a period of time that includes the entire lives of the oldest members of a general population interviewed, with younger members having required other forms of learning (e.g., schooling, conversations with parents, media accounts) to know about events that occurred in the earlier part of the time period. The task for respondents is closest to what memory psychologists call "cued recall" (Lockhart 2000), but in our research the period of recall often encompasses respondents' entire lifetimes—a much longer time span than in most studies by psychologists—and the cues were quite general: the time frame (the 1930s until "today") and the words "national and world events and changes" and "especially important."

The question first developed in 1985 by Schuman and Scott (1989), and then adapted by ourselves and others in later studies reads:

There have been a lot of national and world events and changes over the past 50 or so years—say, from about 1930 right up until today. Would you mention one or two such events or changes that seem to you to have been especially important? [IF ONLY ONE MENTION, ASK: Is there any other national or world event or change over the past 50 years that you feel was especially important?]

83

In all of our studies, the beginning point was given as 1930, yielding the fifty-five-year period used in our initial 1985 research, which was then increased as needed in later surveys (e.g., in 2009–2010, the period was defined as "the past 80 or so years.") In the 1985 survey, older respondents had lived through the Great Depression, and this continued to be true through our 2009–2010 survey, though of course such cohorts had thinned considerably by then.

We call responses obtained from our open question "mentions" or "recall" of an event, using the two terms interchangeably. It was important that the question be open-ended so that the wording would neither constrain nor stimulate any cohort effects that emerged from the investigation. No limitation was placed on the kinds of events that could be mentioned, and the interpretation of "especially important" was left entirely up to respondents. The question did not require memories of events that were personally experienced, and a young person in 2010 could nominate World War II as especially important even though it had occurred many years before her birth.

Because of the centrality of what we call the "standard Events question" to our research, we carried out a number of studies to assess both its robustness and its validity. These are described in appendix D (p. 225), and they provide evidence that variation in the form, wording, and other features of the standard Events question ordinarily did not alter results appreciably. We also note there that we find little difference between using only first mentions of an event, and using both first and second mentions.

Initial results

The events shown in table 4.1 are those mentioned as "especially important" by at least 5 percent of respondents in one or more of the eight American national samples we have available, the first from 1985 and the latest from 2009–2010.[5] The percentages represent the number of

5. Each survey is identified in table 4.1 by the organization that carried it out and the year of administration. Seven of the surveys were administered by the University of Michigan's Survey Research Center (SRC) between 1985 and 2010. (Five of these were SRC monthly surveys.) We include as well NORC's 1993 General Social Survey (GSS) at the University of Chicago, thus varying the survey organization. One of the SRC surveys (NCS 2001–2002), the large National Comorbidity Survey (Kessler et al. 2004), to which we were allowed to add our standard Events question, had its sample unexpectedly divided between those interviewed before the 9/11/2001 terrorist attack (here labeled NCS 2001–2002 Pre-9/11) and those interviewed after that date (labeled NCS 2001–2002 Post-9/11). Comparisons of the two parts by age, gender, education, and race showed a difference only in age (later respondents slightly older), but since our focus is on relations by cohort, age is

Table 4.1 Percentages of Respondents Mentioning Events as Especially Important in Eight Surveys in the United States, 1985–2010[a]

	SRC 1985 Apr–Sep 1985 N=1,410		GSS 1993 Feb–Apr 1993 N=1,606		SRC 1993 Jul–Oct 1993 N=1,189		SRC 2000–2001 Pre-9/11 Jul 2000–Jul 2001 N=3,884		SRC 2001–2002 Post-9/11 Nov 2001–Jan 2002 N=894		NCS 2001–2002 Pre-9/11 Feb 2001–Sep 2001 N=1,216		NCS 2001–2002 Post-9/11 Sep 2001–Nov 2002 N=951		SRC 2009–2010 Aug 2009–Mar 2010 N=1,595	
	(%)	Rank	(%)	Rank	(%)	Rank	(%)	Rank	(%)	Rank	(%)	Rank	(%)	Rank	(%)	Rank
Pre-1985 events																
World War II (1941–1945)	26.0	1	18.1	1	18.7	1	19.7	1	28.2	2	23.5	1	19.1	2	18.9	2
Vietnam War (1965–1973)	19.6	2	8.5	3	12.7	2	7.6	2	10.2	3	11.1	2	10.1	4	5.6	6
Moon landing (1969)[b]	4.8	4	–	–	–	–	3.7	7	1.8	7	5.8	4	3.6	6	3.7	7
Assassination of JFK (1963)	7.9	3	9.2	2	6.8	5	4.0	6	5.8	5	10.8	3	11.4	3	3.6	8
Great Depression (1930s)	5.0	5	3.6	5	3.4	6	6.7	3	9.4	4	3.9	6	2.5	8	8.9	3
Events 1985–2000[c]																
Fall of Berlin Wall (1989)[d]			–	–	11.9	3	4.6	5	0.9	8	5.3	5	2.9	7	3.1	9
Gulf War (1990–1991)			6.4	4	9.9	4	4.7	4	5.7	6	3.4	7	3.7	5	1.1	10

(continues)

Table 4.1 Percentages of Respondents Mentioning Events as Especially Important in Eight Surveys in the United States, 1985–2010[a] (continued)

	SRC 1985 Apr–Sep 1985 N=1,410		GSS 1993 Feb–Apr 1993 N=1,606		SRC 1993 Jul–Oct 1993 N=1,189		SRC 2000–2001 Pre-9/11 Jul 2000–Jul 2001 N=3,884		SRC 2001–2002 Post-9/11 Nov 2001–Jan 2002 N=894		NCS 2001–2002 Pre-9/11 Feb 2001–Sep 2001 N=1,216		NCS 2001–2002 Post-9/11 Sep 2001–Nov 2002 N=951		SRC 2009–2010 Aug 2009–Mar 2010 N=1,595	
	(%)	Rank	(%)	Rank	(%)	Rank	(%)	Rank	(%)	Rank	(%)	Rank	(%)	Rank	(%)	Rank
Events 2001 and after																
9/11 terrorist attacks (2001)									47.4	1			54.6	1	24.3	1
Iraq War (2003–2011)															7.5	4
Financial crisis (2007–2009)															5.7	5

[a]Percentages represent mentions of an event as either first or second in importance, divided by the total number of respondents; for example, 26 percent of respondents in the 1985 survey mentioned World War II as especially important. Responses are not mutually exclusive and therefore totals do not sum to 100 percent. The events listed are those mentioned by at least 5 percent of the sample in one or more years, but we omit events that cannot be precisely dated or that refer to multiple individual events over many years (civil rights, concern about nuclear weapons, communication/transportation, and computers). For this reason, we omit space exploration and the end of communism, replacing them with more clearly datable sub-events—the moon landing and the fall of the Berlin Wall. Also omitted are presidential elections (Bill Clinton and Barack Obama), since the former faded rapidly from collective memory after the 1993 survey and we do not have multiple time points for the latter.
[b]In GSS 1993 and SRC 1993, the moon landing was combined with space exploration and not coded as a separate event.
[c]Blank fields occur when a survey predated an event.
[d]In GSS 1993, the fall of the Berlin Wall was combined with end of communism and not coded as a separate event.

mentions of an event as either a first or second response, divided by the total number of respondents. In five of the eight samples, World War II was the event mentioned most often as especially important—even as late as 2001, fifty-six years after the end of that war. However, it was replaced as the most-mentioned event in three surveys done after the September 11, 2001, terrorist attacks. World War II also decreased in mentions in both 1993 surveys, soon after the dramatic collapse of the Soviet Union and ending of the Cold War, though of the events associated with those changes, we include only the clearly datable fall of the Berlin Wall in the table. Most other events listed in table 4.1 were mentioned often enough to be candidates for testing the critical years hypothesis. (The ongoing financial crisis was mentioned in the 2009–2010 survey, but at low levels; at that point the crisis was not fully recognized by the public.) We concentrate on events mentioned in more than one survey.

Major Forces Opposed to or Confounded with Critical Years Effects

Three forces other than critical years can influence recall of past events, and it can sometimes be difficult to distinguish their impact from effects of the critical years. Consider, for example, the eighty years between 1930 and 2010, the span of time specified for recall of important events in our 2009–2010 survey, which—as shown in figure 4.1—includes many events frequently mentioned in that and earlier surveys.

Event importance

In principle, respondents might consider all events that anyone would judge to be important, and then choose from among them on some objective basis. However, if an omniscient evaluation of "event importance" were the *only* force affecting memory, we would not expect recall to show any relation to birth cohort in a national population: the event's importance should be the same for all cohorts.

---

effectively controlled in our analyses. Thus we have treated the division as having created two separate subsamples. All other surveys were based on independent probability samples, with the GSS and NCS face-to-face, the others by telephone; the distinction for our types of questions has not been shown to produce important differences in results (Holbrook, Green, and Krosnick 2003). (For further details on the surveys, see Schuman and Corning 2012). An additional consideration is the decline in response rates over the period covered by our surveys, but as explained in appendix B (page 221), this should not affect our conclusions in important ways.

4.1   Timeline of major events between 1930 and 2010 recalled in U.S. surveys

Lifetime effects

For all those who lived through a particular historic event, judgments of importance might reflect a "period effect" due to experiencing the event at *any* point in the life course between childhood and old age, rather than during a more limited set of critical years. Such period or *lifetime effects* pose a problem for evaluating memories of events early on the timeline in figure 4.1, because only a small number of cohorts were alive at a time prior to those early events. Unless we have available a wide range of cohorts, including some who experienced the event as younger adults and some who experienced it as older adults, lifetime and critical years effects will be confounded.

For instance, consider World War II (1941–1945), as shown in figure 4.2. The figure uses data from our eight national surveys carried out between 1985 and 2010.[6] The horizontal x-axis shows birth cohorts in five-year groupings, and the vertical y-axis shows the percentage mentioning World War II as an "especially important" event. Note that the figure presents separate plots for each of the eight different surveys, together with a heavy gray line that shows the average of all survey results for each particular cohort (weighted by the number of cases in each survey). Darker segments of the heavy average line represent cohorts who were in their critical years during the war. (For simplicity, in some later figures, only the average line will be presented.)

6. Our charts graph simple percentages, because comparison of a number of such figures with graphing that controlled for education, gender, and race (see Schuman and Rodgers 2004) found at most only trivial differences in the shapes of the curves that are our primary concern. All data points in the average lines are based on multiple survey observations. Data points for the very oldest and very youngest cohorts are omitted from average plots in figures 4.2–4.5 because only one survey observation is available for these two cohorts: the youngest cohort was old enough to take part in surveys only in 2009–2010, and the oldest cohort was no longer present in substantial numbers after 1985. (For information on the size of cohorts in each of the individual surveys shown in figures 4.2–4.5, see appendix C in Schuman and Corning [2012].)

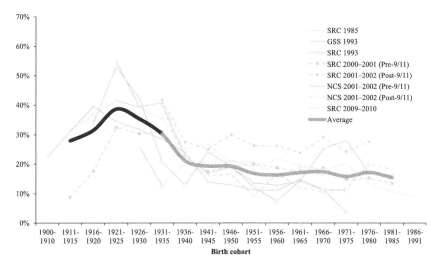

Note: Darker segments of the average line highlight cohorts in their critical years between 1941 and 1945.

4.2   Percentages of each birth cohort mentioning World War II (1941–1945) in eight U.S. surveys, 1985–2010

The plot shows that the cohorts born between 1911 and 1935 were the most likely to mention World War II—a result that fits the hypothesized critical years effect well, pointing to the lasting impact of the war on those who were as young as age ten during the war (that is, born in the 1931–1935 range), and on those around age thirty (born in the 1911–1915 range) when the war ended. (We use the midpoint of the cohort category as the best estimate of its numerical value.) The percentages mentioning World War II are considerably lower among cohorts who were very young children or not yet born at the time of the war.

It is important to recognize that an interpretation in terms of a lifetime effect is also possible in the case of World War II. The only way to identify a critical years effect definitively would be to have a sufficient number of respondents born around the turn of the century (1900) or earlier, in order to show that they did *not* mention World War II in the same proportion. Although we have relatively few respondents born around 1900, there is a downturn for the oldest cohort shown in figure 4.2, born 1900–1910. Thus we have some evidence that the impact of World War II was greater for those who experienced it during their critical years than for those who were exposed to it at later points in the life course—though of course, it would be helpful to have a set of even older cohorts to show that they did *not* mention World War II at the

89

same level. (We will see later that lifetime effects must be taken seriously as an alternative to the critical years hypothesis for some truly transformative events in other countries.)

Recency effects

At whatever point a survey is administered, the most recent notable event is likely to be especially influential in terms of memory. The term *recency* dates from its use by Ebbinghaus (1885) for better memory of the last item read or heard in a list, and most current uses of the term by psychologists refer to short-term memory tasks in research on serial learning (e.g., Bower 2000). However, our own use relates to longer-term memory, where a recent event is recalled more easily than similar events more remote in time. In such cases there often appears to be a recency effect (O'Connor et al. 2000; Bahrick 1984), consistent with common experience, though its strength can be greatly influenced by variations in content and setting. Of course, "recency" is difficult to define when dealing with historical events, since it involves not only time per se but also the impact of other events that preceded a new one.

The September 11, 2001, terrorist attack on the United States is an event we expected to reveal both a critical years and a recency effect, the former because it would have the advantage of primacy for young Americans in 2001, and the latter indicated by frequent recall soon after 2001 (about 50 percent of respondents in two independent samples mentioned the attack—more mentions than any other event in any U.S. survey we draw from, though the comparison does not control for the gap in time between an event and a survey). The fact that the youngest cohorts in figure 4.3 show the most mentions of 9/11 provides prima facie evidence for a critical years effect, since recency alone could not produce the positive association with youth. (Even our youngest respondents in the 2009–2010 survey, aged ten to fifteen in 2001, were old enough to have been greatly affected by the repeated showing of video footage of the attacks on television and discussions by family members and friends.) At the same time—given individuals' tendency to mention events that they themselves experienced—there is a sense in which recent events may exert their greatest impact on the youngest cohorts. The "slice of life" (Ryder 1965: 844) experienced by the youngest cohorts is narrower and includes fewer events, so the likelihood that they will mention an event close in time to the survey is greater than it is for older cohorts. Thus there is no way to completely separate critical years effects from recency effects for the 9/11 attack, especially without a clear

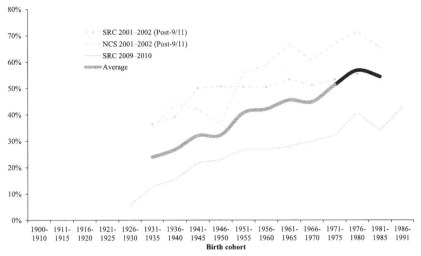

Note: Darker segments of the average line highlight cohorts in their critical years in 2001.

4.3   Percentages of each birth cohort mentioning 9/11 attacks (2001) in three U.S. surveys, 2001–2010

sign of discontinuity in the figure, and it will take additional evidence beyond 2009–2010 to clarify the present results. We anticipate that in future surveys, cohorts born after 1991 (and therefore younger than age ten in 2001) will be less likely to mention 9/11 than those born in the 1971–1991 range. Time will tell.

Improved Tests of Critical Years Effects

In order to distinguish effects due to critical years from *both* recency and lifetime effects, it is useful to consider events that occurred at an interme-diate point on the timeline shown earlier in figure 4.1. Such intermedi-ate events allow us to identify critical years effects with greater certainty because we have sufficient numbers *both* of respondents who were past their critical years when the event occurred, *and* of respondents who were younger than the critical years or not even born at the time of the event. We have two intermediate events from time points in the 1960s: the assassination of President John F. Kennedy and the Vietnam War.

Both events have the advantage of being clearly located in time. The 1963 Kennedy assassination is a precisely datable event. The Vietnam War had clear beginning and ending dates in terms of attention by the

American public (1965 when sustained bombing of North Vietnam be-gan and 1973 when the last U.S. combat troops were withdrawn), but in addition, public concern about the war was extraordinarily intense dur-ing two months in early 1968: the enemy Tet Offensive on January 30 shocked the American public, and then on March 31 President Johnson halted bombing of North Vietnam and withdrew his reelection bid (Karnow 1983). In addition, 1968 was the point at which numbers both of U.S. troops and of U.S. casualties were at their height, and the war was covered by widely watched nightly television news. For both the Vietnam War and the JFK assassination, we have the further advantage of a large number of surveys and thus of multiple replications, as sum-marized by the average lines in figures 4.4 and 4.5.

For these two intermediate events, the critical years hypothesis pre-dicts a curvilinear relation of event mentions to cohort, not simply a skewing to one side or the other as in the case of early and recent events. Such a curvilinear relation is not consistent with any of the alternative explanations described earlier. A lifetime effect would raise the level for all cohorts alive at the time of each event. A recency effect is unlikely be-cause even the first of our surveys in 1985 was administered twenty-two years after the Kennedy assassination and seventeen years after the cru-cial year of 1968 for the Vietnam War. Finally, event importance alone

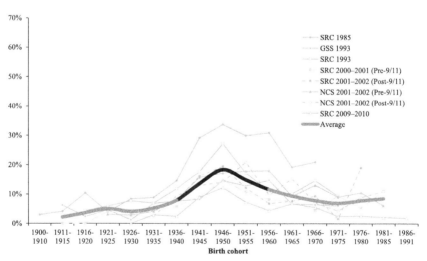

Note: Darker segments of the average line highlight cohorts in their critical years in 1968.

4.4 Percentages of each birth cohort mentioning Vietnam (1968) in eight U.S. surveys, 1985–2010

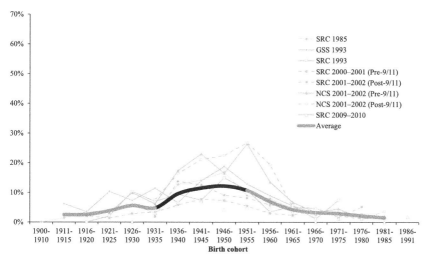

Note: Darker segments of the average line highlight cohorts in their critical years in 1963.

4.5   Percentages of each birth cohort mentioning the assassination of John F. Kennedy (1963) in eight U.S. surveys, 1985–2010

could not explain a curvilinear cohort relation, since it would raise the level of mentions by all cohorts.

Using the averages from our eight different surveys ranging over twenty-five years, figures 4.4 and 4.5 both show the expected curvilinearity. We regard this as important evidence in support of the critical years hypothesis, though since it is limited to two events from the 1960s, it cannot be treated as definitive. Other evidence will be reported that further tests the hypothesis.

There are also interesting differences between the JFK and Vietnam figures that require interpretation, and considered carefully the differences call for some amendment to our specification of the critical years. The curve for Vietnam in figure 4.4 has a single clear peak, with the modal cohort identified as that born in 1946–1950. These individuals would have been on average seventeen years of age at the start of the war in 1965, age twenty at the time of the height of the war, including the impact of the Tet Offensive in 1968, and age twenty-five in 1973 when the war ended for the U.S. military. Moreover, these were just the ages at which young Americans at home would have been keenly aware of their compatriots fighting in Vietnam, and of the possibility of volunteering or being drafted for military service themselves. Thus these ages point to Americans likely to be most attentive to the war for personal reasons. Of course, even men a little younger, as well as the parents and significant others connected to them, were also apt to feel personally affected by the war.

The curve for the assassination of President Kennedy (figure 4.5) does not have a single cohort peak. Instead, it rises for those born in 1936–1940 and thus in their midtwenties at the time Kennedy was shot—a little older than the peak in the Vietnam curve—but the curve remains high even among those born in the late 1950s and still of primary school age at the time of the assassination. The explanation for these early ages helps us better understand the underlying source of critical years effects. The shooting of the president occurred at midday in the United States and was immediately flashed around the country, interrupting television and radio programs. A number of respondents remembered that they learned of the tragic event in class from their teachers. Others were very young children who mentioned not only hearing of the assassination but also seeing how their parents and other adults reacted to the news. "When he died it affected my parents, they were very sad, and as a little kid it made me sad," said a forty-one-year-old man, who was just four years old at the time.

Evidently even without much cognitive understanding of the event, very young children felt its emotional impact vicariously, and that stayed with them over all the subsequent years. Moreover, during that day and evening, there was extensive television coverage of the assassination, and it was the subject of intense discussion everywhere, in homes, schools, and other gatherings. Not only on November 22, but at least through the funeral on the twenty-fifth, there was intense focus on the assassination, with memorable photographs of Jacqueline Kennedy and her children, six-year-old Caroline and three-year-old John, Jr., the latter saluting the flag-draped casket at one point. The state funeral was attended by heads of state from around the world, including the imposing French president Charles de Gaulle, marching in the funeral procession. It is understandable that even children as young as four or five years of age still recalled many years later the day of the assassination and its aftermath.

In two of our national surveys, the question about especially important events was followed by a further inquiry: "What was it about [the assassination of JFK] that makes it seem to you especially important?" Table 4.2 reprints a number of informative responses from the National Comorbidity Survey (NCS) in 2001–2002, given by those who were children age ten or under at the time of the assassination, and there were

Table 4.2 Reasons for Mentioning JFK's Assassination (1963) as an Especially Important Event, Given by Respondents Very Young at the Time (NCS 2001–2002)

Reason (Age at time of assassination)

Reactions of parents and family

"I was real young and listening to the adult reactions as a kid I could sense something major was happening." (Age 3)

"I just remember seeing it on the TV, and how upset it made my family at the time . . ." (Age 3)

"When he died it affected my parents, they were very sad, and as a little kid it made me sad. The whole thing was very awful." (Age 4)

"It was the only time [I] saw [my] mother sit and watch TV. She was also very emotional about the event." (Age 5)

"I was old enough to understand how they could kill our President—it was very traumatic. It was the only president I really knew about. I came home from school and saw my mother crying." (Age 10)

Memories linked to school

"When the president Kennedy was assassinated and Martin Luther King was killed. I was in school when it happened and I remember it from my childhood." (Age 7)

"I just remember I was in the fifth grade when it happened and everyone was crying everywhere I went, I'll never forget it." (Age 8)

Reactions of others in general

"I think watching the reaction of everyone around me and the impact it had on them." (Age 6)

"I saw the effect it had on people—the way people reacted to it. I've never seen such a bunch of somber people in all my life! But then again I hadn't lived prior to that to see what effect the deaths of other people had." (Age 8)

"The way everybody reacted to it." (Age 9)

Awareness of national-level reactions

"I barely remember it but it seems like the whole country shut down and people were crying in the streets. The whole country stopped." (Age 4)

"The whole country and nation was sad, I was in class when that happened." (Age 6)

"It . . . I was 10 years old. It created a lot of controversy. I don't think the American public knows what or why it happened. It was the beginning of distrust of Americans and their government." (Age 10)

Awareness of larger world

"I can remember it and I was only 3 years old, at an early age it brought death and the importance of the presidency to reality." (Age 3)

"For me that was the first time I really became aware of national or international events, everything else was pretty localized for me. Made me think on a larger scale." (Age 7)

"It was just the first thing that I remember of social importance when I was young." (Age 9)

"First time I became aware of national events and I sort of began to feel a kinship with the family." (Age 10)

"It was the first traumatic event of my life. I can't remember anything else so major. For my family and our community. I was 10 at the time, it was probably the first time anything had really shocked me." (Age 10)

---

many more from ages eleven to twelve, well below Mannheim's lower boundary of seventeen.

Thus the graph for mentions of the Kennedy assassination is different from the Vietnam figure in a way that makes good sense and supports the basic idea behind the critical years hypothesis, though calling in this unusual case for an extension of the critical years to an even younger age than late childhood or adolescence. The total range was from ages four or five to almost thirty for an event that was unusually memorable for children. At the same time, both the Kennedy assassination and Vietnam were disproportionately likely to be mentioned by respondents who were within the typical ten to thirty critical years range at the time those events occurred. The two events were given much less frequently by those older than age thirty at the time—Americans who had themselves experienced at a young age such earlier dramatic events as the beginning and end of World War II. For Americans past the age of thirty, these still earlier events probably loomed in memory as more important than even the assassination of a president and the intensity of the Vietnam War in the late 1960s. We believe that it is the *first* big event personally experienced that tends to create an indelible memory.

If we return to the mentions of World War II plotted in figure 4.2, taking seriously the span of roughly four to five cohorts for the critical years effect seen in plots of intermediate events in figures 4.4 and 4.5, we can infer that nearly all the increase in mentions is accounted for by the impact of critical years. In addition, if the plots for World War II and 9/11 (figures 4.2 and 4.3) are viewed together, generational differences in memories emerge in striking fashion. The two curves are nearly mirror images: for World War II, the peak among the oldest cohorts declines to a low plateau for all those too young to remember personal experience of the war, while the impact of 9/11 is lowest among the World War II cohorts but increases steadily for those born later. (Still, the lack of sufficient respondents born during the decades preceding the beginning of the twentieth century leaves some doubt about the critical years hypothesis in the case of World War II, especially since that war affected even the oldest parts of the population, e.g., through shortages and rationing, and to some degree may well have created a lifetime effect.)

Other important events

Three other major events were within the experience of a substantial spread of both younger and older cohorts, as well as distant enough from most survey time points so that the results are not mainly a reflection of

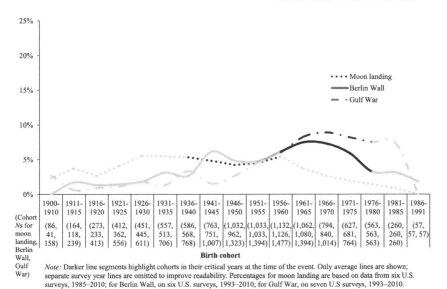

	1900- 1910	1911- 1915	1916- 1920	1921- 1925	1926- 1930	1931- 1935	1936- 1940	1941- 1945	1946- 1950	1951- 1955	1956- 1960	1961- 1965	1966- 1970	1971- 1975	1976- 1980	1981- 1985	1986- 1991
(Cohort *N*s for moon landing, Berlin Wall, Gulf War)	(86, 41, 158)	(164, 118, 239)	(273, 233, 413)	(412, 362, 556)	(451, 445, 611)	(557, 513, 706)	(586, 568, 768)	(763, 751, 1,007)	(1,032, 962, 1,323)	(1,033, 1,033, 1,394)	(1,132, 1,126, 1,477)	(1,062, 1,080, 1,394)	(794, 840, 1,014)	(627, 681, 764)	(563, 563, 563)	(260, 260, 260)	(57, 57, 57)

Birth cohort

Note: Darker line segments highlight cohorts in their critical years at the time of the event. Only average lines are shown; separate survey year lines are omitted to improve readability. Percentages for moon landing are based on data from six U.S. surveys, 1985–2010; for Berlin Wall, on six U.S. surveys, 1993–2010; for Gulf War, on seven U.S surveys, 1993–2010.

4.6   Percentages of each birth cohort mentioning the moon landing (1969), the fall of the Berlin Wall (1989), and the Gulf War (1990–1991)

recency effects: the moon landing in 1969, the fall of the Berlin Wall in 1989, and the Gulf War in 1990–1991. Each event was limited in time and likely to have been a matter of close attention by at least part of the public, so we anticipated evidence of critical years effects in all three cases. All three are shown in figure 4.6, using only averages to simplify and combine their presentations.

The moon landing departs the most from our hypothesis. Although it was mentioned least often by older cohorts—those who were in their fifties, sixties, or beyond in 1969, and also by those below the age of five—it was nevertheless recalled by Americans well beyond our assumed upper critical years boundary of thirty at the time. There is a quite plausible explanation for this exceptional range of birth cohorts: 70 percent of American households had their television sets tuned to the moon landing in 1969 (Edgerton 2007: 268), and given the buildup before the final descent, we can be confident that most people in such households were watching Neil Armstrong leave the lunar module and utter his famous words as he stepped onto the surface of the moon: "That's one small step for [a] man, one giant leap for mankind." Moreover, the first moon landing and moon walk were not merely unusual, but were unprecedented, unlike the Vietnam War, which was not unique for those who had lived through World War II or the Korean War. Thus the moon landing may have seemed remarkable and held special appeal even to those older than age thirty. Furthermore, it had been announced widely in advance, and President Nixon had proclaimed it a holiday, a "National Day of Participation" (*New York Times*, July 17, 1969, 1). Thus, many of those well beyond age thirty could settle themselves in front of their television in order to watch this previously unimaginable feat—quite different from the 1963 Kennedy assassination which had happened suddenly in midday when many adults would have been at work and were not expecting anything unusual.

We can again draw on responses to our follow-up inquiry asking respondents about their reasons for mentioning an event—in this case, the moon landing. In the SRC 1985 survey, we found that older respondents tended to express amazement about space exploits, while those in their critical years at the time of the moon landing tended to take such achievements for granted, speculating instead about further developments to which space exploration might lead (Schuman and Scott 1989). In the more recent NCS 2001–2002 survey, we were also able to code explanations by the 104 individuals who gave the moon landing as their answer to the Events question, and we found further clear evidence that those older than their critical years responded in a way that pointed to the exceptional nature of the event from their standpoint. Responses indicating that respondents felt awe, amazement, and wonder were especially characteristic of those over age thirty at the time, as distinct from younger Americans who may have simply accepted space as a logical frontier for human exploration. The difference by age is highly reliable and is visible in answers such as the following from those beyond age thirty (the respondent's age in 1969 is shown in parentheses):

"The awesomeness that we could get them there and back." (Age 43)

"It was a miracle that they were able to do this." (Age 41)

"The excitement, forethought, and creativity it took to do that." (Age 42)

Younger respondents, on the other hand, gave more answers that accepted space exploits as something to be expected, and they tended to emphasize the new scientific, technological, and practical applications presaged by the 1969 moon landing:

"Discovery . . . discovering what may be out there that we don't know. The future . . ." (Age 18)

"Opened doors to a whole new world of what we are capable of accomplishing." (Age 10)

"Because of the space program things that were invented for it have filtered down to our everyday life: transistors, medical advances. They have enhanced our life—lasers, etc.—and have extended our life. People don't realize it." (Age 30)

Thus responses to the moon landing extended beyond the older end of the critical years that we identified for many other national and world events. The result suggests an extension of the critical years beyond age thirty, and does so in a way that is theoretically meaningful in terms of what those years ordinarily reflect. For a unique event like the 1969 moon landing, one announced well ahead of time and readily experienced by sitting in front of a television set, it is not the exact ages that are crucial, but rather what those ages indicate about the human response to the event.

The fall of the Berlin Wall and the Gulf War in figure 4.6 both show mentions that are in the critical years span, but are not completely confined to it. For the Gulf War the extension is to just several years below age ten, while the extension needed for the fall of the Berlin Wall is to older cohorts—those who were in their late forties when the wall came down. In both these cases what we have identified as the critical years are clearly involved, but for reasons we were not able to fully measure—beyond graphing the age curve itself—the span of ten to thirty is not quite wide enough to encompass the ages of the Americans who paid attention to and recalled these two national or world events. It is possible that in the case of the Berlin Wall, the apparent additional peaking for the 1941–1945 cohort connects the destruction of the wall with its original construction in 1961, when these people were in their critical years and probably aware of its threatening nature. Just one year later, in 1962, this same cohort also lived through the Cuban Missile Crisis—the height of Cold War danger—so the dismantling of the wall may have held particular symbolic significance for them. In any case, it is clear that the ten to thirty span we have identified as the critical years should be treated as approximate.

A resurrected event

In addition to possible effects due to importance, critical years, lifetime, and recency, we can identify one other interesting source of influence on memories of past events: the "resurrection" of an early event because

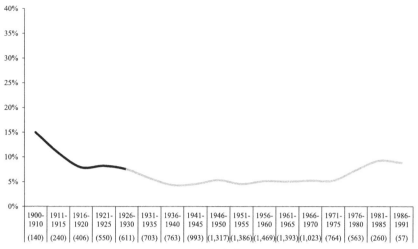

	1900-1910	1911-1915	1916-1920	1921-1925	1926-1930	1931-1935	1936-1940	1941-1945	1946-1950	1951-1955	1956-1960	1961-1965	1966-1970	1971-1975	1976-1980	1981-1985	1986-1991
	(140)	(240)	(406)	(550)	(611)	(703)	(763)	(993)	(1,317)	(1,386)	(1,469)	(1,393)	(1,023)	(764)	(563)	(260)	(57)

Birth cohort

Note: Darker line segments highlight cohorts in their critical years in the 1930s. Only the average line is shown, based on data from eight U.S. surveys, 1985–2010. Cohort *N*s shown in parentheses.

4.7   Percentages of each birth cohort mentioning the Great Depression (1930s)

it appears especially relevant to a current problem. The Great Depression of the 1930s has been referred to by political leaders and economic analysts during entirely new economic crises, especially the one that began in the middle of 2007. Our evidence for the Great Depression, shown in figure 4.7, indicates higher recall for the oldest cohorts in our samples who had lived during the 1930s, but higher mentions also by young cohorts, especially in the 2009–2010 data (not shown separately) gathered early in what was increasingly being called the Great Recession—a label linking it directly to the earlier period. The differences, though not pronounced, are consistent with remembered experience of the Depression by the oldest Americans still living at the time of recent surveys, and the "resurrection" of that now-remote but meaningful event in the minds of young Americans for whom a new economic crisis coincided with their own critical years.[7]

7. We do not consider the role of education in detail here, because our primary focus is on understanding the relationship of collective memories to generation. However, Schuman and Scott (1989: 364) found that the "most powerful background factor that accounts for the lack of historical memory is [low] education." Educational attainment is strongly associated with mentions of most— but not all—the events considered here; see Schuman and Scott (1989) and especially Schuman and Rodgers (2004) for further analysis.

Other frequently mentioned events

Several frequently named events are not included in table 4.1 because they did not lend themselves to systematic analysis in generational terms. For example, "civil rights" was often given as an important change over the past half century, but respondents using that term could have had in mind a variety of different events over a broad time span, and they also sometimes used it to cover the entire period of change. In addition, black Americans were most likely to nominate civil rights, so mentions of that event were dominated by race more than generation in our surveys.

The event identified as "computers" was also not anchored clearly in time, since it refers to a series of technological developments extending over several decades (see also appendix D, section b, p. 225 on the effect of question wording). Other events were mentioned by too few respondents, were too limited conceptually (as in the case of the brief appearance of President Bill Clinton in our 1993 data), or had other characteristics that made them unsuitable for careful testing.

Conclusions about the Hypothesis Based on U.S. Replications

Our evidence for collective memories of eight events, based on multiple replications in the United States, is summarized in table 4.3. In most cases, a given event was disproportionately likely to come to mind as important for respondents if it had occurred when they were approximately ages ten to thirty, a period that includes late childhood, adolescence, and early adulthood. Our basic assumption is that major national and world events occurring during that age range are experienced as "first" events. Since individuals at that point in the life course have few previous experiences to provide perspective, we expect the impact of a first big event to be exceptionally strong. The summary that the table provides is generally supportive of the critical years hypothesis—the more so if the explanations for somewhat deviant ages are regarded as both persuasive and illuminating.

It is useful to divide the critical years hypothesis into two parts, as shown in table 4.3: the effect of experiencing an event at an age *younger* than the ten to thirty range, and the effect of being *older* than that range. The explanations for the two parts are different. At the younger end,

Table 4.3 Summary of Critical Years Effects for Events Mentioned as Especially Important in Eight U.S. Surveys, 1985–2010

Event	Event date	Birth years for critical years cohorts	Does the evidence support the critical years hypothesis . . . [a]	
			at the younger end?	at the older end?
Great Depression	1930–1939	1900–1929	Yes (see text also)	Yes, though not distinct from "lifetime" effect[b]
World War II	1941–1945	1911–1935	Yes	Yes, though not completely distinct from "lifetime" effect[c]
JFK assassination	1963	1933–1953	Yes[d]	Yes
Vietnam War	1968	1938–1958	Yes	Yes
Moon landing	1969	1939–1959	Yes	No; requires extension of effect to older cohorts[e]
Fall of the Berlin Wall	1989	1959–1979	Yes	Yes
Gulf War	1990–1991	1960–1981	Yes	Yes
9/11 terrorist attacks	2001	1971–1991	Yes, though not completely distinct from recency effect[f]	Yes

[a]Conclusions are based on chi-square values (see appendix C) and inspection of figures.
[b]For very early events, when the cohort curve is truncated at the older end because people beyond the critical years have disappeared from the population, a critical years effect is not distinguishable from a lifetime effect.
[c]A downturn is visible for the cohort past the critical years, but that very oldest cohort is present in only the earliest sample.
[d]As explained in the text, our evidence suggests that children even younger than ten were also affected by the JFK assassination. However, using different boundaries to test critical years effects does not change conclusions.
[e]As explained in the text, the moon landing had an impact on cohorts older than the critical years as well as those in their critical years, requiring an extension to older cohorts for unprecedented events.
[f]For very recent events, when the curve is truncated at the younger end because cohorts younger than their critical years are not yet in the sample, a critical years effect is not distinguishable from a recency effect.

those who were very young children at the time generally have limited experience or understanding of major events, while those who were not yet born could not experience the events at all. At the older end, those beyond the critical years range are likely to have had earlier experiences, often of a similar type (war in the case of World War II, the Korean War, the Vietnam War, and so forth), which may tend to diminish the impact of later events.

We do not treat the ten to thirty range as implying precise endpoints, and the exceptions have turned out to be instructive. At the younger end of the cohort dimension, we found that even children aged five or younger could mention the assassination of President Kennedy, quite likely because it occurred in the middle of the school day and could be experienced vicariously through its effect on adults. The unique and extraordinary nature of the moon landing—announced well in advance and easily viewed on home television—probably accounts for its effect on those well beyond age thirty. Although we have evidence for the importance of the approximate range of ages ten to thirty, we treat those ages not as literal boundaries, but rather as a guide to understanding the impact of actual events on the collective memory of Americans. In the next chapter we extend our tests of the critical years hypothesis to eight countries in Europe and Asia, a step that also allows us to consider several other issues important to collective memory, though not directly related to the critical years hypothesis.

FIVE

Exploring Collective Memory in Eight Countries

We were able to draw on data from eight countries beyond the United States: China, Germany, Israel, Japan, Lithuania, Russia, Pakistan, and Ukraine. Most of these countries not only provided further tests of the *critical years* hypothesis, but also addressed other important issues that throw light on the concepts of generations and collective memory.

Problems of sampling and translation, and dependence on others to include our standard Events question as part of their larger research, made the cross-national effort more difficult compared with our U.S. studies. Nor could we carry out the kind of systematic replication possible in the United States. Yet the opportunities provided by greatly different national contexts have proved extremely valuable.

We summarize here important results from each country that bear on the critical years hypothesis and at the same time increase our understanding of other basic issues. The chapter concludes with a full review of evidence—from both the United States and other countries—on the critical years hypothesis.

Germany and Japan

In 1991 our standard question was translated and administered in Germany and Japan, allowing useful comparisons between the two, as well as comparisons with what we had

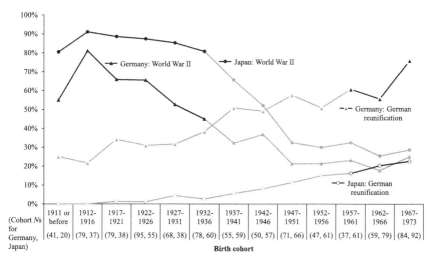

Note: Darker line segments highlight cohorts in their critical years at the time of the event. Data are from surveys in former West Germany and the Yokohama region of Japan, both in 1991.

5.1   Germany and Japan in 1991: Percentages of each birth cohort mentioning World War II (1939/1941–1945) and German reunification (1990)

learned in the United States.[1] In both countries, World War II was re-called especially—and at strikingly high levels in figure 5.1—by older citizens who had lived through the war.[2] The figure shows that the curves for mentions of World War II by birth cohort have a similar shape in the two countries. In addition, for Germany the impact of the reunification then under way is also evident among the younger cohorts, but there was no comparable recent event in Japan at that point. Younger Japanese

1. Both samples were restricted by the local research institutes for reasons beyond our control. For Germany, the sample was only from what had been West Germany prior to reunification in late 1990. For Japan, the sample was restricted to the major metropolitan area of Yokohama. (See Schuman, Akiyama, and Knäuper [1998] for more details and results for both countries, including pp. 432–433 on relevant sampling issues.) The restrictions should not affect the main results for the populations we covered. We cannot be confident that our conclusions apply to the populations omitted (what was originally East Germany and the rural areas of Japan), though given our emphasis on relationships to birth cohort rather than on specific percentages, the conclusions may hold up well for all areas of the two countries (see Druckman and Kam [2011]). We should also note that the two country surveys were not directly connected, and it was a fortunate coincidence that both took place in the same year (1991) and thus allow for their comparison here.

2. Where possible in the cross-national research, we use our standard five-year cohort categories. However—as in the cases of Germany and Japan—we must sometimes use different groupings and/or modify the span encompassed by the very oldest and youngest cohort categories, because of variation in sample size, age distributions, and available data. In addition, we occasionally use ten-year cohort categories in figures presented in this chapter for greater reliability.

did mention German reunification disproportionately, though at much lower levels than Germans. In addition, two other recent events not shown in the figure were mentioned especially by younger Japanese: the Imperial System and the Gulf War, the one occasioned by the recent death of the emperor, widely covered in detail in the Japanese media, and the other by the sudden news about preparations for war in the Gulf and its actual course (figures for these events are shown in Schuman, Akiyama, and Knäuper [1998: 443, 445]).

All the findings are consistent with the critical years hypothesis, and in addition, the World War II results in figure 5.1 provide some evidence that the war is mentioned less frequently by the very oldest respondents in comparison to those just slightly younger. This finding partially precludes competing theoretical interpretations. Furthermore, there were two secondary events—one in Germany and one in Japan—that occurred at points in time that allow for the more complete curvilinearity we found for both the Kennedy assassination and Vietnam using American data (chapter 4). Although not of the magnitude of a major war, each of these secondary events was notable for the respective country. For Germany, this was the reorganization and development of the European Community (EC) as a political institution, especially in the mid- and later 1960s. For Japan it was the 1973 Arab oil boycott, which affected the country severely and became known there as the "oil shock." Each of these intermediate events, as figure 5.2 shows, leads to a curve similar to, though smaller than, the ones we found for Vietnam and the Kennedy assassination, and the peak for each curve is located mainly in the age span of ten to thirty, providing further support for the critical years hypothesis. (For the German sample, the curvilinearity shown in figure 5.2 for mentions of the European Community is reliable, with education, gender, and urban-rural location held constant. For the Japanese sample, the curvilinearity is also reliable, with education and gender held constant.) Thus when we consider these two events, we find clear evidence of critical years effects in both an important European and an important Asian country.

Collective forgetting?

Beyond the successful critical years replications, there is another basic issue about collective memory that both Germany and Japan bring to the fore. Both countries show a striking absence of mentions of events that some might have assumed to be prominent in memory at the time

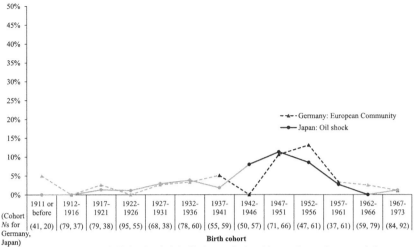

(Cohort	1911 or before	1912-1916	1917-1921	1922-1926	1927-1931	1932-1936	1937-1941	1942-1946	1947-1951	1952-1956	1957-1961	1962-1966	1967-1973
Ns for Germany, Japan)	(41, 20)	(79, 37)	(79, 38)	(95, 55)	(68, 38)	(78, 60)	(55, 59)	(50, 57)	(71, 66)	(47, 61)	(37, 61)	(59, 79)	(84, 92)

Birth cohort

Note: Darker line segments highlight cohorts in their critical years at the time of the event. Data are from surveys in former West Germany and the Yokohama region of Japan, both in 1991.

5.2 Germany and Japan in 1991: Percentages of each birth cohort mentioning the European Community (1967) in Germany and the oil shock (1973) in Japan

the surveys were carried out in 1991. Germans are sometimes thought to feel guilt over the annihilation of Jews (*Judenvernichtung*) by Nazis during World War II, but only 7 of 728 German respondents mentioned Jews at any point in their answers, and those who did were younger than the World War II generation. Older Germans who had lived through the war were much more likely in their responses to the standard Events question to refer to memories about their own suffering under bombing, wartime shortages, and Allied occupation. One interpretation might well be that it was difficult for the German population to report memories that characterized their nation as an extreme victimizer of others.

Yet we also found that only 20 of our 843 Japanese respondents mentioned Hiroshima at any point in their answers, even though Japan in that case represents the victim, not the victimizer (Buruma 1994: 92). When we take the two findings together—the paucity of references *either* to the Holocaust *or* to Hiroshima—we can connect both results to a pervasive finding of surveys around the world: ordinary individuals ("the general public") are usually much more concerned about the impact of events on their own personal lives than they are about events' larger political and symbolic meaning, though the latter occupies much of the attention of intellectuals, political leaders, and academic investigators!

Israel

Israel is a country that was founded on collective memory. In part the memory is said to go back to biblical times; in part to the Holocaust, as well as to exoduses after World War II; and in part to commemoration of its own independence and other recent dates of national significance. Our evidence from Israeli Jews, gathered in 1999–2000, showed, as we expected, opposite relations to birth cohort for the two most frequently recalled events: mentions of the establishment of the State of Israel, which had occurred in 1948, and the assassination of Yitzhak Rabin in 1995, just four years earlier than our survey. Both relations are presented in figure 5.3. The establishment of Israel is mentioned most often by older Israelis and at lower levels by younger people, pointing to a critical years effect (though mentions of the establishment are quite high for all cohorts because of its profound impact on all Israelis). Mentions of Rabin's assassination are also consistent with a critical years effect: it was named especially by those in the ten to thirty age range at the time and much less by older Israelis. As in the case of the 9/11 attacks for Americans, the assassination was too close to the time of the survey to know about those Israelis born after 1995. The establishment of Israel—an early event—also did not allow a full curvilinear shape, as was true as well for World War II

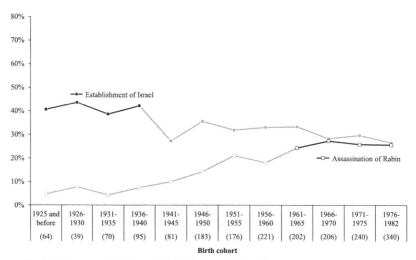

Note: Darker line segments highlight cohorts in their critical years at the time of the event. Cohort *N*s shown in parentheses.

5.3 Israel in 1999–2000: Percentages of each birth cohort mentioning the establishment of Israel (1948) and the assassination of Rabin (1995)

for Americans. Thus the Israeli results are consistent with the critical years hypothesis, though they do not allow a full test.

An exception that also shows the importance of collective remembering

The third event most frequently recalled by Israelis was the Holocaust (data not shown), and at first it does not appear to support the critical years hypothesis, for it shows little relation to birth cohort once we exclude older respondents who had suffered personally due to the Nazi effort to extirpate European Jews. Quite likely, however, this is because remembering the Holocaust has been a commitment by the entire nation: the history of the Holocaust is taught throughout the educational system; an annual observance requires a pause in national life for everyone to remember it; and many other steps have been taken to ensure that memory of the Holocaust remains vivid for all Israelis. Not surprisingly, therefore, mention of the Holocaust is not a function of greater education, setting it apart from most past events in all countries we have studied. Likewise, it is not "gendered," but is recalled at the same levels by men and by women, and it has been learned equally well by those who are children of immigrants and by those whose parents grew up in Israel. Finally, and especially important in a society increasingly divided along religious lines, the Holocaust shows an unusual relation to religiosity: it is mentioned most by those at the orthodox pole but then next most by those at the secular pole, so it is an event that provides considerable unity in memory, in contrast to the division evident in other spheres of Israeli life. Truly, for the Holocaust, "collective memory is not a metaphor but a social reality transmitted and sustained through the conscious efforts and institutions of the group" (again quoting Yerushalmi 1982: xxxiv). Thus in the case of the Holocaust, the failure of the critical years hypothesis is evidence for the *success* of deliberate and fully implemented commemoration and its widespread influence.[3] The exception here proves a larger rule about collective memory.

China

China offers a further valuable source of evidence on generational effects, and with an additional and unusual advantage. The data come from a

---

3. A number of additional results and interpretations from the Israeli study can be found in Schuman, Vinitzky-Seroussi, and Vinokur (2003).

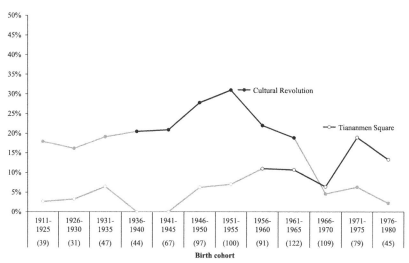

Note: Darker line segments highlight cohorts in their critical years at the time of the event. Cohort *N*s shown in parentheses.

5.4   China in 1996: Percentages of each birth cohort mentioning the Cultural Revolution (1966–1976) and Tiananmen Square (1989)

1996 survey in China, using a sample of villagers in four different counties (Jennings and Zhang 2005). In addition to the intrinsic value of the evidence and the importance of the country, the advantage of this case is that we had no role in planning, executing, or interpreting the results. Ideally, a replication should be entirely independent of the original investigators, who may have inadvertently included features that influenced their results. This replication in China fits that model well. Moreover, Jennings and Zhang changed the time interval respondents were asked to consider, so that for good reason they extended it fifty years into the past, to 1945, rather than back to 1930 as we have typically done. Apart from this change, however, they used our standard Events question.

Of the events mentioned in the China research, two were recent at the time of the survey in 1996: the Tiananmen Square demonstrations and crackdown in 1989, and the focus on national unification (specifically, the issue of unification of Taiwan and China in the 1990s, as well as the anticipated return of Hong Kong to China in 1997). Consistent with the critical years hypothesis, both events were mentioned most often by those in their teens and twenties, though in neither case was it possible to compare this group to still younger respondents, who would have been under eighteen and not included in the sample. Mentions of the Tiananmen Square protests (figure 5.4) show a steep increase among younger cohorts and recall the association of 9/11 mentions with younger ages in the United States (shown earlier in figure 4.3). The earliest event mentioned was the founding of the People's Republic (PRC), and it is most similar to World War II for Americans in the sense that it was mentioned most by the oldest cohorts, but a fully curvilinear trend cannot be seen because still older cohorts are not available in the sample (data not shown). Thus the evidence from these three Chinese events is consistent with the critical years hypothesis, but does not provide a full test of it.

However, another event mentioned does provide such a test. The Cultural Revolution of the 1960s and early 1970s offers an intermediate event, and it displays a clear downturn on either side of the critical years cohorts in figure 5.4, showing the expected curvilinear effect. Thus for this important event where a full comparison to older and younger cohorts is possible, the results by independent investigators fit the critical years hypothesis well. In sum, these data on China provide important further support for the critical years effect.

Lithuania

Results from Lithuania serve as a further test of the critical years hypothesis, and we believe require a modification of it.

We have the advantage of three surveys from Lithuania, conducted in 1989, 1993, and 2009, and we find evidence consistent with a critical years effect for two dramatic events that had distinct beginnings and endpoints—similar to the kinds of events that can stimulate flashbulb memories (Brown and Kulik 1977).[4] Figure 5.5 shows that in both the 1993 and 2009 surveys, the attack on the Vilnius TV tower in 1991—the Soviet military's response to Lithuania's declaration of independence— was most mentioned by cohorts in their critical years during the attack. The 2009 plot also shows the expected downturn in mentions of the TV tower attack among those younger than their critical years at the time. (The 1989 survey predated the TV tower attack, so is not available for figure 5.5. The high level at which the 1921–1930 cohort mentioned the TV tower attack in 2009 is based on just thirty-five cases, making sampling error a likely explanation.)

---

4. Results are reported for ethnic Lithuanians only. Additional results and discussion of the Lithuanian surveys are reported in Corning, Gaidys, and Schuman (2013) and in Schuman, Rieger, and Gaidys (1994).

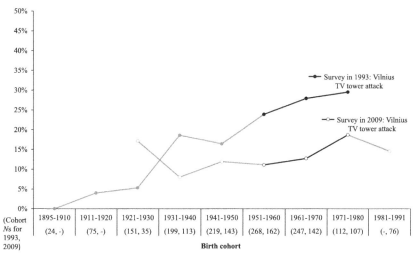

Note: Darker line segments highlight cohorts in their critical years in 1991. Percentages are for the subsamples of ethnic Lithuanians only.

5.5   Lithuania in 1993 and 2009: Percentages of ethnic Lithuanians in each birth cohort mentioning the attack on Vilnius TV tower (1991)

Lithuania's 2005 accession to the European Union was also named most frequently by cohorts in their critical years, though—as for 9/11 in the United States—we cannot definitively interpret this as a critical years effect, because the event was so recent that our samples do not include respondents who were young children or not yet born at the time of the accession (data not shown).

Lifetime effects

However, mentions of an event much larger in scope and scale—Lithuanian independence in 1990–1991—show a different pattern and call for an expansion of our conceptualization of generational effects. Independence was recalled frequently by critical years cohorts, but at least as often by those much older than their critical years, as indicated in figure 5.6 (which also shows mentions of the collapse of the U.S.S.R. from a 1998 Russian survey, discussed below). Although there is a substantial decline in mentions of independence by cohorts born before 1931, those born between 1931 and 1950 and thus well past their critical years at the time of independence were also quite likely to mention it. At the younger end, even the decrease for the very youngest cohort (whose members are included only in the 2009 survey) places it at the level of the rest of the curve. The extended consequences of independence appear to have had an impact on younger cohorts as well.

For Lithuanian independence, we believe it is necessary to allow for the possibility of what we call *lifetime effects*, in which events have a lasting impact on memory for almost *all* those alive and beyond early childhood at the time—not only for those in their critical years. Although independence was a positive event for much of the population, at the same time it was destabilizing and disorienting. Moreover, it was not a unitary event but a cascading sequence of changes whose repercussions were felt over years and in many domains of life. Mentions of independence point to a memory not of a circumscribed event but of an unfolding process—one that might include important episodes like the TV tower attack, but that would also include day-to-day challenges (both positive and negative) of adapting to post-Soviet socioeconomic realities.

Lithuania is thus a case where two different types of events from the same point in history—the Vilnius TV tower attack and Lithuanian independence—show two contrasting effects on memory. The clashes at Vilnius TV tower, on the one hand, occurred over several exceedingly tense and uncertain days, but the conflict was a discrete episode that

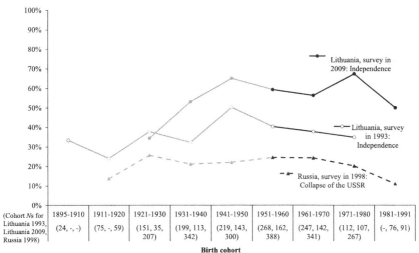

Note: Darker line segments highlight cohorts in their critical years at the time of the event. Lithuanian survey percentages are for the subsamples of ethnic Lithuanians only.

5.6   Lithuania in 1993 and 2009 and Russia in 1998: Percentages of ethnic Lithuanians mentioning independence (1990–1991) and percentage of Russians mentioning collapse of the U.S.S.R. (1991)

ended quickly in the withdrawal of the Soviet military. Some respondents referred to this event as the "attack on Vilnius TV tower," but others referred to the "January events," capturing the brief span of time even in the name itself. Lithuanian independence, on the other hand, is a broader change that fits Sewell's (2005) conception of "transformative" events that reshape daily life and identity through dramatic and permanent change to social structures. The fact that the two events date from the same period in Lithuanian history throws into relief the difference in their nature.

In our 1993 survey, we asked respondents to tell us briefly *why* they named the events they chose as important. Their answers underscore the differences between the two events. In explaining their nomination of the Vilnius TV tower attack, some respondents emphasized the victims, especially those who were killed during the clashes; others mentioned their own shock at the event, and still others identified the attack as a turning point that symbolized Lithuanians' determination to win "freedom at any price." All responses had to do with specific aspects of the event itself, with an emotional reaction to it, or with its symbolic importance.

By contrast, many respondents explained their nomination of independence in very different terms. Some did identify abstract values (such as freedom) or emotions (such as national pride) that the event symbolized for them. But even within this group, some characterized independence as a "return to normal life," and many others gave responses that described it as a long-awaited and/or fundamental historical shift that brought change to virtually all domains of life. For some, it gave meaning to years of dreams and suffering: "our parents have dreamt about it"; "I wasn't in the concentration camp for nothing." Still others invested independence with hopes for a better future, either personal or for Lithuania as a whole, while others expressed disillusionment about the changes: "Life is worse"; "I feel disappointed"; "This is not the independence I was waiting for." Compared to memories of the TV tower attack, memories of independence are not so much a recollection of the "event" itself, but instead center on its consequences or on the contrast between the Soviet and independent periods.

Lithuanians may in fact have experienced *two* transformative events, though we have adequate data only for independence. But fifty years earlier, World War II was probably also a transformative event: it was catastrophic for nearly all Lithuanians, bringing first the loss of independence through annexation by the U.S.S.R., then the German invasion, followed by a second Soviet invasion, occupation, and reassertion of

Soviet control. World War II was recalled by both critical years cohorts *and* older cohorts at about the same levels, though the relatively small number of respondents past their critical years at the time of the war makes it difficult to be confident about that finding (data not shown).

We believe that when an event transforms almost all individual lives and identities in permanent ways, the event can make an indelible imprint on virtually everyone who directly experienced it. Such transformative events appear to be much less common for the United States than for other countries, which probably reflects both its geographic isolation and its political stability in recent years. The difference also cautions us against using only American data to draw general conclusions about the effects of historical experience, reinforcing the value of including cross-national evidence, despite the sampling and other problems it entails.

Two forms of generational effect

The evidence from Lithuania (and, as we show below, from Russia) at a turning point in twentieth-century history highlights the need to acknowledge two different forms of generational influence. When events are sudden and dramatic, as in the case of flashbulb memories, and do not produce substantial change in many individuals' identity or daily lives, they benefit from their special status as "first events" for those in their critical years. However, when events have pervasive and enduring consequences for much of the population, their impact does not seem to be as limited. Instead, they tend to be remembered as important by almost everyone alive and beyond early childhood at the time, producing what we call a lifetime effect. Although transformative events and their consequences seem almost inevitably to span a longer period of time than do many other events, their length alone cannot account for the lifetime effect: in the United States, the Vietnam War produced a classic critical years effect, despite the fact that it extended for nearly a decade, and similarly in China, we found a critical years effect for the decade-long Cultural Revolution. We will see a further version of this basic distinction between two forms of generational influence when we consider American attitudes toward the Gulf and Iraq Wars in a later chapter.

Russia

Our survey in Russia (1998) provides further support for the distinctive generational impact of transformative events. World War II may have had a similar lifetime effect for Russians because of its direct and dramatic impact on individuals' lives and the permanent change it brought to the U.S.S.R. Limited evidence does suggest that older Russians were just as likely to mention the war as those in their critical years (data not shown), but again, because the sample contains few respondents beyond their critical years at the time, we cannot adequately test that explanation.

The Soviet collapse nearly fifty years later, however, was also transformative, and we have a much wider range of cohorts who experienced it. Two events related to the disintegration of the Soviet Union were mentioned by sizable proportions of the sample: Mikhail Gorbachev's reform policy of perestroika, often considered responsible for setting in motion the chain of events leading to the collapse of the U.S.S.R., and the final collapse itself, formalized in December 1991. In the Russian survey, both events were mentioned just as often by older cohorts as by critical years cohorts. Figure 5.6 shows Russians' mentions of the collapse of the U.S.S.R., as well as Lithuanians' mentions of independence (in a sense, the same event from two different perspectives), discussed earlier. The three curves shown in the figure provide visual evidence of lifetime effects: critical years cohorts are no more likely than older cohorts to mention these events. (We find the same results for perestroika and the collapse of the U.S.S.R. in Ukraine.)

Ukraine

We collected valuable data in Ukraine in 2005 at the time of the Orange Revolution, and then again in 2014 after a second major revolution known as Maidan or Euromaidan (after Maidan Nezalezhnosti, or Independence Square, the central square where demonstrations took place), which was followed by continuing political conflict and violence, principally between European-oriented western Ukraine and the Russian-oriented eastern parts of the country.

In order to work with both the 2005 and 2014 data from Ukraine, we must take account of a change in the definition of the country: the loss of Crimea to Russia in February 2014. From a research standpoint the change is not of great significance: in the 2005 survey Crimea constituted just 5 percent of the total sample. It was, however, disproportionately Russian in preferred language (88 percent) and also in self-reported ethnic identification (68 percent). In contrast, Ukraine as a whole in 2005 was more evenly split with regard to language (with much of the population able to understand both languages), and was 80 percent Ukrainian versus 17 percent Russian in self-reported ethnicity (plus 3 percent "other"). Some *oblasts* (administrative regions) in Ukraine are similarly divided by language, but none was close to Crimea in terms of ethnic identification (for example, Donetsk, where fighting has occurred in the East, was 66 percent Ukrainian to 29 percent Russian in our 2005 survey). In our analysis we omit the small amount of data from Crimea in 2005 in order to keep the two Ukrainian samples comparable, but indicate where results from Crimea might affect our overall conclusions.

Armed rebellion in the eastern regions close to the border with Russia was ongoing (though not yet at its height) in 2014 at the time of our survey. Because of the conflict, the experienced survey institute (Kiev International Institute of Sociology [KIIS]) that gathered our data was forced to replace one sampling point in Donetsk oblast with a similar city in the same oblast, but otherwise reported no difficulties in carrying out the interviewing. The refusal rate (24 percent) was about the same and the response rate (48 percent) just slightly below rates for the insti-tute's surveys throughout the year prior. (In both 2005 and 2014 our surveys were carried out by KIIS.)

Critical years effects

In both survey years, responses to our question included very recent events. In 2005, the Orange Revolution, which had occurred just months prior to the survey, was often mentioned. It had appeared ini-tially to move Ukraine toward a more popular democracy, but those re-sults waned over time. Similar tensions over the direction of the country and its ties to Europe and Russia resurfaced during the Maidan protests and violent clashes of 2013–2014, culminating in the forced resignation of President Viktor Yanukovych and his government, as well as related events (in our coding of responses into this category, we also included the annexation of Crimea by Russia and the conflict in eastern Ukraine). Mentions of the Orange Revolution and Maidan are plotted by cohort in figure 5.7, which shows curves from both 2005 and 2014 for the Orange Revolution and from 2014 for Maidan (there is no 2005 plot for Maidan, since that event had not yet occurred). The curve for Maidan in 2014 is very close in shape to that of the Orange Revolution in 2005.

In 2005, over one-third of all respondents—especially the youngest—mentioned the Orange Revolution. By 2014, however, that event had all but disappeared from memory, the victim of its own lack of long-term success, distance in time, and the occurrence of the similar and

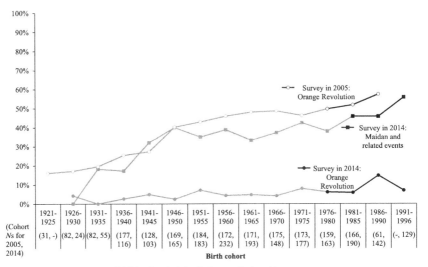

	1921-	1926-	1931-	1936-	1941-	1946-	1951-	1956-	1961-	1966-	1971-	1976-	1981-	1986-	1991-
(Cohort	1925	1930	1935	1940	1945	1950	1955	1960	1965	1970	1975	1980	1985	1990	1996
*N*s for	(31, -)	(82, 24)	(82, 55)	(177,	(128,	(169,	(184,	(172,	(171,	(175,	(173,	(159,	(166,	(61,	(-, 129)
2005,				116)	103)	165)	183)	232)	193)	148)	177)	163)	190)	142)	
2014)															

Birth cohort

Note: Darker line segments highlight cohorts in their critical years at the time of the event.

5.7   Ukraine in 2005 and 2014: Percentages of each birth cohort mentioning Maidan and related events (2013–2014) and the Orange Revolution (2004–2005)

very recent Maidan events. Still, a small but reliable rise is visible at the younger end of the 2014 Orange Revolution curve, for the cohort born between 1986 and 1990 (ages fifteen to nineteen in 2005). The cohort distributions of mentions of these sudden crises are thus consistent with a critical years effect.

Very early events in Ukraine also show curves consistent with our main hypothesis. Figure 5.8 plots two events: World War II (its Soviet name, the Great Patriotic War, was often still used, especially by respondents in the more Russified East) and the famine of 1932–1933, believed to have been engineered by Stalin. (For each event, the curves obtained from our 2005 and 2014 data were very similar, so to simplify the figure, we plot the average percentages across the two survey years, taking into account the number of cases in each survey.) World War II was one of the most frequently mentioned events in both years, and as figure 5.8 shows, it was mentioned most by the oldest cohorts, born well before the war. Later cohorts are less likely to mention it, though still do so at remarkably high levels: there is a plateau for cohorts born in 1941 or after, who would have few if any memories of personal experience during the war, but members of these younger cohorts would have lost family members to the war, and their socialization in the Soviet Union included emphasis on Soviet wartime heroism and sacrifice. The even

earlier famine in Ukraine was mentioned by a much smaller proportion of respondents, but it too was given especially often by the oldest
cohorts, who may have had some memories of it or its effects on their
families. Thus, in spite of the recent occurrence of the two events plotted in figure 5.7, figure 5.8 shows that the oldest respondents in our
samples tended to mention events from their own younger years many
decades earlier.

Chernobyl

The 1986 disaster at the Chernobyl nuclear power plant, which spewed
radiation across Ukraine near the borders with Belarus and Russia, was
not only an entirely different type of event, but also an intermediate
one that predated the end of the U.S.S.R. As figure 5.9 shows, the plot
for the 2005 survey is approximately curvilinear, with mentions of the
event highest among those born in 1966–1975, and thus between the
ages of eleven and twenty at the time of the explosion. Still, the high
points of the curve encompass cohorts born as late as 1985 or even 1990,
indicating that those who were very young children or were born soon
after the event also recall it as "especially important." The explanation
for the younger age seems clear. Children were evacuated not only from

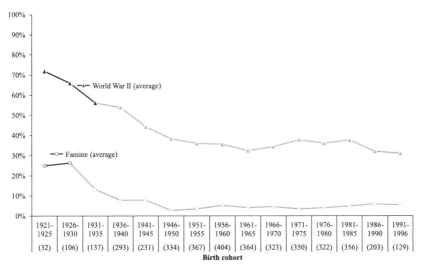

Note: To simplify the figure and improve readability, only average lines are shown, based on data from the two surveys. Total
cohort Ns are shown in parentheses. Darker line segments highlight cohorts in their critical years at the time of the event.

5.8   Ukraine in 2005 and 2014: Percentages of each birth cohort mentioning World War II
       (1941–1945) and famine (1932–1933)

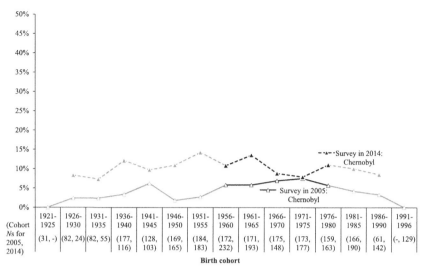

Note: Darker line segments highlight cohorts in their critical years at the time of the event.

5.9   Ukraine in 2005 and 2014: Percentage of each birth cohort mentioning the accident at Chernobyl nuclear power station (1986)

the immediate area of the accident, but also from Kiev and other parts of Ukraine—some sent away by their parents as a precaution. During the years that followed, there was widespread concern about children's physical safety and food and water contamination, since their undeveloped systems were especially susceptible to the effects of radiation. An increased incidence of thyroid cancer as well as other possible health effects was reported, and children exposed to radiation underwent mandatory annual testing (Bromet et al. 2011). Indeed, the peak in mentions for the critical years cohorts is most pronounced among residents of oblasts in the Central region, where Chernobyl is located (data not shown). Thus the 2005 evidence seems consistent with a critical years effect, though with an extension to ages younger than ten. As with the JFK assassination in the United States, a lower boundary for the critical years should be used here. (We have no explanation other than sampling error for the rise in mentions by the 1941–1945 cohort, who were forty-one to forty-five years old at the time of the disaster.)

However, the curve for Chernobyl based on the 2014 survey (also shown in figure 5.9) is quite different in shape. Mentions of the event increased overall, and virtually all cohorts named it as important at roughly the same levels. We think it likely that the disappearance of the critical years effect is due to frequent references to Chernobyl and other

Ukrainian nuclear power plants during the years since 2005, as indicated by various news reports. For instance, during the unrest and conflict of early 2014, the Ukrainian government heightened security in response to threats against its nuclear power plants. Our data provide evidence of public concern: residents of Zaporizhia oblast in southeast Ukraine—far from Chernobyl, but home to the largest nuclear power plant in all of Europe—mentioned Chernobyl at reliably higher rates than residents of any other oblast except for the two most directly affected by radiation from the Chernobyl disaster itself. In addition, other recent events—the twenty-fifth anniversary of the accident, the 2011 Fukushima disaster in Japan, and the near-completion of the new structure designed to contain the damaged plant and its radioactive remains—brought renewed attention to the Chernobyl accident. Moreover, the 2014 survey fieldwork period followed on the heels of the twenty-eighth anniversary of the disaster at the end of April. Each of these factors may have contributed both to the overall increase in mentions of the Chernobyl accident and to the 2014 flattening of the critical years effect observed in 2005.

The importance of region of residence

The effects of region on memory in Ukraine extend far beyond the Chernobyl accident. The most salient regional division, that between East and West, reflects identities—ethnic, linguistic, and political— that shape what is remembered from the past.[5] Although nearly all the events we considered show some effect of region, the four events shown in table 5.1 illustrate the impact of East-West differences especially well, with highly reliable differences in each survey year. (Each of the regional trends would probably be accentuated in 2014 if Crimea, with its heavily Russian population, had been included in the sample.)

As noted earlier, the famine was especially likely to be mentioned by the oldest cohorts who had lived through it. Yet despite those cohorts' gradual disappearance from the population, mentions of the famine show small but reliable *increases* between our two survey years. For Ukrainian nationalists since the late Soviet period, the famine has represented the greatest of the wrongs perpetrated by the Soviet Union on the

5. Ukraine's four major regions are each distinctive, with the most extreme differences between the East and West regions, as shown in a February 2014 survey that found 80 percent support for Maidan in the West, but only 8 percent in the East, and South and Central in between (Paniotto 2014). For simplicity, however, since East and South are similar, we combine them ("East" in table 5.1) and likewise for the West and Central regions ("West").

Table 5.1 Percentages Mentioning Four Events from the Past, by East/West Region (Ukraine 2005 and 2014)

	2005		2014	
Event	East (%)	West (%)	East (%)	West (%)
Famine (1932–1933)	3	6	5	9
World War II/Great Patriotic War (1941–1945)	38	31	48	41
Independence (1991)	6	17	9	24
Collapse of the U.S.S.R. (1991)	34	18	33	13
(N)	(882)	(1,056)	(913)	(1,109)

Ukrainian people (Wanner 1998), and table 5.1 suggests that it still has slightly (but reliably) greater resonance in the more nationalist West.

Table 5.1 also shows substantial increases in mentions of World War II (or the Great Patriotic War) over the years since our previous survey. In contrast to the famine, the war was much more likely to be mentioned by residents of the East. Both the famine and World War II testify to past events' continued currency as symbols—in the one case, of harm perpetrated by a former colonial power, and in the other, of the same power's wartime might and glory. The large increase between the two surveys in mentions of World War II in particular indicates that its symbolic value has been magnified as Ukraine confronts the question of whether its future lies with Russia to the east, or with Europe to the west.

These different regional perspectives on the Ukrainian and Soviet past are crystallized in differing characterizations of what is in a sense the same event: Ukrainian independence and the collapse of the U.S.S.R. In both 2005 and 2014, respondents in the West were much more likely to recall independence than were those in the East. By contrast, residents of the East were more likely to cast their memories in terms of the collapse of the U.S.S.R., in both survey years. Further, especially among those in the West, mentions of independence increased from 2005 to 2014, pointing to its continuing relevance—bolstered perhaps by the recent Maidan events that sought to solidify democratic government and reduce Russia's influence.

Pakistan

We attempted to gather data from one other country—Pakistan, which like Israel was founded in the wake of World War II. However, the sample drawn for us was urban only, had a low level of education and a restricted age distribution (only twenty-four respondents were born before 1945), and few events were mentioned by enough respondents for reliable testing. Apart from a small relation of older age to the establishment of the state, which had occurred also, but much more clearly, with Israelis, we found little in the way of associations with age for the small number of events of any kind recalled. Because the Pakistani data are not adequate for testing the critical years hypothesis, we do not include Pakistan among the survey countries in our summary below.

Conclusions about the U.S. and Cross-National Evidence

Our review of the cross-national evidence indicates substantial support for the critical years hypothesis at the younger end: individuals tend to regard as important those events that occurred when they were at least ten years old, more so than events from early childhood or from before they were born. For reference, table 5.2 summarizes the cross-national evidence on the critical years hypothesis, in the same way that table 4.3 did for the United States. If we consider all events where a comparison can be made at the younger end of the critical years span—whether named by our U.S. samples or by respondents in other countries—we find support for the hypothesis in thirty of thirty-eight cases, or 79 percent. Of the eight cases showing negative evidence, six are events that were either returned to public attention or have retained their relevance over the years since they occurred. We conclude that the critical years hypothesis is well supported by evidence at the younger end. Critical years effects can be swamped by younger cohorts' awareness when events remain highly visible over a stretch of time or return to public view, but such instances are relatively rare.

At the older end of the cohort distribution, evidence supports the critical years hypothesis in 65 percent of cases where that comparison can be made (thirty-one of forty-eight cases), and thus we need to recognize countervailing forces that limit circumstances in which cohorts in their critical years will be more likely than older cohorts to recall an event as important. However, we now believe that at least eleven events brought sudden and decisive change to entire populations on a long-term basis (like World War II and independence in Lithuania, or the collapse of the U.S.S.R. in Russia and Ukraine), producing lifetime effects that appear to override critical years effects. If such lifetime effects are

Table 5.2 Summary of Evidence for Critical Years Effects from Events Mentioned in Surveys in Seven Countries, 1989–2014

			Birth years for critical years cohorts	Does the evidence support the critical years hypothesis . . .[a]	
Country (Survey date)	Event	Event date		at the younger end?	at the older end?
Evidence that supports the critical years hypothesis (may be ambiguous at the younger end)					
China (1996)[b]	Cultural Revolution	1966–1976	1936–1966	Yes	Yes
Germany (1991)	European Community	1967	1937–1957	Yes	Yes
Germany (1991)	Founding of FRG	1949	1919–1939	Yes	Yes
Japan (1991)[c]	Oil Shock	1973	1943–1963	Yes	Yes
Israel (1999)[d]	Peace with Egypt	1977–1979	1947–1969	Yes	Yes
Lithuania (1989, 1993, 2009)[e]	Perestroika	1986–1988	1956–1978	Yes	Yes
Lithuania (1989, 1993, 2009)	Vilnius TV tower attack	1991	1961–1981	Yes	Yes
China (1996)	Tiananmen Square	1989	1959–1979	Yes, though not distinct from recency effect[f]	Yes
China (1996)	National unification	1990–1996	1960–1986	Yes, though not distinct from recency effect[f]	Yes
Germany (1991)	End of Cold War	1989	1959–1979	Yes, though not distinct from recency effect[f]	Yes
Germany (1991)	Reunification	1990	1960–1980	Yes, though not distinct from recency effect[f]	Yes
Germany (1991)	Gulf War	1990–1991	1960–1981	Yes, though not distinct from recency effect[f]	Yes

Japan (1991)	Imperial system	1989	1959–1979	Yes, though not distinct from recency effect[f]	Yes
Japan (1991)	Gulf War	1990–1991	1960–1981	Yes, though not distinct from recency effect[f]	Yes
Japan (1991)	German unity	1990	1960–1980	Yes, though not distinct from recency effect[f]	Yes
Israel (1999)	Peace with Jordan	1994	1964–1984	Yes, though not distinct from recency effect[f]	Yes
Israel (1999)	Rabin's assassination	1995	1965–1985	Yes, though not distinct from recency effect[f]	Yes
Lithuania (1989, 1993, 2009)	EU accession	2004	1974–1994	Yes, though not distinct from recency effect[f]	Yes
Russia (1998)	War in Afghanistan	1979–1989	1949–1979	Yes, though not distinct from recency effect[f]	Yes
Russia (1998)	War in Chechnya	1994–1996	1964–1986	Yes, though not distinct from recency effect[f]	Yes
Ukraine (2005 & 2014)[9]	Orange Revolution	2004–2005	1974–1995	Yes, though not distinct from recency effect[f]	Yes
Ukraine (2005 & 2014)	Maidan and related events	2013–2014	1983–2004	Yes, though not distinct from recency effect[f]	Yes
Evidence that supports the critical years hypothesis (may be ambiguous at the older end)					
China (1996)	PRC Founding	1949	1919–1939	Yes	Yes, though not distinct from lifetime effect[h]
Germany (1991)	World War II	1939–1945	1909–1935	Yes (see text also)	Yes, though not distinct from lifetime effect[h]
Israel (1999)	Establishment of Israel	1948	1918–1938	Yes	Yes, though not distinct from lifetime effect[h]

Table 5.2 (continued)

| Country (Survey date) | Event | Event date | Birth years for critical years cohorts | Does the evidence support the critical years hypothesis . . .[a] | |
				at the younger end?	at the older end?
Russia (1998)	World War II/Great Patriotic War	1941–1945	1911–1935	Yes	Yes, though not distinct from lifetime effect[b]
Ukraine (2005 & 2014)	Famine	1932–1933	1902–1923	Yes	Yes, though not distinct from lifetime effect[b]
Ukraine (2005 & 2014)	World War II/Great Patriotic War	1941–1945	1911–1935	Yes	Yes, though not distinct from lifetime effect[b]
Evidence that is negative at the older end, suggesting lifetime effects					
Germany (1991)	Beginning of economic miracle	1948	1918–1938	Yes	No; effect extends to older cohorts
Japan (1991)	World War II	1941–1945	1911–1935	Yes	No; effect extends to older cohorts[i]
Israel (1999)	Six Day War	1967	1937–1957	Yes	No; effect extends to older cohorts
Israel (1999)	Yom Kippur War	1973	1943–1963	Yes	No; effect extends to older cohorts
Lithuania (1989, 1993, 2009)	Annexation	1939–1940	1909–1930	Yes	No; effect extends to older cohorts[j]

Lithuania (1989, 1993, 2009)	World War II	1941–1945	1911–1935	Yes	No; effect extends to older cohorts[i]
Lithuania (1989, 1993, 2009)	Rebirth	1988–1990	1958–1980	Yes	No; effect extends to older cohorts[i]
Russia (1998)	Perestroika	1986–1990	1956–1980	Yes, though not distinct from recency effect[f]	No; effect extends to older cohorts[i]
Russia (1998)	Collapse of U.S.S.R.	1991	1961–1981	Yes, though not distinct from recency effect[f]	No; effect extends to older cohorts[i]
Ukraine (2005 & 2014)	Perestroika	1986–1990	1956–1980	Yes	No; effect extends to older cohorts[i]
Ukraine (2005 & 2014)	Collapse of U.S.S.R.	1991	1961–1981	Yes	No; effect extends to older cohorts[i]

Evidence that is negative at the younger or both ends, suggesting lifetime effects and/or events of continuing or renewed relevance at the time of the survey

Germany (1991)	Division of Germany	1945	1915–1935	No; effect extends to younger cohorts	No; effect extends to older cohorts[i]
Israel (1999)	World War II	1939–1945	1909–1935	No; effect extends to younger cohorts	Yes, though not distinct from lifetime effect[h]
Israel (1999)	First man on the moon	1969	1939–1959	No; effect extends to younger cohorts	No; effect extends to older cohorts
Lithuania (1989, 1993, 2009)	Independence	1990–1991	1960–1981	No; effect extends to younger cohorts	No; effect extends to older cohorts[i]
Lithuania (1989, 1993, 2009)	Collapse of U.S.S.R.	1990–1991	1960–1981	No; effect extends to younger cohorts	No; effect extends to older cohorts[i]
Russia (1998)	Space exploration	1961	1931–1951	No; effect extends to younger cohorts	Yes

Table 5.2 (*continued*)

Country (Survey date)	Event	Event date	Birth years for critical years cohorts	Does the evidence support the critical years hypothesis . . .[a]	
				at the younger end?	at the older end?
Ukraine (2005 & 2014)	Independence	1991	1961–1981	No; effect extends to younger cohorts	Yes
Ukraine (2005 & 2014)	Chernobyl nuclear accident	1986	1956–1976	No; effect extends to younger cohorts	No; effect extends to older cohorts

[a] Conclusions are based on chi-square values (see appendix C) and inspection of figures. Because of concerns about the quality of the research in Pakistan and the reliability of results, we limited events considered to those mentioned by at least 10 percent—establishment of Pakistan and the 9/11 attacks. Even so, it is not possible to adequately evaluate critical years effects with the urban-only sample, almost entirely born after 1945, so we omit the Pakistani data from this table.

[b] For consistency, the base for percentaging here includes 70 respondents who did not mention any event (although excluding them as Jennings and Zhang [2005] did in their calculations does not alter conclusions.)

[c] In the Japanese sample, respondents who gave no answer to the question are excluded from the base for percentaging because of their large number.

[d] For Israel, the base for percentaging includes 183 respondents who gave no response. Respondents could mention up to three events, but only the first two events are included here, for consistency with the other surveys. The Holocaust is not appropriate for testing the critical years hypothesis, because its deliberate and widespread commemoration means that memories are broadly distributed across age cohorts. Therefore, we omit the Holocaust from this table.

[e] Data for Lithuania are weighted averages over the three survey years, taking account of the number of respondents in each year. Because some events were prominent only briefly, then faded quickly from view, only events mentioned by a weighted average of 5 percent or more are included here. Events mentioned by the Russian and Polish minorities were substantially different, so data are reported for the subsample of ethnic Lithuanians only.

[f] For very recent events, when the curve is truncated at the younger end because cohorts younger than the critical years are not yet in the sample, a critical years effect is not distinguishable from a recency effect.

[g] Data for Ukraine are weighted averages over the two survey years, taking account of the number of respondents in each year. The 2014 data do not include Crimea, which had been annexed by Russia in 2014 prior to our survey. Excluding Crimean respondents from the 2005 data does not affect conclusions.

[h] For very early events, when the cohort curve is truncated at the older end because people beyond the critical years have disappeared from the population, a critical years effect is not distinguishable from a lifetime effect.

[i] For events that bring decisive change to an entire population on a long-term basis, a lifetime effect may appear to override the critical years effect.

treated as expected, then among the older-end comparisons, a total of 88 percent (forty-two of the forty-eight cases) can be successfully interpreted as either critical years or lifetime effects.

———

One unusual feature of the present research has been the many and varied replications we have reported in chapters 4 and 5. We tested the same critical years hypothesis eight times in the United States over the past quarter of a century—in reference to a number of different events—and we also successfully tested the hypothesis at least once in each of seven other countries, including two Asian countries with cultures quite different from those of the United States and Europe, where most of our research has taken place. All the results have been reported in this chapter, whether positive or negative.

We began by presenting the reasons why many national and world events affect a set of people in a way that leads them to retain a strong memory, as evidenced by responses to our general question about "especially important" national and world events between 1930 and the present. Our hypothesis is that individuals within a certain age range at the time the event occurred are the most likely to register and preserve such a memory. Age reflects both opportunities for and constraints on experience. On the one hand, important events that are personally experienced—whether directly or, more likely, by exposure to media accounts and through discussions with family and friends—are vivid enough to be relived mentally at a later point. This would have been the case for those Americans who saw televised footage of planes crashing into the World Trade Center as the overall event was still unfolding, or Lithuanians who heard about the Soviet military's attack on the Vilnius TV tower as it occurred. However, at a much later point, when at least the initial outcome is known and the event has reached a kind of closure, it does not leave the same vivid trace on an individual's mind. Moreover, a later event within the same general category as an earlier one, such as the start of a war for someone who has lived through beginnings of earlier wars, is not so likely to leave such a strong impression or create a memory so easily evoked.

Our initial hypothesis centered on ages ten to thirty as the range most apt to reflect the span when such national and world events are memorable. Children younger than ten in a country like the United States are not likely to attend to most national and world events closely enough to be affected, even when the event is objectively of great importance. And individuals who were born after a momentous event obviously cannot have focused on it as it happened. For example, someone born in 2002 can hardly have a personal memory of the September 11, 2001, attack, even if she later studies it in school and has watched video footage of the twin towers collapsing.

At the other extreme, those older than about thirty at the time a war begins—say, the 2003 Iraq War—may well have experienced earlier striking events that are somewhat similar (for example, the 1990–1991 Gulf War) and therefore will be less affected by a new war, since novelty is one characteristic of a memorable event. (Of course, this assumes involvement in the two wars that is much the same and would not apply to someone who was an observer via television in the one case and a direct participant in the other.)

We found the "failures" of the critical years effect to be as informative as results that fit the original hypothesis. One such exception was the discovery that news of the assassination of President John F. Kennedy was often recalled by individuals who were quite a bit younger than age ten. This was partly due to the news having been broadcast at midday, interrupting other programming, so that even young children were exposed to the event at school or at home. In addition, children who were too young to appreciate the importance of a president's assassination could still observe and grasp the shock and immediate sorrow of adults they happened to be with. Similarly, young children in Ukraine would have observed their parents' fear after the Chernobyl explosion and might remember frequent medical tests and restrictions on what they could eat or drink and where they could play outdoors.

The case of Lithuania revealed a different kind of exception to the critical years effect: the possibility that events can make a substantial impression on those older than age thirty, as well as those younger. The nature of life for Lithuanians changed twice during the long period covered by our survey question: first during the prewar and wartime occupations that brought tremendous destruction and transformed independent Lithuania into a republic within the U.S.S.R., and then again as a result of the political, economic, and social changes set in motion by Lithuania's 1990 declaration of independence. Transformative historical events like these create an enduring sense of rupture in individuals' lives, leaving their mark on nearly everyone alive at the time, not only those in their critical years. Similar evidence from Russia and Ukraine supports our conclusions about such lifetime effects. At the same time,

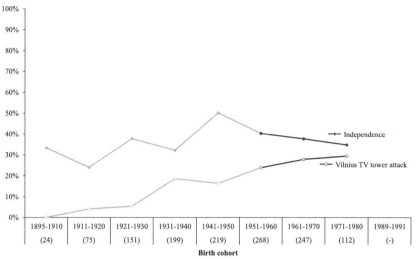

Note: Darker line segments highlight cohorts in their critical years at the time of the event. Cohort *N*s shown in parentheses.

5.10   Lithuania in 1993: Percentages of ethnic Lithuanians in each birth cohort mentioning the attack on Vilnius TV tower (1991) and independence (1990–1991)

other specific events in each of these countries did produce the expected critical years effect.

Two sharply contrasting Lithuanian events are plotted in figure 5.10 for comparison of the cohorts that mentioned them. The plot for the attack on the Vilnius TV tower is highest for the critical years cohorts, then shows a clear downward slope toward the oldest cohorts. The plot for Lithuanian independence is nearly flat, with older cohorts as likely or even more likely to mention it than critical years cohorts. Thus, we need to recognize critical years effects and lifetime effects as two different forms of generational influence on memory. The nature of the event determines which of the two generational effects will occur.

The Holocaust for Israelis is a third exception, where the state's successful commitment to commemoration through schools, holidays, and so forth, resulted in a nearly universal collective memory, broadly distributed across ages and educational levels. Although in this extreme case, the effects of commemoration appear to overwhelm critical years effects, in other cases its effects may be more subtle. We return to the role of commemoration in our final chapter.

A fourth and differently informative exception was the first landing on the moon, a unique event unlike anything previously experienced.

Even for relatively old Americans alive in 1969—well beyond the age of thirty—there was no earlier event with which it could be compared either intellectually or emotionally. Moreover, the anticipated landing was announced and publicized well in advance, and the landing itself was shown dramatically on television, so the spectacular achievement could be seen by almost all Americans and indeed by many others around the world.

In each of these cases, we find that the nature of the event influences which ages are affected and, more generally, whether the relation to generation takes the form of a lifetime or critical years effect. In a sense, the most important outcome of our multiple tests of the critical years hypothesis has been to move us away from identifying a fixed set of years as *the* critical years. Our most general conclusion is that the critical years concept is not, in the end, about a specific set of ages, but rather about the forces that create collective memories of national and world events.

The exceptions to the hypothesized ten to thirty age span, as well as the findings that did fit it, also serve to raise further the question of just what an "event" is, or how it can be defined and delimited. In many cases, the beginning of an event is quite clear, at least to the general population of observers. The ending of an event is often more ambiguous. The assassination of President Kennedy started for most people when television announced and then showed pictures of the shooting. The ending of the event can be said to have occurred after the funeral, or later when the Warren Commission provided a report recounting what had happened, and how and why. But since new claims about the cause and the sequence of occurrences continued and indeed still continue to appear, no ending to the event can be said to be final.

Of the events we have discussed, most of those mentioned by Americans have more or less conventional endings, or at least transitions from the original event to a new though associated one. The American invasion of Afghanistan in late 2001 could be considered a new event, though obviously it was associated with the September 11, 2001, attack, and over time its connection to that precipitating event becomes dim for many people. This was less true of events in countries other than the United States, where, to take the extreme case of Lithuania, the events of World War II and the associated absorption of Lithuania into the U.S.S.R. can be said to have ended only half a century later with the country's return to independence.

PART THREE

Beyond Critical Years Effects

We have seen in previous chapters that collective memories at the individual level are typically influenced by national and world events that occur during the *critical years* of an individual's development, usually within the age range of ten to thirty—the years of transition from late childhood, through adolescence, and into early adulthood. At points we modified the hypothesis to take account of unusual but understandable results that pointed to an earlier age than ten or to a later age than thirty, or in certain national settings produced *lifetime effects* on almost an entire population regardless of age.

In Part III we consider additional issues that relate to the critical years hypothesis, but each one is interesting and important in its own terms:

- the effect of emigration as a type of transition that differs from the transition through adolescence to adulthood;
- the relation of generational effects to the development of new attitudes;
- the similarity between collective memories and personal autobiographical memories;
- the nature and sources of what we call "collective knowledge";
- and finally the basic role of commemoration in preserving and revitalizing collective memories.

Readers may wish to follow their own interests in choosing which chapters to focus on.

SIX

Does Emigration Affect Collective Memory?

There is evidence that, in general, events from transitional periods make an especially strong impression on individuals. For example, alumnae who responded to a request for memories from their first year in college provided memories that clustered in September of that year, frequently referring to the very first day at college, regardless of whether they had graduated two, twelve, or twenty-two years earlier (Pillemer et al. 1988). There may be deeper encoding during such transitions due to "effort after meaning" (Bartlett 1932), or possibly to the fact that transitional experiences serve as informational resources that guide behavior when "scripts governing how to think or behave are violated or missing" (Pillemer 1998: 88). Thus, transitional experiences of *all* kinds may be important for memory. If so, the passage from late childhood through adolescence to adulthood may be simply a universal example in which the effects on memory are easily identified.

Emigration seemed to us a particularly useful transitional experience to study, since it can and does occur at any point in the life course. Moreover, it entails reconstruction of one's life in an entirely new context with unfamiliar cues and expectations. Although Mannheim (1928 [1952]: 293) claimed that emigration should be a less "radical" experience than young people's first encounters with the social and political world, it seemed possible to us that certain emigration experiences might be equally radical— especially when emigration is irrevocable and involves a complete rupture with the emigrant's former social milieu. With this possibility in mind, we examined the destabilizing and disruptive experience of emigrants from the Soviet Union. We expected that their experience of emigration might exert an "emigration effect" on memory similar to that of the critical years in youthful development.

Therefore, in 2000, we used lists from a major refugee resettlement agency in the United States to select a sample of emigrants from the Soviet Union and its successor states. We sent each person a questionnaire that included our standard Events question (p. 83) in both English and Russian, with instructions to choose the language in which they wished to answer (87 percent of respondents completed the Russian version).[1] In order to compare the memories of emigrants to those of Russians who did not emigrate, we are able to draw on our 1998 Russian national survey, discussed in chapter 5.

The nature of emigration for Soviet citizens

Roughly three-quarters of our sample of 1,021 respondents were Jews, a persecuted minority in the U.S.S.R. who were granted refugee status for entry to the United States. The remainder of the sample consisted of non-Jews who emigrated as members of other minority groups, for political or religious reasons, or as family members of Jews. Most emigrants in our sample had left the U.S.S.R. between 1970 and the mid-1990s.

Unlike some other emigrant groups, these refugees could not usually sustain their former identities through ties or frequent travel to their communities of origin (Rumbaut 1989; Morawska 2004). For those seeking to leave the U.S.S.R., emigration was a difficult and risky undertaking, and emigrants who obtained permission to leave would have expected never to return or to see again the friends and relatives they left behind. The émigré poet Joseph Brodsky (1986) related the wrenching story of his parents' repeated, failed applications to visit him after his emigration, and of his own futile attempts to visit them before they died. Another Soviet emigrant captured the sense of finality when he compared emigration itself to death (*New York Times*, July 19, 1998, 13). Those who departed during the 1990s after the disintegration of the U.S.S.R. faced financial rather than political constraints on travel, but they, too, were unlikely to return in the near future. Thus for emigrants

---

1. The sample and other details of the study are described in more detail in Corning (2010).

from the Soviet Union and its successor states, emigration was a disruptive and permanent experience—in a sense, a rebirth. Any influence of emigration on collective memory, we reasoned, should be visible within this group.

Hypotheses about Emigration and Memory

We anticipated that emigrants' memories might reflect American events or other historical content acquired during or after the transition to the United States. Morawska (2004) notes that emigrants from the former Soviet Union show high levels of U.S. citizenship (80 percent in her survey) and participation in American life, and, like other European immigrants, are especially likely to seek employment and education within mainstream rather than ethnic institutions. For those beyond the initial arrival period, American collective memories might serve as desirable markers of familiarity with cultural and political events (Alba and Nee 2003). In addition, collective memories create an important backdrop for social interaction (Coser 1992), and Griswold and Wright (2004) found that internal migrants within the United States acquired substantial local cultural knowledge from their new regions of residence. Thus, we expected that our sample's "shared sense of group and individual emancipation in America and . . . the resulting pride in being a citizen thereof" (Morawska 2004: 1392) might lead them to acquire cultural knowledge of the United States in the form of collective memories.

Furthermore, if the emigration transition leads to increased memories from that time period, we should be able to see an association between the date of emigration to the United States and the date of memories—an "emigration effect" similar to a critical years effect, but centered on the emigration date rather than the critical years of development.

Another possibility is that—even in the absence of a clear association between emigration and event memory dates—the fresh encounters of the emigration transition might diminish or eliminate the critical years effect linked to the developmental period of ten to thirty (which for most of our sample was spent partly or entirely in the U.S.S.R.). On the other hand, if emigrants continue to remember events from their late childhood, adolescence, and early adulthood, this would constitute evidence that the critical years effect is specific to that developmental transition and does not result from other types of transitional experiences, however important they may be to individuals' personal lives.

Emigrants' Memories: Remembering the Soviet Past

The major public events mentioned by the emigrant sample are shown to the left in table 6.1, along with the percentages mentioning each event. We include as well the percentages of the Russian national sample mentioning each event, and refer to those at later points. By far the largest proportion of emigrants named World War II: over fifty years after the war's end, 65 percent of the emigrants mentioned it, often though not always using the standard Soviet term "Great Patriotic War." Twenty-three percent mentioned glasnost and perestroika (the cultural and economic reform programs initiated by General Secretary Mikhail Gorbachev in the 1980s), and 30 percent mentioned the collapse of the U.S.S.R. in 1991. (A few events were mentioned by the emigrants but not by the Russian national sample, and vice versa; these two categories of events are grouped at the bottom of the table. Respondents could name up to two events, so percentages do not sum to 100 percent.)

Content of memories

Our major finding is that events involving the United States barely figured in the collective memories of the emigrants: no individual U.S.-focused event was mentioned by more than a tiny proportion of emigrant respondents, as table 6.1 shows. Indeed, the comparison of events mentioned by the emigrants to those mentioned by the Russian national sample in 1998 (table 6.1) reveals quite similar memories about the Soviet period, with World War II, glasnost and perestroika, and the collapse of the U.S.S.R. mentioned most frequently by both samples. Setting aside events that are of importance to the emigrants but not to the national population (i.e., memories directly related to emigration and to the establishment of Israel), as well as Russia's two wars in Chechnya (both of which took place either around the time of or after most emigrants' departure), the ordering of the four most frequently mentioned events is nearly the same in the two samples, with a reversal only in the percentages naming glasnost and perestroika and the collapse of the U.S.S.R. In sum, the emigrants closely resemble their former fellow citizens in terms of the public events they remember as especially important.

Combining all the various U.S.-related events mentioned by the emigrants, fewer than 3 percent named *any* event that involved only the

Table 6.1 Major National and World Events Mentioned by Emigrants from U.S.S.R. and Successor States and Russian National Sample[a]

	Percent of each sample mentioning		
Event	Emigrant sample in 2000	Russian national sample in 1998	Example responses from emigrants
World War II/ Great Patriotic War	65.4	44.4	"Great Patriotic War," "War 1941–45 with Hitler's Germany," "In 1941 my brother was sent to the front and never returned."
Collapse of U.S.S.R.	30.1	22.2	"Disintegration of the Soviet Union," "Crash of the Soviet system."
Glasnost and perestroika	22.9	25.0	"Beginning of perestroika in Russia under Gorbachev," "Fall of the Berlin Wall," "End of the cold war between U.S.S.R. and USA," "End to the iron curtain."
Space exploration	7.4	11.4	"The first man to visit the cosmos was Yury Gagarin."
Stalin era	5.1	3.0	"Arrest of my father in 1938 (Stalinist terror)," "1937," "Famine in Ukraine in 1933."
Death of Stalin	4.7	2.4	"Death of Stalin and exposing the conse-quences of the cult of personality."
War in Afghanistan	0.8	4.6	"Afghan war," "End of war in Afghanistan."
Other event	16.5	12.3	"Brezhnev coming to the leadership of the country," "Accident at Chernobyl," "Computerization, Internet."

Events unique to the emigrant sample

U.S. events	2.6	–	"Man on the moon," "U.S. President Bill Clinton."
Personal emigration	13.6	–	"Coming to America in 1996," "Arrival in the U.S."
Establishment of Israel	5.1	–	"Creation of the state of Israel."
Possibility of emigration	3.8	–	"Allowing Soviet Jews to immigrate to Israel or USA."

Events mentioned by Russian national sample but not by emigrants

Wars in Chechnya	–	15.9	–
Total	–		
(N)	(999)	(2,000)	

[a]Respondents could name up to two events, so totals do not sum to 100 percent.

United States (table 6.1). Respondents in the youngest cohort, and those who considered themselves "American" (when asked about their ethnic or national identification) were the most likely to mention a U.S. event. Very recent emigrants (those who arrived in 1996–1997) were the least likely to mention a U.S. event, but otherwise there was no association between date of emigration and mention of U.S. events. Since the handful of American events mentioned (the moon landing, the feminist movement, the civil rights movement, the assassination of JFK) mostly took place well before the emigrants' arrival in the United States, these results probably indicate socialization or acculturation influences, to which the youngest emigrants were most exposed through American schooling and greater English-language facility, rather than an emigration effect as such. In general, however, content related to the Soviet Union or its successor states is overwhelmingly dominant in the emigrants' collective memories.

An important difference between the Soviet and American contexts for collective memory lies in the amount of effort invested in the cultural production of officially sanctioned memories. During the Soviet period, the state often sought to harness memory to further its own goals, through commemorative rituals, texts, monuments, and so forth, to which these respondents would have been exposed (Wertsch 2002). Such commemoration may have contributed to the staying power of some Soviet memories, such as World War II or space exploration, but other memories reported by respondents, such as the Stalin era or the death of Stalin, not only were not commemorated, but for political reasons were avoided in the media until the late 1980s. Thus the emigrants' memories do not merely reflect official emphasis and commemoration.

One difficulty in evaluating this evidence on memory content is that the 1980s and 1990s (the period during which the majority of emigrants departed) were distinguished by events of enormous significance taking place in the U.S.S.R., but not by U.S. events of comparable magnitude. Still, there was at least one U.S.-related event from the last decade of the twentieth century that was the focus of much public attention at the time it occurred: the Gulf War, which began in January 1991. (Data from U.S. surveys conducted between July and October 1993 indicate that about one in ten Americans named the Gulf War as one of the two most important events they remembered, and even some nine years after the war, in 2000, about 5 percent mentioned it [table 4.1].) Thus the Gulf War might have made an impression on emigrants as or soon after they settled in the United States, but only a single respondent in the entire emigrant sample mentioned it!

Dates of memories

Despite the absence of American *content* in the emigrants' memories of public events, it seemed possible that the *dates* of events mentioned might show an association with the emigration transition. Even if most memories centered on the emigrants' country of origin, the events they remembered might tend to be those that occurred around the time of their emigration. Clearly such timing cannot account for all memories, since the most frequently mentioned event, World War II, occurred many years before most of the sample emigrated. Two events, however, occurred during the late 1980s and early 1990s, close to the years of emigration for many respondents: glasnost and perestroika and the collapse of the U.S.S.R. Yet there was no association between date of emigration and mentions of either event, even when holding constant other factors. Thus there is no evidence that the critical years effect can be generalized to other kinds of transitions: the emigration period does not produce a clustering of memories similar to that of the critical years.

The persistence of critical years effects

We considered one final possibility: that the experience of emigration might diminish or eliminate the type of critical years effect we reported in chapter 4 for ordinary Americans. Figure 6.1 plots emigrants' mentions of one early event, World War II, and one much later event, Gorbachev's reform program of glasnost and perestroika. The difference in timing of the two events is reflected in the direction of the slope for each plot: World War II is most frequently mentioned by older cohorts, glasnost and perestroika by younger ones. Both plots show a rise among cohorts in their critical years at the time.

   Indeed, for World War II, the tenacity not only of memories but also of terminology and tone is striking. Of those who mentioned the war, one-third referred to the "Great Patriotic War," or used other terms evocative of Soviet media treatments. And even among this mainly Jewish group of emigrants, just 4 percent of those mentioning the war spoke of the Holocaust or of the death toll for Jews specifically, subjects that were not openly discussed during the Soviet period (Tumarkin 1994). In other words, the emigrants' memories do not reflect an American or an American-Jewish perspective on the war (Novick 1999) or even a revised Soviet or Russian perspective that might have been acquired during the late- or post-Soviet period. In terms of their lack of emphasis on the

141

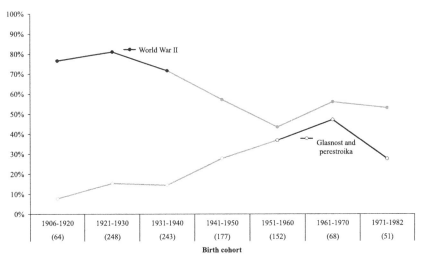

Note: Darker line segments highlight cohorts in their critical years at the time of the event. Cohort *N*s shown in parentheses.

6.1   Emigrants in 2000: Percentages of each birth cohort mentioning World War II (1941–1945) and glasnost and perestroika (1986–1990)

destruction of European Jewry during the war, the emigrants are similar to Russians in the former Soviet Union.

Stalin

Two events related to Stalin show that even subtle differences stemming from critical years experience are visible—a further indication that emigration does not diminish critical years effects. The Stalin era, which extended from 1929 to Stalin's death in 1953, is the earliest of the events mentioned by substantial numbers of emigrants. Given its long duration, we date it using the briefer span of the Great Purges, 1936–1938, that came to symbolize the period. The cohort most likely to mention the Stalin era was in its critical years during the Great Purges, while those most likely to mention Stalin's death specifically were in their critical years in 1953 and thus somewhat younger.

Apart from a brief period of revelations during the short-lived liberalization (the "Thaw") under Nikita Khrushchev, information about the Stalin era was suppressed until the late 1980s. At that point, however, all cohorts would have had ample opportunity to learn about the period from information released about Stalin and the victims of the purges.

Yet mentions of Stalin are concentrated among the cohorts who experienced the Stalin era during their critical years. Similarly, all cohorts would have been exposed to emotionally charged portrayals of World War II as part of the systematic glorification and heroic Soviet war narrative that developed under Leonid Brezhnev, yet the war is especially prominent in the memories of the cohorts who lived through it, not those born later (figure 6.1). Thus neither the subsequent dissemination or restriction of information, nor the experience of emigration, eliminates the critical years effect on memory.

Space exploration

Important Soviet space accomplishments included the Sputnik satellite and the dog Laika, the first animal sent into orbit, both launched in 1957. But the crowning Soviet achievement of the Cold War era was Yury Gagarin's 1961 flight, during which he became the first human to orbit the earth. The emigrants' memories of space achievements fit a critical years effect at the older end, but also extend to younger cohorts who were not even born in 1961. There is no downturn at the younger end, so the results do not completely conform to a critical years effect, but other analysis shows no evidence of distortion resulting from an influence of emigration (and the curve for the Russian national sample's mentions of space achievements is very similar). This result contrasts with findings from our U.S. national sample, where the moon-landing memories also depart from a critical years effect, but in the U.S. case, they extend to cohorts *older* than the critical years (see figure 4.6).

We suspect that the Soviet government's emphasis on space endeavors is responsible for the unusual relation to birth cohort. In the Soviet Union, space achievements represented not only exciting scientific advances, but also victories in the Cold War. Transmitted to the population through schools, works of art, posters, even postage stamps, such accomplishments provided inspiration and excitement, along with confirmation of the superiority of the Soviet system. Even cohorts born after the major aeronautical achievements of the 1950s and 1960s would have been affected by continued commemoration of Gagarin and the work of other cosmonauts and scientists involved in space exploration. Space was mentioned especially frequently by ethnic groups likely to identify positively with the U.S.S.R., suggesting that space achievements were a source of national pride: among the emigrants, non-Jews (mostly ethnic Russians and Ukrainians) mentioned space achievements more than Jews, and in the national sample, Russians did so more than members of ethnic minorities.

Collapse of the Soviet Union

In contrast to other events mentioned by the emigrant sample, there was no sign of a critical years effect for mentions of the 1991 dissolution of the Soviet Union. In fact, critical years cohorts were *less* likely than older cohorts to mention this event. The unexpectedly high mentions of the collapse by older cohorts—which occurred not only for the emigrants but also for the Russian national sample, as discussed in chapter 5—suggest a *lifetime* rather than a critical years effect. Older cohorts especially would have experienced decades of Soviet life with all its frustrations and achievements, and thus may have been more affected both by the "loss of a Soviet master narrative" (Boym 1994: 224) and by changed social and economic circumstances. One emigrant respondent described his memory as follows: "The collapse of the Soviet Union—the country where I was born, finished school and the institute, and worked for 33 years in one place." Another, born in the 1930s, said: "Disintegration of the U.S.S.R. and the whole system in which we lived," and yet another, born in 1906: "Collapse of the U.S.S.R.—disappearance of the usual rules; whether it's a good or a bad thing is hard to say." Just as Lithuanians' mentions of independence evoked its consequences as much or more than the event itself, the emigrants' memories of the collapse of the U.S.S.R. centered on the transformative change it brought about.

Education and Jewish ethnicity

In addition to birth cohort, other social background characteristics were important influences on the emigrants' memories. Respondents with greater educational attainment were more likely to mention World War II, glasnost and perestroika, and the collapse of the U.S.S.R. Jewish ethnicity showed a relation to two events with particular implications for Jews: the Stalin era, characterized by open anti-Semitism, and the establishment of Israel; the latter held personal significance for many emigrants because return to the Jewish homeland provided the Soviet authorities with a face-saving rationale for Jews' departure, thus making it somewhat easier for Jews to obtain exit visas. (Mentions of World War II were not associated with ethnicity; as noted above, the Soviet narrative of World War II did not focus on the threat to Jews.)

Summary of generational effects

There is no doubt that emigration was of crucial importance in these emigrants' lives. In answer to a parallel open-ended question about personal events, 61 percent named emigration as one of the two most important personal events of their lives. (By way of comparison, among married respondents, fewer than half as many mentioned their own marriage or meeting their future spouse.)

Yet despite the losses and challenges of the emigration experience for these refugees, there is no evidence of an emigration effect on memories of national and world events. Instead, the critical years remain a key influence. Table 6.2 summarizes the evidence for the six national events mentioned most frequently by the emigrants, showing that, despite some ambiguity, four of the six events fit a critical years effect. Two events do not entirely fit a critical years pattern, but one, the collapse

Table 6.2 Summary of Critical Years Effects for Events Mentioned by Emigrants from the U.S.S.R. and Successor States, Survey in 2000

Event	Event date	Birth years for critical years cohorts	Does the evidence support the critical years hypothesis . . . [a]	
			at the younger end?	at the older end?
Stalin era	1936–1938	1906–1928	Yes	Yes, though not distinct from lifetime effect[b]
World War II/Great Patriotic War	1941–1945	1911–1935	Yes	Yes, though not distinct from lifetime effect[b]
Death of Stalin	1953	1923–1943	Yes	Yes, though not completely distinct from lifetime effect[c]
Space exploration	1961	1931–1951	No; effect extends to younger cohorts[d]	Yes
Glasnost and perestroika	1986–1990	1956–1980	Yes	Yes
Collapse of the U.S.S.R.	1991	1961–1981	–	No; effect extends to older cohorts[e]

[a]Conclusions are based on chi-square values (see appendix C) and inspection of plots.
[b]For early events, when the cohort curve is truncated at the older end because people beyond the critical years have disappeared from the population, a critical years effect is not distinguishable from a lifetime effect.
[c]The effect extends to slightly older cohorts and is thus not completely distinct from a lifetime effect, but the graphical evidence shows a downturn for the cohort past the critical years.
[d]As explained in the text, space exploration affected cohorts younger than the critical years, possibly because of commemoration and education.
[e]As explained in the text, the collapse of the U.S.S.R. had an impact on cohorts older than the critical years as well as those in their critical years, possibly indicating a lifetime effect.

of the U.S.S.R., may show a lifetime effect, and the other, space exploration, may have been influenced primarily by later exposure through education and official commemoration.

Conclusions

Our evidence indicates that national and world events from a transitional period other than the critical years—emigration—did not imprint themselves on memory, suggesting that more than the mere fact of transition from one significant status or environment to another is involved in the critical years effect. Recent work on adolescence from a life-course perspective portrays the transition to adulthood as a time when young people actively gather and interpret information about the external environment and their own past experience in order to make life choices (e.g., Settersten, Furstenberg, and Rumbaut 2005), which may enhance the importance of experiences at that time.

Moreover, as adolescents approach young adulthood, they also begin to regard themselves as participants in the larger social world. Schwartz (1999: 142) notes the contribution to collective memories of times when "individuals feel society most deeply within themselves." The events adolescents and young adults encounter are not only "first" in the sense of growing awareness; they also represent new opportunities for engagement with the political and social environment, whether young people participate as distant observers, through occasional voting, or through active involvement in political campaigns or military service. While the sense of intense social connectedness that Schwartz (1999) describes may not occur *only* between late childhood and young adulthood, it may be especially likely to occur during those years, as young people begin to participate in the civic life of their communities. The first big event to occur gains in addition because of its primacy (Tulving 2008).

SEVEN

Generational Experience of War and the Development of New Attitudes

If important past events are recalled more readily because they occurred during a person's *critical years* of childhood, adolescence, or early adulthood, they should also be available to be drawn on when an entirely new issue arises and calls for the development of a new attitude. In this chapter, we treat past generational experience as a potential source of influence on the formation of attitudes. We consider the conditions that might stimulate individuals to connect the past with the present—here, when developing attitudes toward appeals for military action by each of two American presidents: George H. W. Bush and George W. Bush.

The United States fought two wars against Iraq during the late twentieth century and early twenty-first century: the brief and highly successful Gulf War of the early 1990s, and the much longer and much less successful Iraq War that began in 2003 and was still seen as uncertain in its outcome after the final departure of the American military in 2011. We distinguish between the two wars by referring to the first as the "Gulf War," as it was called at the time, and the second as the "Iraq War," as it is still called. In each case, views of two earlier major wars—World War II and the Vietnam War—might have been drawn on by Americans of different cohorts for developing attitudes toward one or both of the new wars. The results of our investigations into the two cases turn out to be entirely different, and they support an important theoretical distinction between two meanings of the term "generational effects," already suggested in chapter 5.

The Gulf War in 1990–1991

On August 2, 1990, Iraqi troops suddenly invaded and occupied the small but oil-rich neighboring nation of Kuwait, with all resistance ending in a matter of hours. Within days, President George H. W. Bush declared that the invasion "will not stand," and the international community immediately condemned the Iraqi actions. On August 6, the United Nations Security Council imposed economic sanctions against Iraq. After various attempts by Saddam Hussein to delay withdrawal from Kuwait, all of which the United States treated as unacceptable, the Security Council on November 29 passed a resolution that gave Iraq until January 15, 1991, to withdraw its troops. In addition, it empowered member states to use "all necessary means" to force Iraq out of Kuwait if that deadline was not met.

The United States assembled a coalition of forces to join it in opposing Iraq's occupation of Kuwait, including contributions from thirty-four countries. The U.S. military played the dominant role, however, and a U.S. Army general, Norman Schwarzkopf, was named commander of all coalition forces in the Persian Gulf area. Many Americans probably knew little about Kuwait previously and thus the invasion was an entirely new event toward which they had no readily available attitude. We use the weeks leading up to the Gulf War and the war itself as an exemplar of a situation calling for the construction of new attitudes by Americans.

Four conditions for effects of the past

One condition for a past event to exert an important generational effect in the present is that the past event should have made a lasting impression on the memories of those who experienced it during their youth. Two events that fulfill this condition for Americans were World War II and the Vietnam War. In chapter 4 we found that World War II was the first or second most frequently mentioned event when national samples of Americans were asked between 1985 and 2010 to name one or two "events or changes" from the recent past that seemed to them "especially important." Vietnam was mentioned less often, but nevertheless ranged from second in rank to sixth among all events, and it was never absent from our list of most frequently named events. (The indecisive Korean War, 1950–1953, on the other hand, was not mentioned frequently enough to provide a meaningful ranking; nor was it invoked in the public debate that concerns us here, as were both Vietnam and World War II.) Furthermore, as discussed in chapter 4, mentions of World War II and the Vietnam War both showed effects of critical years experience—clear in the case of Vietnam and at least partly so for World War II.

A second condition for generational effects on attitudes toward current issues is that the impression from the past should be largely consensual, so that most people regard the past event in a similar way, at least at some level of collective memory. There is little doubt that World War II has been widely viewed by Americans as having been a "good war," with clear moral aims and a victorious outcome. It is also true that Vietnam has left a much more negative impression on the public, a sense that it failed to achieve any meaningful goal despite the loss of many lives. There are different and even contrary explanations as to why the Vietnam war was a "mistake" (Schuman 1972), but the sense of a failed military involvement has been broadly held. The consensus at this general level is reflected in the attraction of the Vietnam Memorial: the long list of the dead and the absence of images of victory symbolize something tragic to all who visit it, regardless of different views on the nature of that tragedy (Wagner-Pacifici and Schwartz 1991). As further evidence on both wars, a national survey in 1991 found that 89 percent of the American public regarded World War II as a "just" war, while the corresponding figure for Vietnam was only 25 percent (*The Gallup Poll Monthly*, February 1991).

A third condition for a generational effect on a new attitude is that the current issue must capture public attention so that most people feel a pressing need to develop beliefs about it and accompanying attitudes for or against proposed actions. Just such an issue was provided by the crisis in the Persian Gulf that occurred when Iraq suddenly occupied Kuwait in August 1990. The condemnation by President George H. W. Bush and his decision to send American troops to Saudi Arabia, a major oil country bordering Kuwait, drew immediate public attention, and in the days that followed, all U.S. media outlets focused on the Persian Gulf to the exclusion of almost all other news. Accounts of both the scope of the military effort and the hardships facing troops suddenly plunked down in a vast desert were vividly portrayed on television night after night. Indeed, the Gulf crisis "triggered more network news stories in a shorter period of time than any event in television's history" (Lichter 1992: 224). According to a Gallup Poll in December 1990 (*The Gallup Poll Monthly*, February, 1991), 89 percent of the American public claimed to be following the news from the Persian Gulf "very" or "fairly closely," with only 9 percent saying "not too closely" and a mere 2 percent saying "not at all"—an extraordinary set of figures for any international event! Thus the third condition of a sharp focus on a current political issue by nearly the whole country was met in a stunning fashion by the crisis in the Gulf.

A final condition for broadly felt effects from the past stems from our assumption that many people may not spontaneously dwell on historical analogies in attempting to understand a new problem. Instead, analogies to past events are often made salient by leaders who attempt to shape attitudes toward a particular policy. Exactly this happened with the Gulf crisis: during the course of an open, dramatic, and lengthy debate, prominent figures on both sides of the issue called on lessons of history to explain and justify their positions. On the one hand, President George H. W. Bush—himself a member of the World War II generation—explicitly and repeatedly compared Iraq's leader Saddam Hussein to Adolf Hitler, and Iraq's action to the Nazi conquest of small neighboring countries prior to World War II. Other government leaders echoed the analogy as part of the argument for American military action.

In contrast, those who opposed offensive military force drew heavily on the American experience in Vietnam to explain their view. For example, Senator Bob Kerrey—speaking as a Medal of Honor veteran wounded in Vietnam—told the Senate Armed Services Committee: "I believe that if we launch a military offensive, we will sustain thousands of casualties without military necessity, moral justification, or public endorsement" (Toner 1991: 51). Invocations of Vietnam undoubtedly had different meanings to different listeners, but for most Americans, Vietnam probably suggested the likelihood of many deaths in a war that could turn out to be far easier to begin than to win, though for others it may also have meant the grievous effects of military violence for all sides in a conflict regardless of the outcome.

Thus the public argument turned on which was the better analogy to American military action in the Gulf: the need to stop Hitler at the beginning of World War II, or the Vietnam War, so often characterized as a quagmire (VanDeMark 1995).

Presenting the two analogies

Beginning in October 1990, we asked national cross-section samples in the United States the following three questions each month through most of February:

Now I'm going to read you two comparisons people are making about the current situation in the Middle East. For each, please tell me your first reaction—whether it is a good way to look at the situation, or is it not such a good comparison.

1. First, Saddam Hussein of Iraq is like Adolf Hitler of Germany in the 1930s, and it is important to stop him now or he will just seize one country after another. Is that a good way to look at the situation, or is that not such a good comparison?
2. The second comparison is that getting involved with Iraq in the Middle East is a lot like getting involved in Vietnam in the 1960s, and a small commitment at first can lead to years of conflict without clear results. Is that a good way to look at the situation, or is that not such a good comparison?
3. Which of the two comparisons do you think best fits the Middle East situation with Iraq—the comparison to Hitler and Germany in the 1930s or the comparison to Vietnam in the 1960s?

We randomized the order of the first two questions, so that half of each month's sample received the Hitler question first and half received the Vietnam question first.[1]

The two agree/disagree statements presented initially—the Hitler and Vietnam analogies—have the weakness of giving only one analogy at a time and of being in an agree/disagree format that has been shown to lead to "acquiescence bias"—the tendency of some people to agree with almost any plausible assertion.[2] Thus the function of the two agree/disagree statements was simply to make certain that all respondents were exposed to each historical analogy before being asked the third question, which required a clear choice between the two.

---

1. More details on the sampling and interviewing in relation to steps toward the war can be found in Schuman and Rieger (1992).

2. Such bias shows up in the fact that although the first two items are negatively associated in the total population, as they should be on logical grounds, the association is positive for those with less than a high school degree. This is the classic form of acquiescence by less educated respondents described by Campbell, Converse, Miller, and Stokes (1960).

Although the analogy to Hitler received somewhat more agreement than the analogy to Vietnam throughout the entire period, the forced-choice question showed a fairly even division through December, then a 10-percentage-point jump in favor of the Hitler analogy during the two weeks preceding the U.S. bombing, another 11-point jump in the two weeks after the war began on January 16, and a still further rise of 7 points during February. The key findings emerge when we consider carefully the results presented in figure 7.1, which shows analogy preference by birth cohort prior to the start of bombing and can be seen to divide empirically across two main sets of cohorts. (Approximately 15 percent of respondents did not choose one of the two analogies offered, said "don't know," or did not answer; these respondents are excluded from figures 7.1 and 7.2.)

Our conclusions are based on a step-by-step interpretation of the figure. First, the cohorts on the right side of the figure, born between 1946 and 1970, were in their youth (early childhood to age twenty-seven) between the beginning and end of the Vietnam War (1965–1973). Their relatively greater choice of the Vietnam analogy (as compared to cohorts born in 1945 and before) fits the critical years hypothesis well, but does not exclude other possible interpretations.

Second, most of the cohorts born between 1921 and 1945 were young during World War II, which was of course connected directly to Hitler's

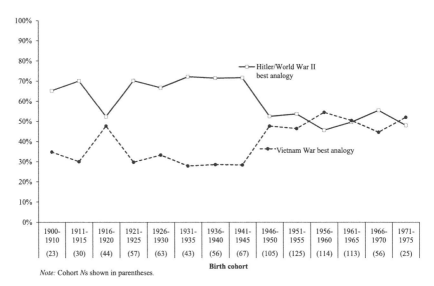

Note: Cohort Ns shown in parentheses.

7.1 Before the war: Percentages of each birth cohort choosing Hitler/World War II and Vietnam analogies for 1990–1991 Gulf War. (SRC 1990–1991)

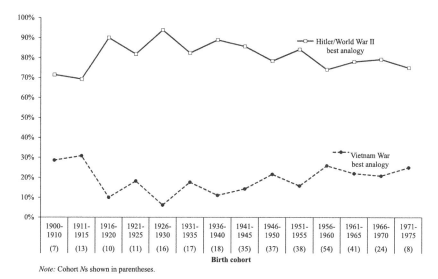

7.2   During the war: Percentages of each birth cohort choosing Hitler/World War II and
       Vietnam analogies for 1990–1991 Gulf War. (SRC 1991)

conquest of much of Europe. Thus their disproportionate choice of the
Hitler analogy is also mainly consistent with the critical years hypothesis. Yet as we saw previously in chapter 4, we cannot rule out a lifetime
effect at the older end of the curve because we do not have available still
earlier cohorts who might or might not have chosen World War II.

However, the third step shows that we do have evidence against a
lifetime interpretation, because all those born between 1921 and 1945
were *also* exposed to the Vietnam War as adults. These respondents had
lived through World War II (or heard about it very soon afterward from
their parents or others) *and* the Vietnam War. Yet as we have just seen,
they tended to choose the Hitler analogy more than the Vietnam analogy. Thus, the critical years experience of the older cohorts tended to be
more important than their experience of the Vietnam War, even though
their Vietnam experience had the added benefit of recency—which we
know to be an important force in memory (Bower 2000).

For this real-life instance—a type of natural experiment where the
American population debated which past to draw on for a lesson about
a serious new issue—the evidence indicates that experience during the
critical years carried greater weight than experience at other times of the
life course. Each set of birth cohorts (World War II and Vietnam) favored
its "own" war as the preferred analogy. Even though the World War II

cohorts had lived through the Vietnam years and had full access to it as an analogy, they nevertheless regarded the World War II comparison as the more applicable one. In sum, this case study of a brief but dramatic point in American history provides useful evidence for the potency of critical years effects on new attitudes.

Once the war began on January 16, 1991, attitudes among all cohorts moved strongly toward the Hitler choice, as figure 7.2 shows, though with some remnant of the earlier difference still visible.[3] This shift reminds us that although past experience can contribute importantly to new beliefs and attitudes, such experience certainly does not entirely control or shape them, particularly in a rapidly changing situation. What actually happens as a result of a new event and its consequences can substantially change beliefs and attitudes of many, if not all, people. We would not wish to argue otherwise.

On February 28, President Bush stated that Kuwait had been liberated and announced a cease-fire, and three days later Iraq accepted the cease-fire resolution passed by the U.N. Security Council. The entire war was over six weeks after its start, widely hailed as a remarkable success for the United States.

We should emphasize that our concern here has been primarily with the effect of analogies on public attitudes. Khong (1992) considers at some length the possibility that the same World War II analogies were not merely a means of winning public support, but had influenced Lyndon Johnson and other leaders personally as they made the decision to escalate the war in Vietnam. From our standpoint, the impact of cohort experience on the general public is not necessarily distinct from its influence on individual political leaders. In this context, though, it is interesting to note that George H. W. Bush himself was a leader socialized by his experience serving in the military during World War II. This was not the case for his son, George W. Bush, who, though he grew up during the Vietnam War, did not join protests at Yale or elsewhere. We have no way of knowing the extent to which George W. Bush's lack of participation in the Vietnam protest movement, or indeed possibly a vicarious identification with his father's World War II experience, may have affected his initiation of the 2003 invasion of Iraq.

---

3. In January 1991, when war seemed imminent, Schuman and Rieger (1992) added a direct question asking whether the respondent would support or oppose U.S. military action if needed. Once the war began, that question was changed to ask whether the respondent supported the military action under way. These two questions are not needed for our present analysis, but are available to others if of interest.

The Iraq War in 2003–2011

Other than constancy in the name of the enemy, the American invasion of Iraq on March 20, 2003, differed in virtually every respect from the Gulf War of 1990–1991. Instead of an American president responding to Iraq's invasion of a neighboring country, the new war began with an American invasion of Iraq itself. Instead of international unity, there was strong dissent from a number of nations. Rather than the war ending in a matter of weeks with unconditional victory, the occupation of Iraq toward the end of 2004—the point at which we first gathered evidence—continued to meet resistance and to experience casualties, some twenty months after the initial invasion. (The war did not end officially for Americans for another seven years, with Iraq still in turmoil at that point.) Moreover, although the decision to invade Iraq had substantial public support at the start, that support steadily eroded over time. A Gallup Poll found 70 percent support for the invasion at the beginning of the war, with only 13 percent strongly opposed, but by December 2004, a Quinnipiac University Poll found that 52 percent thought launching the war had been the wrong thing to do.

Indeed, the vast majority of casualties, both military and civilian, occurred in the weeks and months following a speech by President George W. Bush on May 1, 2003, that declared major combat operations ended. The most serious fighting of the war began on March 31, 2004, when Iraqi insurgents in Fallujah ambushed a convoy led by four U.S. private military contractors. The contractors were killed and their burned corpses were hung over a bridge crossing the Euphrates. U.S. Marines fought in Fallujah in November 2004 and then engaged in the bloodiest battle of the war: the Second Battle of Fallujah, described by the U.S. military as "intense, close and personal, the likes of which has been experienced on just a few occasions since the battle of Huế City in Vietnam" (Ricks 2006: 399–400).

Furthermore, by 2004 the main rationale for launching the war—Saddam Hussein's supposed development of weapons of mass destruction—had been judged a complete mistake, thus undermining the original argument for fighting by American troops. Another important development in 2004 was the revelation of widespread prisoner abuse at Abu Ghraib, which received international media attention in April of that year. First reports of the Abu Ghraib prisoner issue, as well as graphic pictures showing U.S. military personnel taunting and abusing Iraqi prisoners, came to public attention from many news reports. The revelation dealt a blow to the moral justification for the occupation of Iraq in the eyes of many people and was a turning point in the war.

In mid-December 2004, we used the organization SurveyUSA to ask the following forced-choice question about possible World War II and Vietnam analogies. The sample consisted of 4,068 Americans from five states: California, Colorado, Ohio, Pennsylvania, and Texas.[4]

Some people think that what the United States is doing in Iraq is like our fighting in World War II.

Other people think that what the United States is doing in Iraq is like our fighting in the Vietnam War.

Do you see the Iraq War as more like World War II or more like the Vietnam War?

We found that the Vietnam analogy was chosen by almost two-thirds (66 percent) of our total sample, with World War II selected by the remainder (34 percent). Whatever may have been the case at the beginning of the Iraq War in early 2003, by the end of its second year in 2004, the negative analogy of Vietnam loomed as the closer parallel for most Americans.

Our main interest is in the relation of the preferred analogy to birth cohort. Based on the critical years hypothesis, the preference for the Vietnam War over the World War II analogy should have been greater among those who were in their adolescence or early adulthood during the Vietnam War, as compared to those who were older or younger during the Vietnam War period. However, this turned out not to be the case: almost identical large percentages (70 percent) of the Vietnam War cohorts and of the older World War II cohorts (who had also lived through the Vietnam War) chose the Vietnam analogy when asked about the new Iraq War. In other words, most of those who had lived through the Vietnam War at *any* point in their adult lifetime saw it as an appropriate analogy to the new Iraq War. The only cohorts that did not choose the

4. Although a national sample would have been preferable, as well as closer adaptation of the questions used for the Gulf War, there were practical constraints that led to the actual design. As usual, our concern is not with univariate distributions but with the relationships of beliefs and attitudes to cohort, and we have no reason to believe that the basic relations of birth cohort to the Vietnam versus World War II choice would not hold for the nation as a whole. See Schuman and Corning (2006) for evidence that our findings on the Iraq War were consistent with both national partisan differences (Republicans more supportive than Democrats) and regional differences (Texans the most supportive of the five states). In addition, polls by SurveyUSA have had a very good record in predicting the outcome of national elections, and in the present case we were also able to replicate the main findings six months later with an Ohio sample.

Vietnam War analogy were those too young to have been alive at all during the Vietnam period. Therefore, we must reject the critical years explanation for choice of the Vietnam analogy in the case of the Iraq War.

Hypotheses about the effects of generation, or, in our terms, cohort experience, can be stated in two versions. First, the lifetime hypothesis suggests that, when an important event occurs, it will make a stronger impression on all persons alive at the time than on those not born until a later point. The second, more sharply focused critical years hypothesis states that (as we saw in chapters 4 and 5) an important event experienced during the years of late childhood, adolescence, or early adulthood makes such a strong impact on memory that it is more readily recalled at a later point by those who experienced it during their youth than by other cohorts. The results of the present study of preferred analogies to the first two years of the Iraq War support the lifetime model rather than the critical years model, unlike the earlier Gulf War.

We believe that the difference between the sudden and sharp public debate about future military action in the Gulf War in 1990, together with its quick success in early 1991, and the increasing disillusionment with the Iraq War almost two years after the American invasion in 2003, accounts for the different cohort effects. The Iraq War involved prolonged experience by an American population that had initially supported the invasion but had learned painfully that both its rationale and its outcome were very different than had been first believed. Many of these cohorts had also experienced something similar during the Vietnam War. Regardless of their ages during Vietnam, almost all those who experienced the Vietnam War during their own lifetimes now used it to interpret their negative experience with the new Iraq War.

Our lifetime interpretation of these results is similar to one offered by Osborne, Sears, and Valentino (2011) for an unanticipated lifetime effect in Democratic Party identification by cohorts in the South who lived through the 1960s civil rights strife: the length as well as the intensity of the struggle during those years seems to have affected all cohorts, not only those in their "impressionable years," as the investigators had expected. It is likely that for some events, as was indeed the case for Lithuanian collective memories of independence from the Soviet Union (chapter 5, pp. 112–113), the main distinction is between those who were deeply affected at *any* point in the life course and those not born until later years. The latter, Americans who had not lived at all during the Vietnam era, could not and did not rely on Vietnam to the same degree when asked to choose an analogy from the past for the Iraq War.

Conclusions

It might seem as though our results from the 1990–1991 Gulf War and those from the later Iraq War point in different directions: the one showing an effect due to experience during the critical years, the other much less so. But considering both time periods and both sets of findings together indicates that they are not inconsistent.

First, attitudes assessed in the months leading up to the Gulf War were especially influenced, we believe, by critical years experience during World War II *or* the Vietnam War for the cohorts growing up during one or the other time period, as our Figure 7.1 showed. Their previous experience was the only basis they had for predicting what a new war in an unfamiliar part of the world would be like.

Second, we believe that attitudes toward the later Iraq War were influenced not mainly by experience during World War II *or* during the Vietnam War, but primarily by events in the Iraq War itself from its start in early 2003 through the end of 2004 when our data were collected. Those fresh and quite recent events showed Americans that their initial assumptions at the time of the American invasion were largely false in three respects:

first, the rationale for the invasion—that Saddam Hussein possessed weapons of mass destruction—had turned out to be incorrect;

second, the moral basis of the American military effort was undermined by the shock of Abu Ghraib;

third, and perhaps most important of all, the belief in a speedy victory with almost no American casualties (as had happened in the Gulf War) was seen by the end of 2004 to be unfounded.

At that point in time, the Iraq War already looked more like the Vietnam experience than like the U.S. experience in World War II. All these outcomes were recent and salient when our survey took place at the end of 2004. Thus it is no surprise that the predominant response was that the Iraq War was more similar to the Vietnam War than to World War II, and furthermore that the still continuing events in Iraq affected the judgments of most Americans.

In addition, because the Gulf War occurred suddenly in a time of peace in 1990, respondents to a survey who turned to a past collective memory for guidance at that point should have recalled World War II if they had lived through that war during their critical years, as did

President George H. W. Bush, or the Vietnam War, as did Senator Bob Kerrey and others of his cohort. But during the first two years of the Iraq War, its widely reported failures clearly resembled those of Vietnam as recalled by those who had experienced that earlier war, *regardless* of their age at the time, so the difficulties in Iraq would have mostly brought the Vietnam experience to mind.

In sum, the Gulf War and the Iraq War were not at all parallel experiences for Americans. Collective memory can have an important effect on new attitudes, but the extent and way in which individuals relate collective memories to the present and the attitudes they develop will always be influenced significantly by ongoing events.

EIGHT

Autobiographical Memory versus Collective Memory

We have dealt thus far entirely with collective memories of historical figures or of national and world events—memories by Americans and others of events such as World War II, the fall of the Berlin Wall, and the 9/11 attack on the United States. However, at the same time that we and other social scientists have been exploring collective memories, a number of psychologists have been carrying out research on "autobiographical memories"—recall by individuals of personal events from their own lives. These personal memories have often been studied by presenting a set of single words ("word cues") to respondents and asking for personal associations prompted by the words (following Crovitz and Schiffman [1974]), or by asking other types of more direct questions about their past.

Autobiographical and collective memories were brought together—or rather, what we call collective memories of national events were treated as one form of autobiographical memory—in an important article by Rubin, Rahhal, and Poon (1998), entitled "Things Learned in Early Adulthood Are Remembered Best." Despite the words "early adulthood" in the title, the thesis of the article was that events occurring between the ages of ten and thirty are the source of a large proportion of later autobiographical memories of all kinds. Along with evidence on personal memories, the article included figures showing results for national and world events first published by Schuman and Scott (1989) and included by us in chapter 4, as well as still other evidence on memories for sports, films, and other experiences that date mostly from the ten to thirty age range.

When describing the distribution of early ages that gave rise to their results, Rubin, Rahhal, and Poon (1998) and other memory psychologists have characterized what we call the *critical years* as creating a "reminiscence bump" (Rubin and Schulkind 1997). The term starts from the fact that disproportionate memories from the early years of life (including what we refer to as memories of national and world events) partly reverse the usual finding by psychologists that recall is greatest soon after a person learns something new, followed by a consistent decline in remembering over time (Bower 2000). Thus individuals are especially likely to remember recent events, but a distribution of events remembered over the life course shows that the steady decline in the number of memories with distance in time is interrupted by a "bump," which indicates that many memories seem to date from the ten to thirty age span. Such a bump has been reported many times in a wide range of psychological research and is often considered one of the most consistent results from studies of autobiographical memory (Glück and Bluck 2007). The term "reminiscence bump," often shortened to the catchier "bump," has appeared with great frequency in psychology journals to describe the early developmental years populated with events recalled by adults who are in their older years.

However, the evidence reported by Rubin, Rahhal, and Poon (1998) comparing personal memories and collective memories of national and world events came from different investigators, in different disciplines, using different data collected at different points in time. The authors did not, and at that point could not, look closely at the exact location in age for both types of memory. A subsequent lack of cross-disciplinary investigation of the relation of different types of memories to age has been reinforced by the separation of journals by discipline, so that readers of research on autobiographical memory are often unaware of research on collective memory, and vice versa. In addition, the different terminology—"reminiscence bump," popularized by psychologists, versus "critical years," used by sociologists, including ourselves—has created a further barrier.[1]

---

1. References to sociologists apply also to political scientists, who in writing about political socialization use still another term, "impressionable years," as essentially synonymous with "critical years" (Sears and Levy 2003). Neither "impressionable years" nor "critical years" is regarded as reflecting an instinctual process, as in some animal studies (e.g., Burley 2006), but instead is seen as due to the increased exposure and sensitivity to larger national and world events that children experience as they enter adolescence and early adulthood.

Here we report research that compared the two types of memory when—for the first time—both were obtained from the same large sample: a cross-section of Americans ages eighteen and older in 2011. We find that both forms of memory do come from a broad age span characterized by psychologists as showing a "reminiscence bump" for personal events and by us as indicating critical years for memories of national and world events. But within that period, there are important differences in the specific ages to which the two types of memories are linked—differences that point to distinctions valuable to recognize and interpret. In addition, the distinctions lead us to consider past reports of research on memory for musical events and for sports figures, and all of this evidence points to the possibility of differences in the interests and preoccupations that characterize various developmental stages. We are able to put together the different forms of memory and the ages sensitive to each in order to arrive at a broader theory of what is remembered from which ages, and why.

Autobiographical and Collective Memories

Using a national sample of U.S. adults in June 2011, we presented both psychologists' inquiries about autobiographical events (with word cues employed to elicit personal memories) and our own inquiry about collective memories of important national and world events (employing the standard Events question drawn on in chapters 4 and 5 and reproduced below). Thus we repeated the original Rubin, Rahhal, and Poon (1998) comparison, but did so with the *same* individuals answering both types of questions.

In order to ensure adequate precision for the age distributions of both kinds of memories, we obtained a large probability sample (N = 2,085) of U.S. adults, which has the additional advantage of including variation by age, education, gender, and other social-background characteristics. Probability sampling of such a clearly defined population facilitates later replication in the same population, whether to assess reliability or to try out changes in wording—both of which we did and report at a later point in this chapter.[2]

2. For additional analysis and details on the study, see Schuman and Corning (2014). Data in this chapter were gathered for us through the KnowledgePanel survey series (administered initially by Knowledge Networks and then by GfK), which used probability sampling to create a large national panel. Panel members agree in advance to respond to later questionnaires by Internet (with equipment furnished if needed), and they are then randomly allocated for a particular survey such

Since posing questions about both collective and autobiographical memories to the same individuals might produce different results depending on which question was asked first, we randomized the two sequences of questions and examined the possible effect of question order. We found that the order did not change the basic patterns reported in this chapter for either type of memory. An unrelated question on respondent's place of birth was also included as a "buffer" between the two types of memory questions, but it had no effect either alone or in combination with question order, and thus we do not deal with it further here.

To assess autobiographical memory, respondents were given eight simple words one at a time (flower, horse, fire, bird, lake, window, book, friend) and asked to respond by indicating "a specific event from your own life that each word brings to mind. It may or may not be an event you think of as important, but it should have happened at a specific point in your life, whether recent, long ago, or at any other time." Examples of responses to the word cues "fire," "bird," and "window" were: "Roasting marshmallows over a camp fire," "An owl I found that was sick," "Chipping ice from windows in winter." After describing each memory, respondents indicated how old they recalled having been at the time of the personal event they remembered.

The associations with age that we obtained using each of the eight word cues are presented in figure 8.1. A reminiscence bump or critical years effect is apparent for each word, and since the distributions are quite similar, we averaged them and will refer mainly to that summary, shown in figure 8.2, though the evidence in figure 8.1 is valuable for showing the close replication across the different word cues. Studies of the reminiscence bump in memories of personal events ordinarily limit their examination to respondents beyond the bump age itself, because for people in their teens and twenties the period of the reminiscence bump coincides with the period of recency, so that the two effects are confounded. In both figures 8.1 and 8.2, we follow Conway and

as ours, which minimizes self-selection in terms of survey content. The final sample drawn for our survey was stratified to reflect U.S. national distributions for age, education, and other basic demographic variables, and should be representative of Americans ages eighteen and older in 2011, rather than being a convenience or purely self-selected sample as in most autobiographical memory studies. (The carefully reported two-stage response rate was .16 for recruitment into the panel, and .64 for completion of the survey, levels fairly typical of good national surveys at that time. Independent analyses of response-rate data based on initial probability sampling have indicated that variables not clearly related to taking part in a particular survey are seldom affected by nonresponse [see appendix B, page 221], as suggested also by the success of most final preelection polls in the 2008 and 2012 presidential elections in the United States.) In addition and very important is the fact that the coverage and response rates for our survey were the same for *both* types of memory and are therefore quite unlikely to account for any differences in results.

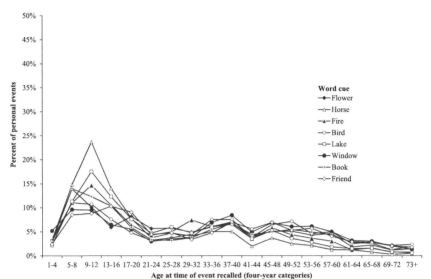

Note: Data points show personal events recalled from each age as a percentage of memories for each word cue; base *N*s for each word cue range from 1,509 to 1,557.

8.1   Personal events recalled from each age in response to eight word cues

Williams (2008) in restricting our sample to those aged thirty-five and older, though in fact neither using the full sample, nor limiting our focus to people over sixty-five, leads to changes in the figures that would affect our conclusions.[3]

The bump in figure 8.2 is in the range covered by the ages of approximately five to twenty, with the peak at nine to twelve. (Although the figures show ages one to four, there are very few claims of recall from those ages, which fits the assumption that this is the period of childhood amnesia; such responses may be either erroneous in dating or otherwise very unusual.) The range is similar to that reported by Jansari and Parkin (1996), using a sample of students and employees at a British university, and also by Janssen, Rubin, and St. Jacques (2011), using a large Internet sample. Indeed, Rubin and Schulkind (1997) suggest that the bump may well go back to age five—"that is, back to the childhood amnesia component" (529). Our evidence supports such an extension to earlier than

---

3. The gradual decrease in height at the tail of the curve for memories dating from older ages results in part from the natural decline in the numbers of adults within the population who are old enough to remember events from each older age category. For example, all respondents included in the figure can remember events from their early thirties, but only those aged seventy and older can recall events from their late sixties.

the ten to thirty range often given for the reminiscence bump and also fits our findings in chapter 4 about the early ages of memories of the 1963 assassination of President John F. Kennedy due to its occurrence during the day and its impact on adults close to young children.

To examine collective memories, we adapted the standard Events question used extensively in our earlier chapters:

There have been a lot of national and world events and changes over the past 50 or so years—say, from about 1930 right up until today. Would you mention one or two such events or changes that seem to you to have been especially important?" [IF ONLY ONE MENTION: Is there any other national or world event or change over the past 50 years that you feel was especially important?]

The total period of time defined by the question changed depending on the date of the survey, but 1930 has always been the starting point. In our 2011 comparison of collective and autobiographical memory, the total period indicated was "80 or so years," in order to include the 1930s.

Responses to the collective memory question were used to create dichotomous variables showing mention of a particular event as especially important versus no mention of the event. Specific events given

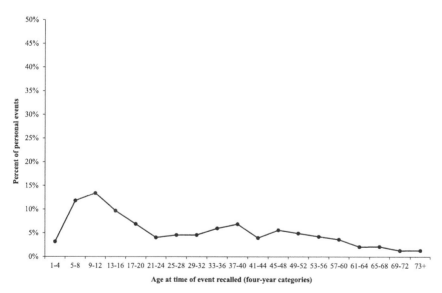

Note: Data points show personal events recalled from each age as a percentage of the total memories recalled, averaged across eight word cues; the base *N* is 12,273 memories (produced by 1,575 respondents).

8.2   Personal events recalled from each age (average across eight word cues)

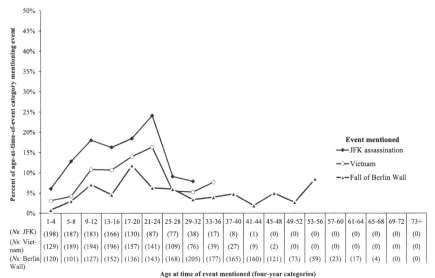

	1-4	5-8	9-12	13-16	17-20	21-24	25-28	29-32	33-36	37-40	41-44	45-48	49-52	53-56	57-60	61-64	65-68	69-72	73+
(Ns: JFK)	(198)	(187)	(183)	(166)	(130)	(87)	(77)	(38)	(17)	(8)	(1)	(0)	(0)	(0)	(0)	(0)	(0)	(0)	(0)
(Ns: Vietnam)	(129)	(189)	(194)	(196)	(157)	(141)	(109)	(76)	(39)	(27)	(9)	(2)	(0)	(0)	(0)	(0)	(0)	(0)	(0)
(Ns: Berlin Wall)	(120)	(101)	(127)	(152)	(136)	(143)	(168)	(205)	(177)	(165)	(160)	(121)	(73)	(59)	(23)	(17)	(4)	(0)	(0)

Age at time of event mentioned (four-year categories)

Note: Data points show percentages of respondents in each age group mentioning each event. Total number of survey respondents was 2,085; base Ns for each age group and event are shown in parentheses. Only data points with base Ns of at least 30 are plotted.

8.3   Percentages mentioning three national and world events as important, by age at time of event

as important in this 2011 comparison included World War II (1941–1945), the assassination of President Kennedy (1963), the Vietnam War (1965–1973), the fall of the Berlin Wall (1989), and the September 11, 2001, terrorist attacks—all events we have considered in earlier chapters. Because of the ambiguities involving lifetime and recency effects inherent in early events like World War II and recent events like 9/11, as discussed in chapter 4, we prefer a conservative approach here that focuses on intermediate events not so open to alternative interpretations. For this purpose, the Kennedy assassination, the Vietnam War, and the fall of the Berlin Wall are especially valuable, because each shows the predicted critical years effect as part of a curvilinear distribution that largely precludes competing lifetime or recency interpretations. (Results for World War II and 9/11 are consistent with conclusions based on the other three events, however.)

Respondents' ages at the time of each event named can be readily calculated, and when mentions of the event are distributed by age at the time of the event, a critical years increase or reminiscence bump is visible, as shown for three events in figure 8.3, with peaks in the late teens and early twenties similar to those reported in chapter 4. (Since our focus here is age at the time the events occurred, the x-axis in figures 8.3, 8.5, and 8.6 omits respondents who were infants or not born at the time of an event.) Despite the different dates of the three events themselves, the ages are largely within the often-cited reminiscence bump or critical years age span of ten to thirty. But it is important to note that collective memories peak in the later years of that range, between seventeen and twenty-four for each event.

It is necessary to keep in mind that the questions typically used to obtain autobiographical and collective memories are framed differently. The x-axis in figures 8.1 and 8.2 shows each respondent's remembered age at the time of the personal event he or she had reported in response to a word cue, and percentages are based on the total sample drawn for the survey. The distribution by ages at the time of each national and world event shown in figure 8.3 reflects the proportions of respondents within each age-at-time-of-event category who mentioned each event. This difference precludes a straightforward analysis using cross-classification, and our approach therefore compares the ages of respondents at the time of the personal events they remember and their ages at the dates of the national and world events they recall as especially important.

Comparing the Results for the Two Types of Memories

Our most important finding from this comparison of personal and collective memories is that the reminiscence bump for autobiographical memories elicited by word cues tends to be located at younger ages (especially five through sixteen or a little older) than the critical years for memories of important national and world events (approximately seventeen to twenty-four), even though both kinds of memories fall within the broad age span of childhood, adolescence, and early adulthood that has often been called the reminiscence bump period—in our figures, approximately ages five to thirty.

A replication

A separate replication seemed desirable with regard to the word-cued associations, all of which came from our single 2011 survey. We believe it is the entire orientation of the word-cue task presented to respondents that accounts for the difference between the age location of the word-cued associations and the collective memories, and not simply inclusion of the word "important" in the latter question and not the

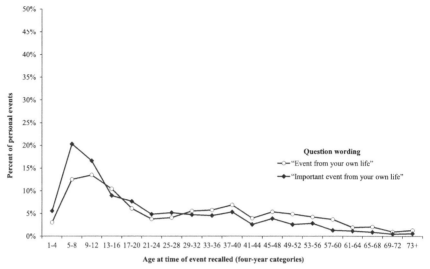

Note: Data points show personal events recalled from each age as a percentage of the total "book" and "fire" word-cued memories recalled, averaged across two word cues; the base *N* for question wording that includes "important" is 2,010 memories (produced by 1,040 respondents), and for wording that omits "important," 3,063 memories (produced by 1,563 respondents).

8.4   Personal events recalled from each age (average across two word cues) with and without "important" in the question

former. However, to test this hypothesis, in our second survey (N=1,406) in September 2011, we repeated two of the original word cues, but added the adjective "important" to the word-cued memory instructions, with the rest of the instructions essentially unchanged:

On the next screens, you will see two different words. Please briefly describe a specific important event from your own life that each word brings to mind. It should have happened at a specific point in your life, whether recent, long ago, or at any other time.

As figure 8.4 shows, the autobiographical word associations do not move closer in age to the collective memories when the word "important" is added as an adjective within the instruction to give personal word associations.[4] The location of autobiographical memories is replicated almost perfectly despite this change; if anything, the replication

4. Only two word cues could be used in the replication because of limited resources, but results of the first study shown in figure 8.1 indicated that two words were adequate for this further comparison. Both words we chose, "book" and "fire," were ones that might prompt memories from a wide range of ages.

points to a slightly earlier age for the reminiscence bump than the original inquiry.

A second more exact replication

Our two experiments on memories of personal events and memories of national and world events had the advantage of comparing responses from the same individuals within the same large sample. However, we still started from different question frames to obtain the two sets of memories: autobiographical memories were prompted by word cues, and memories of national and world events were elicited by our standard Events question. In order to eliminate this remaining source of variation, we carried out a further experiment in 2014 that employed exactly the same word-cue approach to obtain *both* types of memories. A random half of a national sample was presented with five different word cues and asked to provide a personal memory prompted by each word. The other half of the sample was presented with the same five word cues, but asked to provide a memory of a "national or world event that happened during your lifetime." Thus the question frame was held constant, and *only* the type of memory—personal versus national and world—varied.[5]

The results for the replication of memories of personal events in the new experiment are virtually identical to those from 2010 shown earlier in figure 8.2, so a new figure need not be presented here. The peak or bump again appears mainly at ages five to twelve. When we used the same word cues to elicit memories of national and world events, respondents mentioned a wide range of different events, so they are best considered one at a time. The word cues "fight," "black," and "friend" prompted events that were given by sufficient numbers of respondents for analysis and were clearly datable. Again, we focus on intermediate events (discussed earlier in chapter 4), which took place during the lifetimes of most respondents. In response to "fight," 6 percent mentioned the Gulf War (1990–1991); 13 percent mentioned the Vietnam War

5. The five words were: window, black, fight, friend, and fire. Two had been used in our previous experiment and three were new. In addition, we included "during your lifetime" for the national and world events version of the question because the personal events version is by definition constrained to each respondent's own lifetime. We could also have kept the question frame constant by starting with the direct question used originally for national and world events and using it to ask about personal events, but since it emphasized the word "important," it might have led respondents to recall such landmark personal events as graduation or marriage, rather than leaving the content open.

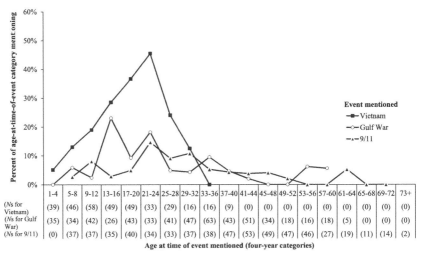

Note: Data points show percentages of respondents in each age group mentioning each event. Total number of survey respondents was 606; base *N*s for each age group and event are shown in parentheses. Only data points with base *N*s of at least 10 are plotted.

8.5 Percentages mentioning two U.S. military conflicts and the 9/11 attack, in response to word cue "fight," by age at time of event

(which we date using 1968, the year of most intense attention), and 5 percent mentioned the September 11 attacks (2001). Figure 8.5 plots the relation to age of mentions of these three events.

Despite the very different locations in time of the events, each was most likely to be mentioned by those who had been in their mid-to-late teens and early twenties at the time it occurred. The Vietnam War shows a clear peak among those aged from twenty-one to twenty-four in 1968, and the peak for 9/11 is also visible among those aged from twenty-one to twenty-four at the time of that event. In the case of the 1991 Gulf War, the peak is a little earlier, located among those aged between thirteen and sixteen, with a secondary peak for those between twenty-one and twenty-four at the time. In each case, respondents in their mid-to-late teens and twenties are the most likely to recall the event—definitely older than the peak ages for personal memories.

Figure 8.6 plots mentions of two events unrelated to military conflict. The word cue "friend" elicited mentions of the large-scale international aid song releases, concerts, and related events from the mid-1980s: 3 percent of the sample named benefit concerts such as Live Aid and Farm Aid, both in 1985, the hugely successful single "We Are the World," performed at the Live Aid concert, or charity events such as Hands Across America (1986). Mentions of these songs and events peak among those aged twenty-one to twenty-four at the time, though mentions are also high among those in their later twenties and early thirties. The word cue "black" prompted mentions of events connected to Martin Luther King for 10 percent of the sample: his assassination in 1968, the march on Washington in 1963, and the Selma to Montgomery march in 1965. Mentions of King peak for those who were ages thirteen to sixteen in 1968, with a gradual drop-off among those in their twenties at the time. In sum, the findings for each of the national and world events we are able to consider provide additional evidence that memories of national and world events tend to date from later ages than do memories of personal events, which cluster in the ages of five to twelve (figure 8.2).

Our replications support the conclusion that autobiographical and collective memories in the present comparison tend to be located at different ages: purely personal autobiographical memories in the earlier years, mainly ages five to late teens in terms of our categories, and national and world event memories in the later years, mainly ages seventeen to twenty-four. The figures do show some overlap, and there are no doubt individual differences in development for both kinds of memories, and also situational differences in exposure to external events that can affect collective memories (for example, quite young children being affected by a parent drafted into an ongoing war). But superimposing

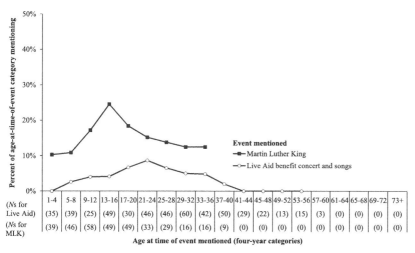

Note: Data points show percentages of respondents in each age group mentioning each event. Total number of survey respondents was 606; base Ns for each age group and event are shown in parentheses. Only data points with base Ns of at least 10 are plotted.

8.6   Percentages mentioning Martin Luther King and Live Aid benefit concerts and songs, in response to word cues "black" and "friend," by age at time of event

the personal events in figure 8.2 on the national and world events in figures 8.3, 8.5, and 8.6 presents a clear difference in ages for the two types of memory, whether using modes or other ways of judging the degree of separation.

We did not attempt in our research to discover explanatory correlates (such as emotional content, reaction time, etc.) of word-cued personal memories, but note that most such systematic attempts have not produced clear results (notably Rubin and Schulkind 1997; Janssen and Murre 2008). We also did not discover differences in the location of the bump by education, gender, or race; and consistent with most, though not all, past reports on word-cued memories (e.g., Jansari and Parkin 1996; Rubin and Schulkind 1997), memories with positive and negative content show similar curves in our data.

Evidence on Age for Other Types of Memories

Autobiographical personal memories and national and world memories are obviously different in content. It is useful to consider other investigations of content involving memory from early years, drawing on previously published research. Evidence from two specialized inquiries on memory of music and sports points to what seems to be an intermediate age location between that for word-cued personal associations and that for collective memories of national and world events.

Music

In earlier research, we asked respondents in a 1993 national survey to nominate "an event, a performer, or a style having to do with music over the past half century or so that you especially liked," and followed with "How old were you when [that] made an impression on you?" (Schuman, Belli, and Bischoping 1997: 73–74). The findings were clear, as shown in table 8.1: the median age of reported impression, irrespective of the kind of music named, was sixteen, and although the age of impression increased slightly with the present age of the respondent, the more striking result was that almost all the median ages were in the teens. Smith's (1994) study of musical tastes based on a national sample revealed similar results, and Janssen, Chessa, and Murre's (2007) broader study that included music along with books and movies arrived at similar critical years for music (see especially their figure 1). In summary, we take the midteens as the best estimate of recall of preferred music.

Table 8.1 Median Age of Music Impression By Present Age (SRC 1993)

Question: "Would you mention an event, a performer, or a style having to do with music over the past half century or so that you have especially liked? . . .
How old were you when [that] first made an impression on you?"

Present age	Median age of impression	(N)
18–23	14	(57)
24–29	13	(92)
30–34	15	(102)
35–39	16	(121)
40–44	15	(103)
45–49	17	(88)
50–54	16	(66)
60–64	17	(57)
65–69	16	(36)
70–74	19	(37)
75–80	27	(26)

Sports

Janssen, Rubin, and Conway (2012) asked Dutch respondents to give the names of the five football (soccer) players they thought were the best of all time. (Respondents were first shown a list of 190 players known to have been judged excellent, and they were also allowed to add names to the list.) The authors write:

The results were clear-cut. The mode of the age of the participants at the midpoint of the nominated players' careers was 17. The mode did not change much when the different selection criteria were used. It remained at approximately the same value with players who were still active or with players who had retired, with the most popular or with less popular players, with Dutch or with foreign players, and with male or with female participants. (174)

The modal age of seventeen for remembered sports figures is very close to that for memories in the realm of music, as reported above.

Both sports and music are pursuits where interests and preferences are often established during the teenage years and rehearsed frequently thereafter. Interests that are strong in the teen years may be linked to what is most apt to be recalled from that same period, thus producing a reminiscence bump or critical years effects.

Life scripts

Although most of the early studies by psychologists that gave rise to the term "reminiscence bump" used word-cued associations, over the past decade research on the bump has increasingly focused on the concept of "life scripts" (e.g., Berntsen and Rubin 2002, 2004; Rubin and Berntsen 2003; Dickson, Pillemer, and Bruehl 2011; Thomsen, Pillemer, and Ivcevic 2011). Life scripts are thought to be "culturally shared representations of the timing of major transitional life events" (Berntsen and Rubin 2004: 427) that structure and help explain the bump in autobiographical memories by guiding respondents to focus on the adolescent and early adult years when attempting to recall positive events. These studies—which generally locate the reminiscence bump between ages fifteen and thirty—have tended to gather data on autobiographical memories through direct questions. In some cases, for example, life-script studies have asked respondents when their most important experiences occurred or when they felt happiest, most afraid, most proud, most in love, and so forth, but often they have asked respondents about their expectations for the timing of such experiences in the life course of a hypothetical person. Furthermore, some studies that do not stress the specific concept of life script also ask similar direct questions. Thus, Holmes and Conway (1999) instructed participants recruited near Bristol University "to list private events from their own lives which they considered to be important," and found a bump for ages twenty to twenty-nine that referred to such major areas of life as marriage, divorce, work, and education. It does not seem at all surprising to us that, within an adult sample, such direct questions focusing on the "importance" or emotional significance of past events leads to mentions of life changes—for example, high school or college graduation, marriage, or a first important job—that date from a later period in comparison with word-cued associations.

Koppel and Berntsen (2014) propose the existence of a general cognitive "youth bias" and provide evidence that the impact of cultural life scripts extends to public as well as personal events: respondents most frequently expected a hypothetical person to experience the most important *public* event of his or her life between the ages of eleven and thirty. Their research suggests that cultural expectations about the importance of youth—and, we might add, perhaps also general cultural assumptions about the importance of first experiences—may guide the retrieval of memories of all kinds.

Critical Years, Multiple Bumps, and the Primacy of Events

The term "reminiscence bump" is used widely, well beyond the studies described here, and the age range identified for the bump (or the critical years) extends from early childhood, as young as age five, to at least the age of thirty. We can make sense of such a range of usage by recognizing that different types of questioning about memory can legitimately produce different memory content, and that the different content tends to be connected to different ages. This conclusion is consistent with some seventy-five years of experimental research on survey questions, which has shown repeatedly that relatively small changes in question form, wording, and context can have important effects on answers (Cantril 1944; Schuman and Presser [1981] 1996; Sudman, Bradburn, and Schwarz 1996). Our experiment reporting the effects of question framing on responses about Abraham Lincoln (chapter 3, p. 67) also provides support for the importance of how questions are framed and worded. Such experimental evidence on the question-answer process has been largely neglected in much of the psychological research on autobiographical memory. In sum, different questions or procedures lead to different "bumps" or critical years spans, with none necessarily more legitimate than another.

In addition, it is likely that memories within a particular domain tend to come from the point in the life course at which events in that domain are especially interesting and meaningful to many individuals, and as a result may have benefited from frequent rehearsal. Simple early memories tend to be sparked by free word-cued associations; memories for sports and music—activities important to teenagers—tend to date from the teens; and the late teens and twenties seem to be the source of memories having to do, on the one hand, with serious personal relationships and other early adult concerns, and on the other hand, with larger national and world events encountered via the mass media. Acknowledging these differences in memory as legitimate, and as linked to the type of questioning used, reconciles conclusions from different research reports.

Neither we nor other writers have provided a still further theoretical explanation for which specific event is remembered within a particular reminiscence bump. In the case of collective memories of national and world events, it seems likely that the first national or world event that most people would consider important has a particularly strong impact on those who are in adolescence or early adulthood. Thus a major war, an economic crash, or a singular event like the 9/11 attacks should be most easily remembered from this stage of life because there is nothing earlier that is meaningful for comparison. The event itself becomes a kind of baseline.

At the purely personal level of early childhood, with memories elicited by word cues, even a simple first experience such as "roasting marshmallows over a camp fire" can turn out to be memorable. The event may not be judged important later in life by the same individual (Rubin and Schulkind 1997), but it may well have *seemed* important when it first occurred in childhood, leading to its memorable quality at the time, its rehearsal with friends and family (Rundus 1971), and its long-term recall in the form of the top-of-the-head word associations we found. The same subjective importance may be attached to experiences connected with both sports and music during the teenage years. In still later years, it makes sense that what seems important to most individuals when directed to think in personal terms are milestone experiences involving their education, work, and social relationships.

Thus it is possible that there is no general explanation for the location of a particular bump or critical years span beyond the occurrence of the first event that seemed important to individuals at that stage of life and in that domain. Tulving (2008: 38) offers a general proposal in the form of a "law of primacy," writing: "Most traditional explanations of primacy do not explain primacy as much as they explain primacy away. After they are finished there is no real phenomenon left to explain."

Tulving maintains instead "that primacy is primary" and that "it reflects a basic property of the brain." Thus, within a stage of life that makes most individuals open to a particular type of event, we can speculate that it is the first such event—whether a childhood experience, sports activity, form of music, milestone experience, or national or world event—that appears important and thus registers most strongly for later recall. Indeed, in chapter 1, we saw that the significance of Christopher Columbus to Americans was maintained in part because of his "firstness."

Finally, based on our main results, it seems best to continue to use the broader term "critical years" to refer to the overall ten to thirty age span or its approximation for early memories, reserving the term "bump" for particular peaks that have unusual psychological significance within that larger time span.

NINE

Collective Knowledge: Findings and "Losings"

In chapter 4 on the *critical years* hypothesis, we quoted part of a longer sentence by Karl Mannheim ([1928] 1952: 296) that reads:

I only really possess those "memories" that I have created directly for myself, only that "knowledge" I have personally gained in real situations. This is the only sort of knowledge which really "sticks" and it alone has real binding power.

In our earliest research, we interpreted Mannheim's claim to refer to "collective memory," and our evidence consisted of responses to an open-ended question about "especially important" national and world events from a past set of fifty or more years. (See the standard Events question wording in chapter 4, p. 83.) We did not treat the events that individuals mentioned as "right" or "wrong," but as indicating what they recalled as important from the past. We call this "collective memory" in a general sense, and in chapter 4 we were successful in showing that collective memory is rooted in the national and world events that individuals experience during their youth.

In a later study in 1991, we decided to test what Mannheim had conjectured about knowledge—perhaps taking his statement more literally than he had intended. We hypothesized that correct knowledge about national and world events should be acquired and remembered especially when individuals learn about events by experiencing them during their critical years of late childhood, adolescence, and early adulthood—typically the ages of ten to thirty, as discussed in chapter 4.

Therefore, in a survey in 1991, we presented a set of terms or names related to specific political, social, and cultural events that had occurred over the previous sixty or so years, and asked each respondent to say: "which ones you have heard of at all, and, if you have, what they refer to in just a few words." We scored the answers for each term as correct, partly correct, or incorrect (the latter usually occurring in the form of "don't know" responses), and have subsequently treated this as a distinct type of collective memory, which we call "collective knowledge." (We drew on the same kind of evidence in chapter 2 in order to assess knowledge about Sally Hemings and Ann Rutledge.)

For example, one of the terms, the "Tet Offensive," was scored as correct if it was said to be an attack by the enemy in Vietnam (e.g., "The Communists attacked us in Vietnam."). It was scored as partly correct if it was said to be an American attack on the enemy during the Vietnam War, and was scored as incorrect if the respondents said they did not know what it was or misidentified it completely (e.g., as a battle during the Korean War). The categories of correct, partly correct, and don't know/incorrect were represented by scores of 2, 1, and 0, respectively.

The initial data came from the 1991 Detroit Area Study (DAS), with a sample of 1,042 respondents from the metropolitan Detroit area (the city plus the large surrounding suburbs). (A number of comparisons with national samples [e.g., the General Social Survey in 1993] indicate that on almost all issues, the two are virtually indistinguishable in the shapes of associations they produce, and only a little different in absolute levels.) Table 9.1 shows the DAS 1991 results, plus results when the question was repeated using a national cross-section sample (SRC 1993), thus replicating the original knowledge test in a different survey two years later. Moreover, in line with our emphasis on replication, we included another event, "Woodstock," along with the Tet Offensive in both surveys.

Findings

As can be seen from table 9.1, the results for the two events are almost identical between the two samples, despite the difference between the national population and that of metropolitan Detroit, as well as the gap of two years between the original research and the second set of interviews. These are just the kinds of literal replications across different

Table 9.1 Events from the Past: Distribution of Knowledge Scores

Event	Approx. date	Incorrect (%)	Partially correct (%)	Correct (%)	Total (%)	(N)	Example of response scored as "correct"
		Knowledge score					
Tet Offensive (DAS 1991)	1968	70	15	15	100	(1,000)	"Communists attacked us in Vietnam"
Tet Offensive (SRC 1993)	1968	66	16	18	100	(1,951)	
Woodstock (DAS 1991)	1969	25	14	61	100	(1,000)	"That's the hippies' concert"
Woodstock (SRC 1993)	1969	24	15	61	100	(1,950)	
Village of My Lai (SRC 1993)	1969	64	17	19	100	(1,010)	"The American army shot women and children; one fellow was court-martialed"
WPA (DAS 1991)	1938	64	7	29	100	(1,000)	"FDR gave work to people in the 1930s"
Watergate (DAS 1991)	1973	14	37	49	100	(1,000)	"When Nixon broke the rules"
John Dean (SRC 1993)	1973	67	21	12	100	(1,511)	"Did a lot of testifying in Watergate hearings, blew the whistle on everyone"
Christa McAuliffe (DAS 1991)	1986	49	6	45	100	(1,000)	"In the space shuttle disaster"

samples and different time points that we look for in order to feel confident in our results when no change is expected.

Even stronger and more impressive evidence appears in figure 9.1 when we look at those who could correctly identify the Tet Offensive. The curvilinearity in accurate knowledge by birth cohort appears much the same in the two surveys, and is also similar to the curve for simple "mentions" of the Vietnam War as an especially important past event (see figure 4.4 in chapter 4). Indeed, the peak for knowledge about the Tet Offensive occurs among those who were born between 1941 and 1950, and thus about age twenty-three in 1968 at the time of the Tet attack. This was the most intense point of the Vietnam War, as we indicated in chapter 4.

As a still further sign of validity, the curve for men is clearer than the curve for women, as we expected given the greater importance of the Vietnam conflict for men because of pressure from the draft (data not shown). Table 9.1 also presents results for the village of My Lai (the site of a massacre by American troops)—a quite different event in Vietnam

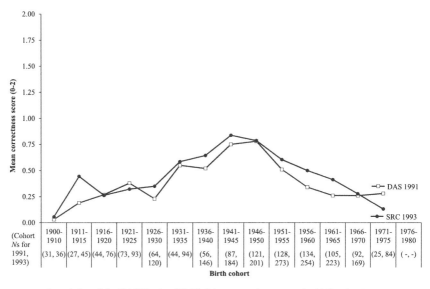

9.1   Knowledge of the Tet Offensive (1968): Mean correctness score by birth cohort
(DAS 1991 and SRC 1993)

that also took place in 1968. Additional evidence supporting our belief in a critical years effect for collective knowledge occurs in the curve for the village of My Lai, which looks much the same as that for Tet in terms of the ages found for answers judged to be correct. Curves for both Tet and My Lai replicated in a 2009 national survey. The curve for Woodstock is also much as expected in both the DAS 1991 and the national survey. In sum, all the results fit together beautifully, giving us considerable confidence in our hypothesis about collective knowledge.

In a further analysis about an earlier period, we found additional meaningful cohort patterns in knowledge of the "WPA," the acronym for the Works Progress (later Work Projects) Administration, the largest of the New Deal programs instituted in the 1930s. Responses scored as correct (for example, "FDR gave work to people in the 1930s") showed a reliable relation to education, but an even stronger relation to cohort (earlier birth cohorts gave correct answers disproportionately). Moreover, the effect of birth cohort differed depending on education. For those with little education, being old enough in 1991 to have had some personal experience with the WPA (e.g., "My uncle had a job with the WPA") was the crucial source of knowledge, but among those with a college education, a fair number of those too young to have had direct or indirect experience with the WPA could nevertheless identify the program correctly. Thus direct experience with the WPA was needed for knowledge by those with little education, but those with greater education compensated for their lack of personal experience by means of education—probably reading or hearing a teacher speak about the WPA. Again, this was the kind of complex result that made very good intuitive sense. Other researchers, too, have reported evidence of a "reminiscence bump" when knowledge of public events is evaluated for accuracy, though using a highly educated, self-selected sample (Janssen, Murre, and Meeter 2008).

Losings

Given findings like those just noted, why do we treat the evidence for a critical years effect on collective knowledge as more uncertain than our evidence for collective memory in chapter 4 (for example, in the summary table 4.3)? One reason is that knowledge of some other events—"Watergate," for example—did not show a similarly meaningful association with age at the time it occurred (roughly 1973–1974 when Nixon resigned as president). At first we thought this might be due to the broad importance and wide use of the term "Watergate" itself, so that knowledge of it could not be expected to be limited to those in or close to their critical years in the early 1970s. For that reason, in a new survey, we substituted for Watergate a related term that we thought was less likely to be widely familiar, the name John Dean, but this term also failed to show the expected relation to birth cohort.

Another name we used was that of Christa McAuliffe, who theoretically should have been disproportionately known to the cohorts who were in their critical years in 1986 at the time of the *Challenger* disaster. Our 1991 survey results showed that roughly equal percentages of most cohorts were able to identify Christa McAuliffe—perhaps because the event was still quite recent at that point in time—though the youngest two cohorts were slightly less knowledgeable. A 2009 replication indicated a much clearer decline in knowledge among younger cohorts, especially those too young to have had any direct memory of the *Challenger* disaster, and knowledge of the science teacher/astronaut among the oldest cohorts had decreased dramatically compared to 1991. Still, even respondents who had been as old as fifty in 1986 were just as knowledgeable about McAuliffe as those in their critical years, so the

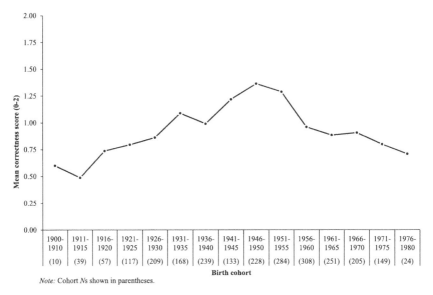

9.2   Knowledge of Laika (1957): Mean correctness score by birth cohort (Russia 1994)

results do not conform to a classic critical years effect, either for the sample as a whole or for women alone. If the older boundary is extended by two decades, the curve does fit a revised critical years shape, but without additional replication or other evidence this cannot be taken as positive support. In sum, these and other results failed to demonstrate "construct replication," and thus we feel uncertain about the critical years hypothesis when applied to collective knowledge.

We also tried to test the effect of critical years on knowledge using Russian survey data (Schuman and Corning 2000). Again, our initial results from data first collected in 1994 seemed compelling. For example, the dog Laika, the first mammal sent into orbit in a *sputnik* (satellite) in 1957 as part of the Soviet space program, was known best by Russians who were children approximately seven to eleven years old at the time (figure 9.2). It was entirely plausible that a dog traveling across the sky in a spacecraft and ballyhooed by the Soviet government would have made a considerable impression on young children. Older cohorts would be expected to be a little less knowledgeable about Laika, as would younger cohorts who grew up after the event had occurred. These results seemed quite sensible to us. In addition, knowledge of some other events was greatest among those young at the time, as expected. For example, Katya Lycheva (an eleven-year-old girl sent by the Kremlin as a peace emissary to the United States in 1986, in response to an earlier twelve-year-old American girl, Samantha Smith, who visited Moscow as an ambassador for peace in 1983) was best known to those aged ten to seventeen in 1986, and particularly to young girls in that age range. This appeared to be another very meaningful finding about critical years and actual knowledge.

Unfortunately, when we tried to replicate the results for both Laika and Katya Lycheva in a survey in 2010, no critical years effect appeared in the figures we produced. This was a failure in literal replication, because the change in time—at least for Laika, whose flight took place thirty-seven years before the original survey and fifty-three years prior to the replication attempt—did not seem great enough to account entirely for the disappearance of the original relation. Perhaps these two quintessentially Soviet symbols had faded in meaning for critical years cohorts in the decades since the Soviet collapse. Or, it is possible that the second survey—which was administered by a different organization and which we were not able to supervise ourselves—was poorly done, but in the absence of direct evidence of such a problem, that explanation is unsatisfying, and we lacked resources to attempt another replication.

Thus all told we remain too uncertain of our full set of results on critical years and collective knowledge to state conclusions with confidence at this point. We have a mixture of tantalizing *findings* combined with what, at present, we think of as later *losings*. Additional research by ourselves or others is needed to test further the critical years hypothesis when extended from collective memory, as defined and described in earlier chapters, to the important sphere of collective knowledge.[1]

We should emphasize that this uncertainty about the application of the critical years hypothesis to collective knowledge does not cast doubt on either the concept of collective knowledge itself or its assessment. On the contrary, measuring knowledge by asking people to identify individuals and events from the past, and scoring answers in terms of correctness (including "don't know"), has a great deal of "face validity" and is supported well by much other evidence (for example, the correlations between correctness scores and educational level). Here we have been investigating a much more novel point: whether knowledge is affected in important ways by experience during the critical years. That issue calls for additional research.

---

1. Detailed evidence from the American data can be found in Schuman, Belli, and Bischoping (1997), and similar evidence from Russia appears in Schuman and Corning (2000).

The Complexity of Ignorance

As in other parts of our research, we were concerned in our study of knowledge to draw qualitatively on what respondents had to say. Here we illustrate the kinds of mistakes that people made when they did *not* answer knowledge questions correctly in terms of the scoring criteria we used. We found the wrong answers to be often illuminating, worth recording and bearing in mind for future research on what is called "semantic memory" (Tulving 1972), or more simply for us, "collective knowledge"—though perhaps some of these examples reveal what might better be understood as a form of "collective ignorance."

The conception of memory as a collection of accurate records of past events has long been questioned by both psychologists and sociologists (Bartlett 1932; Halbwachs [1950] 1980) and is now largely abandoned. Initially, the "recordings" themselves are inevitably incomplete due to the impossibility of capturing literally what occurs with even the simplest event. Next, what is remembered over time is likely to be increasingly simplified, with subtle connections lost, broad characterizations stressed, and some merging of similar or related memories—not to mention the influence of others' accounts and reconstructions. There is also differential recognition and acceptance of one's ignorance, so that when invited to report the past, people vary considerably in their willingness to use associations and imagination to supplement their knowledge, and they may even guess entirely about happenings of a few days, months, or years past. All these factors making for inaccuracy are compounded by the fact that for complex occurrences remote from current interests, people may have paid only casual attention to all sorts of significant features and feel no great concern to assess critically what springs to mind in response to a question about the past.

The deficiencies on the part of respondents to a survey—and on the part of investigators as well—appeared in fascinating ways in our study of collective knowledge. One name that we presented to our DAS 1991 sample was that of Joe McCarthy. We asked respondents for an identification, and scored the answers as follows:

<u>Correct</u>: Must indicate that he hunted communists (or was reputed to do so), e.g., "He went after communists."

<u>Partly correct</u>: Mentions communists or politics but not very clear, e.g., "Conducted hearings after World War II."

<u>Don't know, or clearly incorrect</u>

Initially, we did not give much attention to the nature of the wrong answers beyond treating them as incorrect, and we made no distinction between those that contained substantive content—however wrong—and those where the respondent simply said he or she did not know. At a later point, however, we decided to examine the nature of the answers scored as incorrect and found them to be of considerable interest.

First, and somewhat humbling, a number of answers scored as incorrect turned out to reflect the initial narrow vision of the researchers, rather than the ignorance of the respondents. Starting from the assumption that the only possible correct answers to "Joe McCarthy" in 1991 had to be about the Wisconsin senator who claimed to pursue communists but was later censured for making wild and unsubstantiated accusations, we scored all other answers as incorrect. Yet in retrospect it became clear that the response "Manager of the New York Yankees" identified a well-known figure from the past half century and thus was an entirely legitimate answer that should have been scored as correct for the five people who gave it. Nothing in the question required the name to involve matters of state or of politics. Our first lesson thus had to do with a kind of ignorance of our own.

A little further from national life and indeed not even within the ken of the researchers at the time were media personalities from the metropolitan Detroit area, including J. P. McCarthy, a radio host and disk jockey on a local station who was well known locally and described by twenty-two respondents, and there was also a second J. McCarthy on radio and fairly well known locally. "Joe McCarthy" was connected to these local celebrities mainly by respondents who were on the young side—definitely younger than the main researchers—and who were living within the Detroit area, rather than in the insulated setting of Ann Arbor. Was their mention a mark of the lack of worldliness of the respondents, or was the initial incorrect scoring better treated as a sign of the researchers' academic provincialism?

Wrong Answers That Were Meaningful

Inversions

Most of the other answers were more clearly incorrect, even if we broaden our latitude of acceptance, yet on closer examination they carry important meaning about the past and about how it is transformed by memory and thus communicated to the present and the future. Especially striking were the "inversions," in which people had some knowledge of

185

a symbol, but the knowledge was "backward" in a way that led to a more glaring mistake than even a plea of "don't know"   an error of commission rather than omission. Thus, nine people knew that Joe McCarthy was connected to communism, but inverted the connection in a way that would have amazed the senator were he alive today:

"Yes, a senator accused of being a communist."

"Yes, Red communist senator."

"Indicted for communism, a Senator?"

"Yes, communism, a senator accused of communism."

"Yes, Joe McCarthy was a communist."

"They thought he was a communist but it was never proven."

"Communist leaning."

"Yes, Senator, communist."

"Communist of the movie industry."

These answers provide vivid testimony to the danger that history presents of its own kind of "guilt by association." The name Joe McCarthy and the negative term "communist" had been preserved, but changed into a positive association quite unlike the original negative relationship between the two terms. Evidently there is a real risk in being repeatedly linked to a negative symbol like "communist," no matter the original nature of the relationship. The true character of the linkage may be lost over time, even though the symbol lives on and retains its negative tone! Such answers do not deserve to be simply relegated to a category of "incorrect," lest their qualitative richness be lost entirely.

More generally, being defended as *not* a "racist" or *not* a "sexist" (or *not* something else) may have some of the same long-term danger as being attacked directly as a racist or a sexist, for all that may remain in the minds of a later generation is the association to the term "racist" or "sexist," not the context in which it occurred. (This type of inversion is reminiscent of a story told about Senator McCarthy, which may well be apocryphal but was not without some resonance for those familiar with his behavior. McCarthy was said to be holding a committee hearing on the menace of communism in America and began to berate a witness before the poor man had a chance to say a word. One of McCarthy's aides leaned over and whispered to the senator that this particular witness had been invited to testify because he was widely known as an *anti*communist. To which McCarthy is said to have replied: "I don't care what kind of a communist he is!" And the senator went on hectoring the witness.)

Inversions were also common with other symbols that we presented in this assessment of knowledge. The Tet Offensive was often correctly associated with the Vietnam War, but described as an offensive by the U.S. Army against the communist enemy, rather than the other way around—perhaps because Americans tend to think of their own military as always the winning force in war.

A different but especially meaningful type of inversion occurred when "Rosa Parks" was identified by five respondents as a black woman who gave up her seat on a bus, rather than refusing to move from her seat. All five of these inverters were white, and four of them were old enough (two were in their eighties) to have grown up in a time when blacks were assumed to be submissive in just such a situation. Our large black sample made a smaller proportion of errors on Rosa Parks generally and no inversions at all, probably because it was the dramatic *action* that Rosa Parks actually took (refusing to move!) that made the event memorable for them.

Name associations

Although interviewers always read the full name of a figure we asked to have identified, frequently only part of the name was seized on and used to develop a response. Fifteen people identified McCarthy as a World War II general, and we believe they had Douglas MacArthur in mind. MacArthur's fame overlapped in time with that of Joe McCarthy, since MacArthur played a leading role in the Korean War in the early 1950s, as well as during World War II. Hence respondents—all in their twenties and thirties and thus too young to have their own memories of either person—had the right period, more or less, just the wrong man. "MacArthur" and "McCarthy" are close enough to invite such a mistake by those vague about an earlier period of history, even if the first names "Joe" and "Douglas" are pretty far apart.

Also close in sound to Joe McCarthy was the name Paul McCartney, identified clearly by three respondents (e.g., "Singer with the Beatles"), and Eugene McCarthy, referred to by six people ("He ran for president in the '60s"), the latter being the only case where the last name was exactly the same. We should note that here as elsewhere there is good reason to believe that the mistakes probably reflect associations that respondents are likely to carry through life and are not limited to the setting of a survey interview. Thus when these people hear the name Joe McCarthy without much context on television, or come across it in a newspaper or at a website, they are likely to make much the same connection as in a survey interview. Hence they bring to the experience a very different set of ideas than had been intended by the television speaker or the original writer.

In the same vein, a number of people identified "John Dean" as a former secretary of state, presumably based on the association of "Dean" to either Dean Acheson or Dean Rusk, perhaps in these cases aided by a vague but correct sense that all the names had something to do with the government. Further afield in terms of vocation, though not in wording, were frequent characterizations of John Dean as an actor who died young (James Dean?), or a little less often as a singer (Jimmy Dean?). The name Dean may be distinctive enough to make respondents think the person must be someone they are familiar with, unlike names like Smith or Jones, and thus to assume that whatever Dean comes to mind is apt to be correct.

Temporal displacements

Some of the errors noted above also involved temporal mistakes, as when Eugene McCarthy, a man of the sixties, was substituted for Joe McCarthy, a man of the fifties. A variant of the same kind of error occurred when foreign-sounding words were asked about, and respondents tried to keep the same exotic frame of reference but displaced it to another time and location. Thus the Tet Offensive was identified by a number of respondents as having occurred during the Korean War. As part of our analysis, we were able to show that such respondents tended to be old enough to have reached their teens or early twenties during the Korean War period, so their mistake was in the spirit of a critical years effect—a kind of further confirmation of the hypothesis that had guided our research.

Other more distant responses

There were some forty other answers to the question about Joe McCarthy that seem to be more clearly wrong—but were noteworthy for the degree to which people try to make sense of a name likely to be well known but not known well by them. Here are some samples in response to Joe McCarthy:

"Director of the FBI at one time."

"Yes, mayor of Detroit."

"Yes, boxer."

"Prosecuting the mafia, the mob."

"Yes, beginning of anti–civil rights movement."

"Yes, film industry."

Apart from the last response, which may connect McCarthy to the Hollywood blacklist, we have not been able to figure out the origin of each of these particular errors, but it is entirely possible that even in these cases there was some meaningful connection to the name McCarthy that we missed.

Finally, we found that the term WPA seemed to invite people to come up with words that fit the letters, though we doubt that much more than guesses were ever involved:

"World Peace Association."

"World War II Workers Party."

"'We pay afterwards' plan for people needing help."

"The Women's . . . No, I guess I don't really know."

The last example represents a reasonable start, followed by a kind of self-restraint that is lacking in the following attempt by an imaginative respondent to explain the Tet Offensive:

"The line in football where you have three backs and you split a wide receiver to the right. A handoff to the running back."

Conclusions at Present

We have attempted in this book to provide sufficient replication or other evidence so that our conclusions will hold up when further tested. Especially in the case of the U.S. data dealt with in chapter 4, there are enough replications to feel reasonably confident that the main findings will not become "losings." In this chapter, we reported examples of both findings and "losings" when we attempted to extend the critical years hypothesis to collective knowledge of some important past events in the United States and Russia. The initial findings were often empirically supportive and intuitively persuasive with regard to the relation of knowledge to the critical years, and there were some reassuring instances where replication was successful across time, across survey vehicles, and across constructs intended to test similar theoretical points. But though the failures in replication were usually explicable one by one, there were enough that we remain uncertain about whether the critical years hypothesis can be applied widely and directly to what people actually *know* about the past. For now we do not have sufficient confidence that collective knowledge is grounded in the critical years to allow us to firmly state a conclusion.

However, we also profited by learning about the nature of the mistakes that respondents made. Academics tend to assume that the meaning a symbol carries for them is much the same for others. In particular, someone fascinated by politics may think that the name Joe McCarthy must convey the same meaning to everyone. With a little experience at listening to those who are younger and not especially schooled in history, one comes to realize that many people are poorly informed about a name or other symbol that resonated widely at an earlier time. But even then it can be surprising to learn some of the associations exemplified here. That "Joe McCarthy" could be remembered as a senator who was a communist himself is probably the greatest paradox, but only a little more so to those immersed in political life than is his being overshadowed today in the minds of some by the 1950s manager of the New York Yankees, or indeed the senator's reemergence as a member of the Beatles.

TEN

Commemoration Matters: The Past in the Present

We have taken "collective memory" for granted in previous chapters by assuming that it is always available in the form of beliefs about the importance of past national and world events, and can even be carried along by emigrants as they confront entirely new problems. But memories fade, become distorted, or may be replaced by new competing memories (Baddeley, Eysenck, and Anderson 2009). Therefore, both societies and individuals make use of commemoration to preserve, restore, and revitalize memories that are slipping from consciousness or indeed may have even disappeared. The word "commemoration" comes from Latin (com [together] + memorare [to remember]), and thus to commemorate means to remember together. Every group, large or small, has some form of commemoration.

Commemoration helps to spur recall and prompt rumination, retelling, and other forms of retrieval that facilitate the retention and transmission of memories (Roediger, Zaromb, and Butler 2009). It also imbues past events with present meaning, helping to restore "the mnemonic quality of historical knowledge, to bring it back to popular consciousness, and to reconnect it with the realm of lived experience" (Assmann 2001: 6823). The reconnection to present experience is often accomplished by defining an event's significance to members of a group and reaffirming their identity in the process. In this chapter, we consider the commemoration in the United States of two important though very different past events: the 9/11 attacks in 2001, and the 1969 Woodstock Festival. We also look at how individuals undertake forms of commemoration on their own.

The 9/11 Attacks on the United States

We took advantage of the tenth anniversary of the September 11 attacks in 2011 to conduct a type of natural experiment. The date of the anniversary and the associated national commemoration intersected with our fieldwork to create naturally occurring quasi-experimental conditions: the fieldwork period between August and September 2011 encompassed the several weeks before, during, and after the tenth anniversary of the original attacks, allowing us to assess the effects of the commemoration on the American population. Moreover, we were able to track media coverage of commemorative activity that waxed and waned during those same weeks.

We asked our standard open-ended Events question to a national cross-section sample of 506 Americans in interviews conducted from late August through September 2011:

There have been a lot of national and world events and changes over the past 80 or so years—say, from about 1930 right up until today. Would you mention one or two such events or changes that seem to you to have been especially important? [IF ONLY ONE MENTION, ASK: Is there any other national or world event or change over the past 80 years that you feel was especially important?]

We were able to examine change in the events that respondents judged important on a day-by-day basis over the commemorative period. Our concern is with mentions of 9/11 as one of the two "especially important" events in response to the question.[1] First, however, we examined changes in commemorative activity.

Assessing commemorative activity

To gauge variation in references to commemoration, we conducted keyword searches from August through September 2011 within three sources: the *New York Times*, *USA Today*, and television evening news broadcasts. The *Times* is based in New York City, close to ground zero

---

1. The question was included near the beginning of the SRC monthly survey. Additional information on survey administration, our media search results, and analyses other than those reported in this chapter can be found in Corning and Schuman (2013).

and not very far from the two other attack sites in Washington, D.C., and Pennsylvania, so we expected the newspaper to attend closely to the commemoration, and to any implications for the country and for individuals. Furthermore, the *Times* is widely regarded as the leading U.S. newspaper and tends to play an agenda-setting role for other media outlets (McCombs 2004). In order to include more popular media sources, we also searched the Vanderbilt television archive (which contains evening news reports from ABC, CBS, NBC, CNN, and Fox News), and we searched the national newspaper *USA Today*, which, after the *Wall Street Journal*, had the second largest circulation in the United States in 2011 (Vega 2012) and was readily available in almost every locale. It is important to note that we do not assume that our respondents read or watched the specific sources of news we examined. Instead, we use the three news sources as a general indicator of the extent of commemorative activity to which the entire American population would have been exposed.

It may seem obvious that commemoration surrounding 9/11 would affect collective memory, but even in the case of the tenth anniversary, we cannot safely make that assumption. It is noteworthy that, in 2001, during the several weeks after the attacks occurred, over half of a national sample we had obtained did *not* mention 9/11 as a first or second "especially important" event! Thus, we could not be certain that the public as a whole would be particularly attentive even to a commemoration on the scale of the tenth anniversary of 9/11. Indeed, while 42 percent of a national sample said they followed the tenth anniversary coverage, only 27 percent claimed to follow it more closely than any other news (Pew Research Center for the People and the Press 2011).

Furthermore, the resonance of 9/11 commemorations may have decreased over time; commentators have noted fatigue and even cynicism in response to the plethora of memorials (e.g., White 2004; Sturken 2007). Although a national sample telephone survey at the time of the first anniversary in 2002 indicated that "virtually every American plans to do something to remember the events of 9/11, honor the victims, and/or pay tribute to those involved in the rescue and recovery work" (Pew Internet and American Life Project 2002: 15), in a similar survey nine years later, just 50 percent planned to mark the occasion in some way (ABC News/*Washington Post* Poll 2011).

Commemoration of the tenth anniversary of 9/11

Commemorative events and ceremonies surrounding the tenth anniversary of 9/11—the dedication of the new World Trade Center memorial,

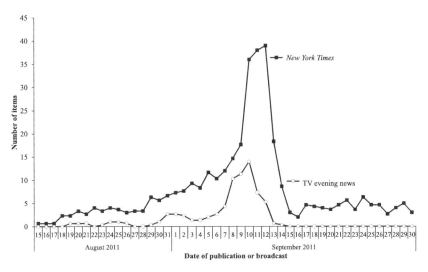

10.1   Number of items related to 9/11 in two news sources during the tenth anniversary, August–September 2011 (three-day moving averages)

official ceremonies attended by both President Obama and former president George W. Bush, and other tributes throughout the United States—were widely reported by the media. In addition, coverage included many of the media's own commemorative efforts. For its "Portraits of Grief" series in 2001, the *New York Times* had interviewed friends and family members of those who died in the attacks. On the tenth anniversary, the *Times* reinterviewed a small number of those friends and relatives for "Portraits Redrawn." *USA Today* conducted interviews with twenty individuals, highlighting the ways in which 9/11 had altered their lives: most had been directly affected, having lost friends or family in the attacks, but others were more distant observers who nonetheless were changed by 9/11. For example, the newspaper traced the journey of one young man whose experience of seeing the 9/11 attacks on television in high school led him to enlist in the Marines, study Islam and Middle Eastern cultures, and eventually, become a Muslim (Hampson and Moore 2011).

Media coverage from the *New York Times* and television evening news programs is shown in figure 10.1, which plots keyword counts—our measure of commemorative activity—for each day during the commemorative period. (The very similar plot of *USA Today*'s coverage is omitted to keep the chart more readable.) To smooth out day-to-day fluctuation, each data point plotted is a three-day moving average—that is, the count for each day is shown as the average of itself, the count for the day be-fore, and the count for the day after. The counts vary in sheer number across the two sources because of differences in available space (the *New York Times* prints a much larger number of articles each day than can be included in TV evening news), but they both follow the same general pattern: coverage beginning roughly two weeks before the day of the anniversary, intense coverage from September 6 to 12, followed by a decrease and a return to normal levels from September 15 on.

Recall of 9/11 at the tenth anniversary

Figure 10.2 shows our survey results for the corresponding 2011 fieldwork period, again using three-day moving averages. The plotted line represents the percentage of respondents interviewed each day who named 9/11 as one of two national or world events they consid-ered "especially important." Because of the small number of interviews each day, there is considerable variation from one day to the next, but the plotted line shows a fairly steady rise through September 13 and a substantial drop thereafter, following quite closely the curve of media coverage in figure 10.1. (September 11 fell on a Sunday in 2011, and

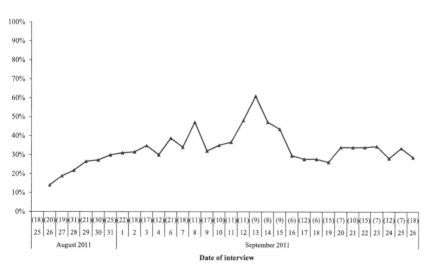

Notes: Ns for each interview date shown in parentheses.

10.2   Percent of respondents mentioning 9/11 during the tenth anniversary, by date of interview (three-day moving averages; SRC August–September 2011)

respondents' mentions of the attacks increased slightly on the day itself, but then continued to a peak on September 13, presumably as respondents watched, read about, or discussed the various commemorations over the course of several weekdays.)

In order to simplify the comparisons of the percentages mentioning the 9/11 attacks over time, we divide the total period into three sub-periods corresponding to the intensity of anniversary coverage. We define the "Early" commemorative period as the ten days from August 25 to September 3, the "Peak" commemorative period as the two weeks from September 4 to September 17 (the period of greatest coverage), and the "Late" commemorative period as the ten days from September 18 to 27.

During the Early period of the tenth anniversary, 25 percent of respondents nominated 9/11 as one of the two most important events of the past eighty years; by the time of the Peak period, that percentage had increased to 40 percent (a highly reliable difference), and it then declined to 32 percent in the Late period (though that decrease was not reliable). Among the other events nominated in 2011, only two showed reliable change from the Early to the Peak period: mentions of World War II dropped from 29 percent to 19 percent, and mentions of the Vietnam War declined from 8 percent to 2 percent, a total percentage point decrease roughly equivalent to the Early to Peak increase in 9/11 mentions. Since both World War II and Vietnam refer to major military conflicts, it seems likely that respondents who would otherwise have mentioned these events may have been influenced by the commemoration to focus on 9/11 instead.

Further evidence from 2009 and 2010

We were not able to continue interviews beyond the end of September, but we can draw for additional evidence on earlier surveys conducted in August–September 2009 (992 respondents), and February–March 2010 (603 respondents). The 2009 survey encompassed the eighth anniversary period, and the 2010 survey enriches our analysis by providing a data point midway between the eighth and ninth anniversaries. In comparison to the tenth anniversary, the eighth anniversary commemorations were much less extensive, so we expect a weaker impact on recall of 9/11. Although the increase in mentions of 9/11 from Early (20 percent) to Peak (26 percent) period in 2009 is smaller than in 2011, the increase continued into the Late period (30 percent), where it was reliable in statistical terms. In other words, in both 2009 and 2011, commemoration strengthened public perception of 9/11 as an "especially important" event, but the effect was particularly strong for the tenth anniversary in 2011.

There is also some indication of enduring effects of commemoration. In 2011, mentions of 9/11 decreased rapidly in the week immediately following the anniversary, but then stabilized. In 2009, mentions of 9/11 continued to increase after the anniversary, remaining higher into 2010 at a point well after the eighth and also prior to the ninth anniversary. Commemoration's effects thus appear to persist, restoring memory as it ebbs or possibly even cumulating over the years, since each commemoration represents a kind of rehearsal of memories. Of course, that cumulation cannot continue indefinitely, since even with substantial commemoration, memories should dwindle with the disappearance of cohorts who experienced an event during their lifetimes. (Still, the impact of extensive commemoration should not be underestimated: as discussed in chapter 5, the Holocaust has successfully been kept alive for Israelis by purposeful commemoration on a national scale, despite the decreasing proportion of Israelis who witnessed the Holocaust themselves.)

Social background and memory of 9/11

As we have shown in preceding chapters, memory is not solely an individual affair, but is shaped by "social frameworks" (Halbwachs [1952] 1992). Individuals know the past "with and against other individuals situated in different groups" (Schwartz 2008: 11), and our data on memory of 9/11 provide support for this idea. In both 2009–2010 and 2011, younger respondents—those in their *critical years* of ten to thirty at the time of the event—were the most likely to mention 9/11, replicating results from our survey conducted soon after the attacks in 2001. As we saw in chapter 4 (figure 4.3), older cohorts who had lived through earlier important events—such as World War II, the Kennedy assassination, the war in Vietnam—were less likely to mention 9/11. The collective memory of cohorts who experienced the attacks during their youth may well emerge as a full, curvilinear critical years effect in future studies by ourselves or others. Indeed, the 9/11 attack is a prime candidate for testing the critical years effect in the future, for it was a very widely known and dramatic event, yet also an event much more limited in duration than a war or a severe economic recession. For these reasons, it should be recalled years later by those in their critical years much more than by those older or younger or not born at the time.

The effect of the tenth anniversary commemoration on mentions of 9/11 was stronger for blacks than for whites, and we found a similar effect for the eighth anniversary commemoration in 2009. These commemorations may have been particularly powerful in enhancing the importance of 9/11 for blacks because President Obama—the first African American president—played the lead role in both ceremonies. In addition, on both occasions, President Obama emphasized the unifying power of national identity. At the tenth anniversary memorial service, he noted that Americans include "people of every conceivable race, religion and ethnicity—all of them pledging allegiance to one flag; all of them reaching for the same American dream—*e pluribus unum*, out of many, we are one" (Obama 2011). At the eighth anniversary service, the president also recalled the sense of national solidarity that transcended social divisions after the attacks in 2001: "On a day when others sought to sap our confidence, let us renew our common purpose, let us remember how we came together as one nation, as one people, as Americans united" (Stolberg 2009). For black Americans, the attention devoted to the attacks by President Obama, combined with his messages of national solidarity, may have temporarily increased the prominence in memory of a recent national calamity. The finding underscores the importance of group identification as a pathway through which commemoration operates.

Conclusions

Our evidence showed that increases in collective memories of September 11 corresponded closely to the timing and intensity of media coverage during the tenth anniversary of the terrorist attacks, and we found similar evidence for the eighth anniversary. Commemoration of the September 11 attacks appeared to influence whether respondents deemed 9/11 important to remember. We thus have some evidence that memories are constructed, not simply retrieved: commemoration can, at least temporarily, make certain events salient, affecting what individuals regard as "deserving of remembrance" (Schwartz 2001). Similar evidence of the effect of the "media agenda" on collective memory at a time of commemoration is provided by Kligler-Vilenchik, Tsfati, and Meyers (2014) in their study of mentions by Israelis of the establishment of their state.

Our results emphasize the importance of investigating the distribution of public responses to commemorative efforts, rather than assuming that the public as a whole will accept or reject a memorialization. In the case of 9/11, we find evidence that the sense of unity and solidarity within a group that commemoration engenders—Durkheim's "collective effervescence" ([1915] 1968)—can sometimes affect which identities will shape memory. Blacks more than whites were influenced by the commemorations to consider 9/11 an important event—presumably because for blacks the commemorations increased a sense of national identity, symbolized by the first African American president. Our findings on the impact of commemoration point to the importance of understanding collective memory not as a static property but as a dynamic process.

The Woodstock Festival

Unlike the 9/11 attacks, the Woodstock Festival—a three-day-long outdoor music extravaganza in August 1969—represents not a national calamity but a cultural landmark. Despite a lack of consensual attitudes regarding the festival's sex, drugs, and peace activism, the music of Woodstock has become an institution in its own right (*Rolling Stone* included the festival among its fifty moments that changed the history of rock and roll [Cave et al. 2004]), and the fortieth anniversary in 2009 was widely recognized.

As a cultural event, Woodstock received very few nominations in response to our standard Events question, so we cannot study it as we did 9/11 and earlier events like those discussed in chapter 4. However, we adopted another approach in order to estimate its continued vitality as a collective memory. In the 2009 survey, we examined "collective knowledge" of Woodstock, using the same type of inquiry we reported in chapter 2 with regard to Sally Hemings and Ann Rutledge, as well as in chapter 9. Respondents were asked to identify a set of terms, introduced with the statement:

For the next question, I'll read you a few words and names from the past that come up now and then, but that many people have forgotten. Please tell me which ones you have heard of, and, if you have, what they refer to in just a few words.

The term "Woodstock" was included along with ten other words and names (e.g., "the WPA," "Rosa Parks"). After reading each term, interviewers prompted respondents for a brief definition by asking, "Who is [name]?" or "What does [word] refer to?" Responses were recorded verbatim by the interviewer and later evaluated in terms of correctness (65 percent gave a correct identification of Woodstock; see table 2.1, p. 54, for the full list of terms and percentages giving correct/partially correct identifications). The correct responses become our operational measure of knowledge, and in that sense a form of memory. We focus here on the percentages giving a definition scored as "correct"—that is, those who identified it as a musical event or some kind of gathering or festival. (No equally direct question was possible for the 9/11 attacks, since it is likely that all but a few Americans had some knowledge of that event, but we did include a term that referred to a specific aspect of the event, and should reflect greater knowledge: "Mohammed Atta," the name of the ringleader of the attacks and the hijacker who flew one of the planes into the World Trade Center. We draw on those results briefly below.)

Woodstock at the fortieth anniversary

The Woodstock Festival took place in New York on August 15–18, 1969. Its fortieth anniversary in 2009 was marked by references, retrospectives, and commemorations of all kinds, including a six-CD anthology of music recorded at the festival; museum exhibits; books; a film, *Taking Woodstock*, directed by Ang Lee; television specials; and considerable coverage of both the original and commemorative events in newspapers, magazines, and on television. Figure 10.3 shows that media coverage of Woodstock began in August, increased through the anniversary, and then declined sharply, except for a small secondary peak. The trajectory of increase and decline spans about three weeks, similar to that shown for 9/11 in figure 10.1, though with much lower absolute numbers of news items.

Our survey fieldwork took place over the course of two months in 2009, from late July to late September. We again drew on the results of our media search to divide interviews into those conducted during the Early (July 23–August 6), Peak (August 7–29), and Late (August 30–September 22) commemorative periods.

From the Early to Peak period, the percentage of respondents giving a definition of Woodstock scored as "correct" increased by nearly 8 percentage points and remained stable into the Late period. When birth cohort, education, region, and race are held constant, the effect of the commemoration remains reliable. The lack of decrease from the Peak to the Late commemorative period may be due to the late August release of the film *Taking Woodstock*, though mentions of September 11 also did not decline soon after the Peak period in 2009–2010.

Social background factors and knowledge of Woodstock

Knowledge of Woodstock was greatest for cohorts born after 1941, especially the 1956–1960 cohort, who were ages nine to thirteen (the early

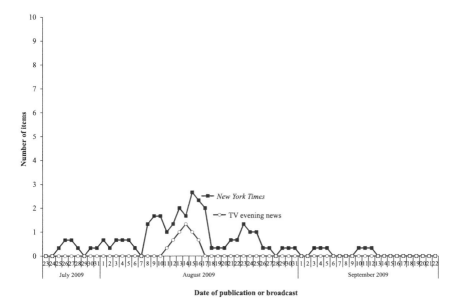

10.3   Number of items related to Woodstock in two news sources during the fortieth anniversary, July–September 2009 (three-day moving averages)

critical years) at the time of the original festival. College graduates were also more likely to know about Woodstock than respondents without a college degree, while knowledge of the festival was lower among blacks and other nonwhites than among whites, even when holding education constant. Blacks, on the other hand, showed greater knowledge than whites about another symbol from the 1960s in our questionnaire, in this case a figure linked to the civil rights movement: Rosa Parks. Each of these differences was highly reliable.

Education and the effect of commemoration

In light of the association between college education and knowledge of Woodstock, it seemed possible that the impact of commemorative activity might depend on education—that is, that the contribution of commemoration to knowledge might be greatest among those least likely to know about the festival to begin with. Indeed, as figure 10.4 shows, commemoration had virtually no impact among college graduates, but a sizable effect among nongraduates. Apparently, for those without a college degree, the fortieth anniversary commemorations provided knowledge that college graduates routinely acquired during their college years

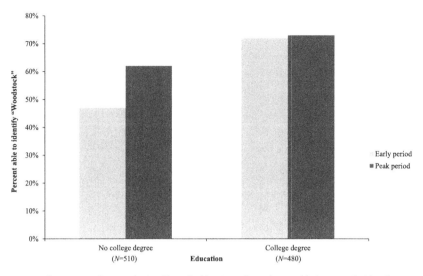

10.4   Percentage of respondents with and without a college degree able to correctly identify "Woodstock" during the fortieth anniversary, by Early and Peak commemorative period (SRC July–September 2009)

(whether through formal learning or through cultural references absorbed from peers). In other words, the commemoration helped to compensate for lower levels of knowledge among nongraduates, but had little impact on those already likely to be familiar with the event. The effect was strongest for the Peak period, but extended into the Late period as well (data not shown).

In contrast, we did not expect—and did not find—differences by educational level in the effect of commemoration on memory of 9/11. Nearly all respondents would have known about 9/11, so any failure to mention that event was unlikely to result from lack of knowledge related to educational level.

Commemoration or remembrance and knowledge of two other names

In addition to Woodstock, another name included in 2009 was that of the 9/11 terrorist Mohammed Atta. Atta was not nearly as well known as Woodstock: less than one-quarter of the sample was able to identify him correctly, though, as was true for Woodstock, knowledge of Atta was greatest among respondents with more education. There was no apparent effect of the 9/11 eighth anniversary commemorations on knowledge of Atta—perhaps not surprising, since the commemorations focused on the victims and first responders, not the perpetrators: Atta's name did not appear even once in the *New York Times* in September 2009.

We considered one additional occurrence that is more a public remembrance than a commemoration: Lieutenant William Calley's apology in August 2009 for his role in the 1968 My Lai massacre. Calley's speech was not the focus of much public attention, but the *Times* ran a report and an editorial; CNN and ABC evening news covered it briefly; and it was reported in some other newspapers. We found no relation of Calley's apology either to knowledge of the My Lai massacre or to mentions of Vietnam as an "especially important" event.

Commemoration, Judgment, and Behavior

Recall of Events versus Judgment of Events

Our results for Woodstock indicate that major commemorations contribute to greater awareness of events on the part of those less knowledgeable about them. In addition to knowing about an event, however, mentioning an event as important in answer to our standard Events question requires two steps—first recall, and then judgment of importance, though the two may occur almost simultaneously. One question, therefore, is whether commemoration only helps to bring fading events more readily to mind, or whether it also affects individuals' subjective judgments of an event's importance. Clearly, commemoration alone is not sufficient to make an event seem important: although the fortieth anniversary commemorations of the Woodstock Festival surely made that event more readily retrievable from memory, not a single respondent nominated it as first or second in importance in answer to our Events question (although a handful did volunteer it as a third event).

We can begin to address this issue with the case of 9/11. We assume that the minimum condition for memory—knowledge—was already met, since nearly all adult Americans would have known about the attacks. Our standard Events question asked respondents to mention both a first and a second event they considered "especially important," so we can examine how commemoration affected mentions of 9/11 in first or second place. We focus on respondents with critical years experience of 9/11, because our overall data on memory indicate that they are a group for whom 9/11 was likely to be prominent in consciousness and thus easily recalled. Since the critical years cohorts were less likely to need commemoration as a prompt to recall, any change observed in the order of mention of 9/11 by this group should be at least partly due to change in judgments of importance.

In general, we find that extremely important events are more apt to be mentioned in first place (see appendix D, p. 225). And indeed, during the eighth anniversary commemoration in 2009, first-place mentions of 9/11 more than doubled among the critical years cohorts, from 16 percent during the Early period to 35 percent during the Peak period, while second-place mentions seemed to decline slightly, from 11 percent to 8 percent. Our interpretation is that the commemoration influenced judgments, leading some respondents who might have mentioned 9/11 in second place or not at all to move it to first. At the tenth anniversary in 2011, both first- and second-place mentions of 9/11 by the critical years cohorts were already at very high levels during the Early period (35 percent) and remained stable into the Peak period (36 percent); second-place mentions again showed a possible though not reliable decline from Early to Peak (18 percent to 15 percent). Taking the 2009 Early period levels as a baseline, we surmise that in 2011, the critical years cohorts may have been affected by awareness of the upcoming anniversary and early references to it by peers and the media even prior to the major commemorations. Thus for critical years cohorts, not only the commemorative ceremonies but the fact of the anniversary itself appeared to increase mentions of 9/11, particularly in first place.

In contrast, for other cohorts, commemoration appeared to affect *both* first- and second-place mentions of 9/11, especially at the time of the tenth anniversary. Moreover, at no point in our 2009 or 2011 surveys did first-place mentions of 9/11 by these older cohorts exceed 21–22 percent: their levels never approached the 35 percent first-place mentions by critical years cohorts. More than this one event is needed for firm conclusions, but our evidence suggests that commemoration enhances not only recall, but also judgments of importance.

Individual Commemorative Behavior

The tenth anniversary commemorations of 9/11 were organized and executed by local and national governments, and many were broadcast nationally as well. Listeners and readers who paid attention to the commemorations were influenced by the moving ceremonies, probably in ways well beyond their answers to a single survey question. However, the larger public did little to create or develop these commemorations, and indeed half of a national sample interviewed in the weeks before the anniversary indicated that they themselves would not do anything specific to commemorate the anniversary (ABC News/Washington Post Poll, August 2011).

Anniversaries aside, when ordinary individuals are motivated to seek out ways to commemorate an important event, what kinds of actions do they engage in? And which individuals are most likely to participate in commemorative activity? To address these issues, we can consider questions that were included in DAS 1991 (see p. 178) about World War II and the Vietnam War. These questions were asked at a point in time when there were still numerous Americans who had lived through both of those major wars.

The DAS 1991 survey included the standard Events question. At a later point in the hour-long interview, interviewers said:

Sometimes we remember or learn about events of the past in different ways. What about World War II—have you ever kept pictures or some other objects in your home, gone to a reunion, made a special visit to a memorial, or done anything else like that to help you remember World War II?

A similar question was asked about the Vietnam War. The answers were coded as shown in table 10.1.

Combining all forms of commemoration, the likelihood of engaging in commemorative action is clearly and reliably related to subjective importance as measured by the standard Events question, for both World War II and Vietnam. Furthermore, commemorative behavior for each war shows a clear relation to cohort in figure 10.5, with those in their critical years at the time of each war the most likely to commemorate it—pointing to critical years effects on actions as well as on collective memory. The results are not attributable to male veterans, for there is no gender difference for Vietnam commemoration and only a small difference (11 percentage points) for World War II. Similar results are found when the sample is divided into those who have ever served in the military and those who have not. (We cannot completely control for military service during each war, but World War II had a fairly wide age range for those in the armed forces.) The association between critical years experience and commemorative activity underscores the role of personal relevance and meaning in memory practices—a point apt to

Table 10.1 Percentages of Respondents Reporting Commemorative Behavior for World War II and Vietnam (DAS 1991)[a]

Question: "Sometimes we remember or learn about events of the past in different ways. What about World War II (Vietnam)—have you ever kept pictures or some other object in your home, gone to a reunion, made a special visit to a memorial, or done anything else like that to help you remember World War II (Vietnam)?"

World War II (N=1,042)	(%)	Vietnam (N=1,039)[b]	(%)
Arlington National Cemetery, Tomb of the Unknown Soldier	2.6	Vietnam Memorial/The Wall	8.1
Other memorial or museum	6.7	Other memorials	2.3
Grave sites (other than Arlington)	0.5	Grave sites	0.2
Reunions	1.1	Reunions	0.3
Memorabilia (e.g., father's uniform; helmet; medals; gun; pictures)	16.2	Memorabilia, pictures	7.5
Any Holocaust-related memoria (e.g., pictures, memorials, reunions)	1.7	—	—
Media (books, TV, films, newspapers)	7.2	Media (books, TV, films, newspapers)	5.2
Other (e.g., learned about it in school)	4.9	Other (e.g., learned about it in school)	6.9
None	59.1	None	69.5
Total	100.0	Total	100.0

[a] Only the first of two coded mentions is shown here and used when collapsing the percentages for analysis.
[b] The N for Vietnam is smaller because of missing data.

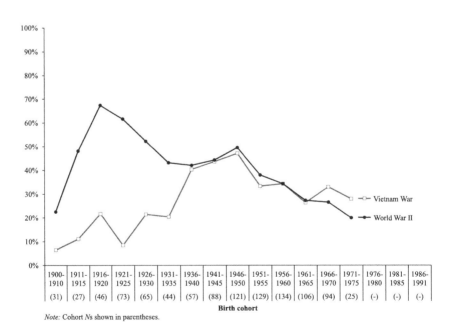

Note: Cohort Ns shown in parentheses.

10.5   Percentages of each birth cohort engaging in commemorative behavior related to World War II and the Vietnam War (DAS 1991)

be lost if we focus only on cultural resources for commemoration and neglect to investigate individual engagement.

These results show not only that many Americans pursue commemoration on their own, preserving commemorative symbols themselves or visiting places set aside for commemoration by others, but that this behavior is consistent with the critical years effects that we have reported for collective memory more generally.

Conclusions about Commemoration

Commemoration provides an opportunity to observe the intersection of cultural resources for collective memory and individual beliefs and actions. Using data from ordinary Americans, we explored the correspondence between anniversary commemorations, on the one hand, and collective memory or collective knowledge of the events commemorated, on the other, showing that individuals can and do respond in several ways to commemoration.

First, anniversary commemoration can increase knowledge about a past event. The timing of the rise in collective knowledge of the Woodstock Festival—a now long-ago cultural event—matched the timing of the festival's fortieth anniversary commemoration.

Second, commemoration can increase the likelihood that a past event will be recalled and judged "deserving of remembrance," as indicated by our 9/11 findings. Increases in collective memories of September 11 corresponded closely to the timing and intensity of media coverage of the attacks' tenth anniversary, and we found similar evidence for the eighth anniversary. The visual correspondence between the two September 11 figures—the one showing media coverage (figure 10.1) and the other showing survey respondents' nominations of 9/11 as "especially important" (figure 10.2)—is compelling.

We did not have resources to continue our 2011 study beyond the end of September, but we note that the largest drop in mentions of 9/11 occurred during the week following the anniversary, and there is no sign of any further major decrease during subsequent weeks. In addition, we found some indication for the eighth anniversary of 9/11 that the effects of commemoration lasted for at least several months. Such persistence suggests that commemoration's effects help to resist the erosion of memory over the years. Loss of collective memory of 9/11 in the future should occur mostly as cohorts from the September 11, 2001, time point disappear from the population.

Third, we have some evidence to indicate that commemoration serves not only to inform and to remind a group about past events, but also to instruct, by identifying events that are "deserving of remembrance." Especially for the critical years cohorts who were most likely to mention the September 11 attacks, commemoration and even the anniversary year itself appeared to enhance the subjective importance they attached to the attacks. For members of other cohorts, commemoration's main role may be simply to restore fading events to memory.

Fourth, commemorative spaces and objects—memorials, museums, memorabilia—provide opportunities that allow individuals not merely to respond emotionally or psychologically but to become active participants in collective memory. We presented evidence to show that individuals take advantage of such opportunities, preserving commemorative symbols and visiting commemorative sites. As Wagner-Pacifici and Schwartz (1991) show, many visitors to the Vietnam Memorial leave messages or other personal remembrances, and this occurs at other memorial sites as well (for example, Newtown, Connecticut, after the 2012 school shooting). Our data indicate that commemorative behavior appears to be undertaken disproportionately by those who were in their critical years (approximately ten to thirty) at the time the commemorated event occurred.

Even when individuals are simply responding to commemoration rather than actively participating in it, we find that the effects of commemoration are unevenly distributed across the population. The ways in which commemoration works in conjunction with education and race indicate the different roles it can play. Commemorative activity on the anniversary of Woodstock—an event both temporally and psychologically distant—helped to level disparities in familiarity with the term by increasing knowledge among those who had not acquired it as a result of education or its correlate, "cultural capital" (Bourdieu 1973). In the case of 9/11, we find evidence that the sense of unity and solidarity within a group that commemoration engenders—"collective effervescence," in Durkheim's words, or "emotional energy" (Collins 2004)—can sometimes affect the identities that shape memory. Blacks more than whites were influenced by the commemorations led by President Obama to consider 9/11 "deserving of remembrance"—perhaps because for blacks the commemorations increased a sense of national identity. Thus, when commemoration evokes particular identities, it may shift collective memories as well. In this sense, our evidence underscores the degree to which collective memory is a dynamic process not only in terms of the content conveyed by the cultural resources—such as commemoration—that sustain it, but also in terms of what different individuals glean from those resources to shape their beliefs about the past. Collective memory cannot be fully understood without attending to both elements and to the connections between them. Commemoration, when successful, unites the past and the present.

Closing Reflections

Each of us lives through two histories. One is personal: we grow up, go to school, make friends, find a job, get married (or remain single or are divorced), have or do not have children, grow old, die. The other history we live through is that of the larger society that changes almost independently of our personal life: the events summarized by such words as war, assassination, civil rights movement, moon landing, terrorist attack. For the most part, our two lives remain separate: children play and people marry on the same day that a president is elected or a dictator dies, and the two events hardly touch for many of us.

At times, though, personal biographies and national and world events do connect. Even a person who only follows televised images of a war or a political demonstration can be caught up vicariously in the affairs of the nation. A young person drafted to fight in Vietnam in the 1960s or a Reserve Officer sent to Afghanistan in 2015 suddenly finds his or her personal fate caught up in the fate of nations. A person who joins a group protesting military action finds her interests revolving around that protest and can sometimes be led to take actions far removed from the rest of her life. A photograph from the mid-1980s (p. 211) shows the eighty-five-year-old mother-in-law of one of the authors: she had just been arrested at a military base in a demonstration against U.S. involvement in Central America. Judging from the size of the police officer taking her to jail for the night, she must have been regarded as a pretty tough cookie, though in fact her commitment was to Quaker pacifism.

Arrest of Margaret Miles for participating in a demonstration against U.S. involvement in Central America, 1980s

She saw her personal beliefs and the course of the nation's policies as so interconnected as to call for action on her part.

The arrest of an eighty-five-year-old protestor suggests a unique intersection of personal biography with national or world events. But it is the *social* accumulation of many such intersections that gives shape

211

to generations and collective memory. The idea that each individual's experience encompasses certain historical events in ways that are shared by others within the same cohort led us to what we call the critical years hypothesis. We were stimulated by Karl Mannheim's 1928 essay "The Problem of Generations"—still well worth reading nearly a hundred years after its first publication in German. But we have gone beyond Mannheim's method and conclusions in a number of significant respects. Mannheim defined seventeen to twenty-five as the ages when events make their strongest impression on individuals, but whatever the appropriateness of that span for Germany at the time (and Mannheim did not provide any systematic evidence), it was only half the range needed to understand generational memories of national and world events in the United States during the quarter century we cover. Moreover, we found important exceptions to even that extended range, such as an unusual event that was remembered by children very young when it occurred, or a transformative event like Lithuanian independence that affected and was remembered by almost the entire population alive at the time.

Although we have been mainly concerned with generation, it is only one of many dimensions along which the personal and the national intersect to influence collective memory. A person's other commitments and affiliations also determine which events are experienced and how they are interpreted and remembered. Columbus is not the same historical personage for an American Indian and for a descendant of European immigrants. World War II is not interpreted in the same way by a person in East Ukraine and a person in West Ukraine—even if they both lived through that war. A commemoration led by President Obama is not the same commemoration for an African American and for a white American. Just as generation determines the historical events that are experienced, social groups—the many others with whom we experience events and then remember them—influence the meaning of past events and thus their place in collective memory.

Throughout our work, two interrelated ideas about collective memory have both oriented us and been supported by the evidence we found. The first is the idea that the past is not a realm only of history books, but is connected to ordinary individuals and to their lives, beliefs, and commitments in the present. The second is the idea that when ordinary people encounter commemorations, holidays, textbooks, or any such representations of past events that have been created by elites or others in positions of power, they can (and often do) accept those representations—but they may also reject, ignore, or reinterpret them.

By investigating the multiplicity of ways in which people make sense of and draw on past events, we have been able to learn about the social forces that affect how individuals absorb, participate in—and even influence—collective memory.

───────

Our emphasis in this book is in part on the variety of methods—or, better, *approaches*—that can be used to gain different vantage points on generations, collective memory, and the critical years hypothesis. (The word "method" is often taken to imply statistical analysis, but that has *not* been our focus.)

Readers can find our main results and conclusions at the end of each chapter, as well as at the end of Parts I and II, so rather than summarize further here, we instead consider the range of approaches we employed to obtain evidence. In doing so, however, we refer to some of our main results and indicate some possible future directions to pursue.

Scholarly work by historians has been important to us at many points. For example, writing by scholars about Columbus's first landing in the Americas proved essential as we developed our own research, and we then studied later accounts of how Columbus was remembered up to and beyond the four hundredth anniversary in 1892. Only with this history at hand were we able to appreciate our own findings based on interviews with samples of present-day Americans. Similar historical scholarship informed our chapters on Jefferson and Sally Hemings, and on Abraham Lincoln. When we turned to the critical years hypothesis and more recent events, we also depended on writing by others to understand, for example, the Great Depression of the 1930s in the United States, the impact of World War II on Germany and Japan, and present-day divisions within Ukraine—the last-mentioned helping us to appreciate why some Ukrainians could still recall with great intensity the experience of famine from the early 1930s.

Much—though not all—of our evidence about collective memories in our own time comes from personal interview surveys with national samples carried out in the United States. In addition, we were able to conduct surveys in eight countries with different histories, where people face different problems—and those different histories were essential to extending our understanding of generational effects. Both in the United States and cross-nationally, however, our use of survey interviews was unusual in important respects. First, we relied a great deal on open-ended questions that invited respondents to answer in their own words—especially for our primary categorization of "important" national and world events. In this way, we attempted to ensure that we recorded their beliefs and attitudes rather than mirroring our own preconceptions.

Often, we sought further explanations and insight by asking follow-up "Why" questions—again, encouraging people to answer in their own words. These descriptions and explanations helped us interpret puzzling results, such as the very young ages reported for memories of the Kennedy assassination in 1963, the much older ages for memories of the moon landing in 1969, and the lifetime effect we found for memories of Lithuanian independence in 1990–1991. Elsewhere, too, we drew on qualitative explanations that interviewers recorded, finding, for example, that a number of respondents who lacked correct knowledge of a past event engaged in what might be called "historical inversion" when they identified Senator Joe McCarthy as a famous communist.

We sometimes integrated other systematic methods for obtaining information into our survey approach. To learn how Lincoln is thought of at present, we included in a survey a randomized experiment that varied the framing of a key question, but held constant all other influences. When we found a difference too large to be accounted for by the random allocation of interviews to one question or the other, we were able to attribute it to the difference in the way the questions were framed. We adopted a similar experimental approach in order to directly compare the ages most common for collective memories with the ages most common for autobiographical memories.

"Natural experiments"—where an external event created quasi-experimental conditions that made possible a useful comparison—were important to our work. For example, events at the time of the Gulf War (and later the Iraq War) provided an opportunity to learn whether respondents of different ages were influenced by different past wars (World War II versus the Vietnam War). As another example, our study of the 9/11 and Woodstock commemorations took advantage of the way the survey fieldwork coincided with the tenth and fortieth anniversaries of those events.

The most important step we took to build confidence in our results was to treat *replication* as an essential component of our research wherever and whenever possible. Replication can occur in different forms, however, and be used for different purposes. Often we used literal replication to learn whether a discovered relationship may have resulted from chance, just as flipping an ordinary coin one hundred times can lead to an unusual result (say, sixty heads). For example, our study of how different question frames affect reported beliefs about Lincoln was based largely on a theoretical hunch. When the experiment yielded reliable and sensible results, it was tempting to simply accept the finding. But since conceivably the result might have been due to an unusual but appealing chance patterning, we repeated the experiment, and only when an equally strong positive result occurred again did it seem reasonable to conclude that the finding was trustworthy. (Unhappily, we ourselves have taken seriously and published results that seemed convincing at the time, but that, because of non-replication, we now qualify in chapter 9 on collective knowledge. It is important to add that confirmation of an empirical result does not guarantee that one's interpretation of it is correct.)

Replication was very useful in other ways, too. In our study of beliefs about Columbus, our initial neutral question showed—to our surprise—that few if any Americans seemed to have been affected by the revisionist protests leading up to the 1992 Quincentenary. We therefore reworded our question to invite more negative views of Columbus, and asked it in a new survey, but again the results revealed little criticism of Columbus. So we rephrased the question yet a third time to try to encourage negative views, and only when we still received few critical responses did we conclude that most Americans around the time of the Quincentenary saw 1492 and Columbus in entirely positive terms, no matter how we phrased our inquiry. This was an instance of construct replication, where we reformulated our measure from one version to another in order to be sure that the concept itself was being adequately captured.

The same Columbus research illustrated still another reason for replication. After concluding that our measurement of views about Columbus in the decade after the Quincentenary was robust, we repeated our initial neutral question sixteen years later, and at that point, some twenty years after the five hundredth anniversary of 1492, we finally obtained clear evidence of both a decrease in heroic views of Columbus and an increase in critical views. Moreover, the most negative views came mainly from young Americans, many recently of school age. Thus change in the American population's beliefs appears to be taking place through cohort replacement—which indeed is the most important way in which long-held beliefs change in a society.

Replication of each of these kinds was fundamental to our conclusions about the critical years hypothesis. We first found evidence for the hypothesis in 1985, and then in succeeding years through 2010 we replicated our basic result in seven more U.S. surveys. We attempted—and often (though not always) succeeded—in replicating critical years effects in surveys carried out in Germany, Japan, Israel, China, Lithuania, Russia, and Ukraine. Even in a sample of emigrants from the Soviet Union to the United States, we found that events from emigrants' critical years continued to be prominent in memory despite the importance of the emigration experience itself.

In addition to providing confirmatory evidence, replication also helped us to broaden our understanding of generational effects. When we discovered results in Lithuania that did not conform to the critical years hypothesis, we amended the hypothesis to accommodate what we now call a lifetime effect, which appears to occur when an event is so important and pervasive that almost everyone in the population is affected. This was the case with independence in Lithuania, the collapse of the U.S.S.R. in Russia and Ukraine, and possibly World War II in all three countries. (Of course, further replication is needed to assess our lifetime hypothesis.) Our efforts at replication did not merely confirm or disconfirm what we already believed, but provided evidence and ideas we had not envisaged and helped to define the boundaries of our findings and conclusions. Quite likely future work by ourselves and others will improve or amend our understanding still further.

Surveys were not our only source of systematic evidence. When studying commemoration of two events, the September 11, 2001, attacks and the 1969 Woodstock Festival, we tracked newspaper and television reports through content analysis in order to determine the degree of correspondence between coverage of the anniversaries and mentions of the original events in survey interviews. Content analysis of a large sample of high school textbooks also allowed us to identify positive and negative cultural representations of Columbus and American Indians, and to study change in those representations over several decades.

Some things cannot be summarized with numbers, and just as we used answers offered by respondents in their own words to survey interviewers, we drew on all kinds of readily available qualitative evidence—from congressional speeches and presidential proclamations, to notable monuments, paintings, and films, to book jackets and advertisements. Each kind of evidence contributed to our understanding of the ways in which collective memory of past events and people is embodied by physical objects.

In these and many other ways, we drew on both quantitative and qualitative evidence, often striving to use connections between them in order to understand individuals' memories and responses to representations of the past. Throughout our research, method and substance have been joined, each stimulating and drawing inspiration from the other.

Future Research

We have surely not succeeded in answering all of the questions we raised about generations and collective memory—and even where we have arrived at some answers, they inevitably raise new questions. For example, if we could continue to ask our basic question about Columbus over the next several decades, to what extent and at what rate would his reputation continue to decline?

An important larger challenge for the future is to test the critical years hypothesis by using it to predict new results. We considered the impact of a very significant recent event—the September 11 terrorist attack on the United States—soon after it occurred in 2001. The youngest respondents in our sample were the most likely to recall 9/11 as especially important, but at that point we could not adequately distinguish the effect of critical years from the effect of recency (pp. 90–91). We anticipate that once even younger cohorts enter our samples, they will be less likely to name 9/11 as important, since events that they have personally experienced will loom larger for them. Recency will also tend to have disappeared.

We agree with Watts (2014) that the scientific status of a theory depends not only on it being intuitively plausible, but on its ability to survive testing through careful prediction (which is indeed closely related in its scientific function to replication). Theories of evolution and, more recently, of catastrophism, have been able to withstand such testing in recent years (see Weiner 1994; Kolbert 2014).

While our own hypothesis is far more modest in nature than theories of evolution or catastrophism, we intend to test it further using the 9/11 attack as an important example. Although our research extended a decade after 2001, our samples of adult respondents did not yet include people who were very young or not yet born at the time of the attack. Our investigation of collective memory of the assassination of John F. Kennedy (pp. 94–96) showed that the critical years effect extended to children who were quite young at that point, because of the time of day of the shooting and the fact that the shock and sorrow of adults was readily visible even to small children. In the case of 9/11, the event's emotional impact on adults, as well as the graphic images that dominated television and other media, may have created a similar extension of the critical years effect to quite young children. Until our samples include respondents born after 2001—who do not have their own early memories of watching televised images of planes crashing into the World Trade Center, or of seeing their parents or others affected by the news—it may be difficult to detect a clear downturn in mentions of 9/11. Recognizing these complications, we wrote on p. 91 that "Time will tell."

Still, even at this early point, we plan to carry out a partial test of the prediction by gathering further evidence during 2015, using our standard Events question in order to determine which cohorts remember the 9/11 attack as an important event. Whatever the outcome, we hope to report our results in some form in the near future.

Appendix A: Statistical Testing and Its Limitations

When discussing results of statistical tests in our book, we use the term "reliable" to identify differences that are at $p<.05$ and "highly reliable" when $p<.01$, though in most such cases the value is often .001 or less.

We often rely on bivariate analysis with chi-square tests—for example, to carry out the statistical testing of critical years effects described in appendix C. When it is important to control the effects of other variables (that is, to hold constant one or more variables while evaluating the effects of a key variable of interest on the dependent variable), we sometimes use logistic regression analysis.

More generally, we believe that traditional statistical testing should be treated with caution. One potential pitfall is the selective use of p-values that increases the probability of rejecting the null hypothesis—a particular concern when carrying out many significance tests, as has been necessary in our research, which includes studies in many different countries at many different points in time. For this reason, we regard statistical tests as just one component of our analysis, which, as we have discussed, also relies on visual display of data and especially on replication of results.

Appendix B: Survey Response Rates

Response rates to national surveys declined considerably between 1985 (the date of our first survey) and 2014 (the date of the most recent survey included in this book), but the evidence from Pew experiments is that such decrements seldom have important effects on questions unrelated to volunteerism and civic activity. In addition, conclusions about relationships between variables (the focus of the research discussed in this book) are even less likely to be affected than are univariate percentages associated with particular responses. (See Pew Research Center for the People and the Press [2012]; Druckman and Kam [2011]; Abraham, Helms, and Presser [2009]; Groves and Peytcheva [2008]; Keeter, Kennedy, Dimock, Best, and Craighill [2006]; and Curtin, Presser, and Singer [2000].)

SRC monthly survey sampling has adapted to the shift within the U.S. population from landlines to cell phone use. Since 2012, the Surveys of Consumer Attitudes have been gradually introducing cell phone numbers into the monthly survey sample. Of the surveys on which we draw, only the sample for the SRC July 2014 survey includes cell phones, thus affecting the comparison (discussed in chapter 1) between that survey and the landline-only 1998 survey, which took place before the proliferation of cell phones. In the July 2014 survey, cell phone numbers made up roughly two-thirds of the initial sample.

Appendix C:
Formal Tests of Critical
Years Effects

The visual support for the critical years hypothesis is substantial, but it can be difficult to establish just where a rise in the curve begins or ends. The graphical evidence we present in the figures is supported by formal statistical tests that help to establish whether those in their critical years at the time of each event are more likely to remember it than those either older or younger.

To carry out this more careful testing, we adopt Schuman and Rodgers' (2004) approach, taking age ten as the lower boundary for the critical years window and thirty as the upper bound. For each event, we first categorize respondents in terms of whether the event preceded, intersected with, or followed their critical years. For example, to identify the birth cohorts of respondents who were in their critical years at the time of World War II, we subtract ten and thirty (the boundary ages of the critical years) from the event beginning and end dates of 1941 and 1945, identifying cohorts born from 1911 to 1935 as in their critical years at some point during the war. Older cohorts who were beyond their critical years at the time are all those born in 1910 or earlier, while younger cohorts are those born in 1936 or later. We then compare the percentages that mentioned World

War II in each of the three categories. Since multivariate analysis with controls leads to essentially the same conclusions as bivariate analysis (Schuman and Rodgers 2004), we simplify the approach by using percentages and chi-square tests. The results of these tests, and visual inspection of the plotted curves, are the basis for conclusions in tables 4.3, 5.2, and 6.2.

Appendix D: Robustness of Standard Events Question

a. Question wording

A split-sample experiment tested the possibility that the location of the words "to you" in the standard open Events question (p. 83) might emphasize either objective or personal importance. The experiment (included as part of the 1990 Chicago Metropolitan Area Study, N=1,026) highlighted personal importance by moving "to you" to the end of the question for a random half of the sample. No reliable difference occurred for the relations to cohort or other key variables. Furthermore, translations of the question into national languages in China, Lithuania, Germany, Japan, Russia, Ukraine, and Israel inevitably altered both syntax and connotations of words, yet results similar to those in the United States were often obtained.

b. Question form

Schuman and Scott (1987) reported that both the univariate percentage and the magnitude of the correlation with age of the response "the invention of the computer" increased if the question was given in a closed form. However, no changes occurred for other events (World War II, the Vietnam War, the JFK assassination, and space exploration) included as part of the experiment. The authors believed that in 1986 the computer was not salient for the general public and thus could be affected by question form more than were other answers. The comparisons in Schuman (2008: 59–61, figures 2.1–2.5) provide visual evidence that the relation of event mentions to cohort is generally the same as when the open-ended question form is used, except in the case of computers. In later surveys the percentage of computer responses to the open question increased appreciably and its expected negative relation to age was obtained.

c. Number of responses encouraged

In a split-sample national experiment in February 2004, respondents were encouraged to name up to six events. We found decrements in codable responses with each subsequent probe. By the fourth request we had lost more than half the sample, and many mentions could not be used because of small numbers. The order of events changed little regardless of the number of probes, nor was there any appreciable difference in relations to cohort.

d. Advantage of two responses over one

Obtaining two codable events from the respondent provides a more stringent test of the critical years effect, since respondents have two opportunities to mention events that did not occur during their critical years. It also enables study of associations among events. As would be expected on the basis of the importance of cohort effects, factor analysis indicated that inter-item correlations are influenced more by time period than by genre (e.g., the Great Depression and World War II, which were adjacent in time, are more highly correlated than are World War II and the Vietnam War, both of which involved U.S. participation in major wars).

e. Difference between first and second responses

We do find that certain very important and frequently given events (such as the September 11, 2001, attack on the United States) are more apt to be named as a first mention than as a second mention. Despite this tendency, both the first mentions and the total mentions almost always give the same results when used in associations with other variables. In particular, using only the first mention instead of total mentions does not change conclusions about the relation of event mentions to cohort.

References

ABC News/Washington Post Poll. 2011. iPOLL Databank, Roper Center for Public Opinion Research, University of Connecticut. Retrieved September 22, 2012 (http://www.ropercenter.uconn.edu/ipoll.html).

Abraham, Katharine G., Sara Helms, and Stanley Presser. 2009. "How Social Processes Distort Measurement: The Impact of Survey Nonresponse on Estimates of Volunteer Work in the United States." *American Journal of Sociology* 114: 1129–1165.

Alba, Richard, and Victor Nee. 2003. *Remaking the American Mainstream: Assimilation and Contemporary Immigration.* Cambridge, MA: Harvard University Press.

Alwin, Duane F., and Ryan J. McCammon. 2007. "Rethinking Generations." *Research in Human Development* 4: 219–237.

American Heritage Dictionary. 1992. 3rd ed. Boston: Houghton Mifflin.

Appiah, Kwame Anthony, and Henry Louis Gates, Jr. (2005) *The Encyclopedia of the African and African American Experience.* New York: Oxford University Press.

Assmann, Aleida. 2001. "History and Memory." Pp. 6823–6829 in *International Encyclopedia of the Social and Behavioral Sciences*, edited by Neil J. Smelser and Paul B. Baltes. New York: Elsevier.

Assmann, Aleida. 2007. "Response to Peter Novick." Pp. 33–38 of *Bulletin of the German Historical Institute.* Washington, D.C.

Axtell, James. 1992. "Columbus Encounters: Beyond 1992." *William and Mary Quarterly* 49: 335–360.

Baddeley, Alan. 1990. *Human Memory: Theory and Practice.* Boston: Allyn and Bacon.

Baddeley, Alan, Michael W. Eysenck, and Michael C. Anderson. 2009. *Memory.* New York: Psychology Press.

Bahrick, Harry P. 1984. "Semantic Memory Content in Permastore: Fifty Years of Memory for Spanish Learned in School." *Journal of Experimental Psychology: General* 113: 1–31.

Barger, Herbert. 2009. "The Truth about Thomas Jefferson and Slave Children." Retrieved November 4, 2013 (religionnewsblog.blogspot.com/2009/06/truth -about-thomas-jefferson-and-slave.html).

Bartlett, Frederic C. 1932. *Remembering: A Study in Experimental and Social Psychology*. Cambridge: Cambridge University Press.

Bennett, Lerone, Jr. 1954. "Thomas Jefferson's Negro Grandchildren." *Ebony* 10: 78–80.

Berntsen, Dorthe, and David C. Rubin. 2002. "Emotionally Charged Autobiographical Memories across the Life Span: The Recall of Happy, Sad, Traumatic, and Involuntary Memories." *Psychology and Aging* 17: 636–652.

Berntsen, Dorthe, and David C. Rubin. 2004. "Cultural Life Scripts Structure Recall from Autobiographical Memory." *Memory and Cognition* 32: 427–442.

Blight, David W. 2001. *Race and Reunion: The Civil War in American Memory*. Cambridge, MA: Harvard University Press.

Bodnar, John. 1992. *Remaking America: Public Memory, Commemoration, and Patriotism in the Twentieth Century*. Princeton, NJ: Princeton University Press.

Boorstin, Daniel J. 1962. *The Image: A Guide to Pseudo Events in America*. New York: Atheneum.

Bourdieu, Pierre. 1973. "Cultural Reproduction and Social Reproduction." Pp. 71–112 in *Knowledge, Education and Social Change: Papers in the Sociology of Education*, edited by Richard Brown. London: Tavistock.

Bower, Gordon H. 2000. "A Brief History of Memory Research." Pp. 3–32 in *The Oxford Handbook of Memory*, edited by Endel Tulving and Fergus I. M. Craik. Oxford: Oxford University Press.

Boym, Svetlana. 1994. *Common Places: Mythologies of Everyday Life in Russia*. Cambridge, MA: Harvard University Press.

Brodie, Fawn M. 1974. *Thomas Jefferson: An Intimate History*. New York: Norton.

Brodsky, Joseph. 1986. *Less Than One: Selected Essays*. New York: Farrar, Straus and Giroux.

Bromet, Evelyn J., David P. Taormina, Lin T. Guey, Joost A. Bijlsma, Semyon F. Gluzman, Johan M. Havenaar, Harold Carlson, and Gabrielle A. Carlson. 2009. "Subjective Health Legacy of the Chornobyl Accident: A Comparative Study of 19-Year Olds in Kyiv." BMC Public Health 9:417–428.

Brown, Roger, and James Kulik. 1977. "Flashbulb Memories." *Cognition* 5: 73–99.

Browne, Janet. 2002. *Charles Darwin: The Power of Place*. Princeton, NJ: Princeton University Press.

Burley, Nancy Tyler. 2006. "An Eye for Detail: Selective Sexual Imprinting in Zebra Finches." *Evolution* 60: 1076–1085.

Burlingame, Michael. 2008. *Abraham Lincoln: A Life*. 2 vols. Baltimore, MD: Johns Hopkins University Press.

Burns, John F. 2004. "Drawing from Its Past Wars, Britain Takes a Tempered Approach to Iraqi Insurgency." *New York Times*, October 17: N12.

Burns, Ken. 1996. *Thomas Jefferson*. Public Broadcasting Company.

Buruma, Ian. 1994. *The Wages of Guilt: Memories of War in Germany and Japan.* New York: Farrar, Straus and Giroux.

Callender, James. [1802] 1999. "The President, Again." Originally published in *Richmond Recorder*, September 1, 1802. Reprinted, pp. 259–261, in *Sally Hemings and Thomas Jefferson: History, Memory, and Civic Culture*, edited by Jan Ellen Lewis and Peter S. Onuf. Charlottesville: University of Virginia.

Campbell, Angus, Philip E. Converse, Warren E. Miller, and Donald E. Stokes. 1960. *The American Voter.* New York: Wiley.

Cantril, Hadley. 1944. *Gauging Public Opinion.* Princeton, NJ: Princeton University Press.

Cave, Damien, Matt Diehl, Gavin Edwards, Jenny Eliscu, David Fricke, Lauren Gitlin, Matt Hendrickson, Kirk Miller, Austin Scaggs, and Rob Sheffield. 2004. "The Moments: Mud, Nudity, Rock and Roll." *Rolling Stone* 951: 122–123.

Chase-Riboud, Barbara. 1979. *Sally Hemings: A Novel.* New York: Viking Press.

Coates, Eyler Robert, ed. 2001. *The Jefferson-Hemings Myth: An American Travesty.* Charlottesville, VA: Jefferson Editions.

Cohen, Martin. 2005. *Wittgenstein's Beetle and Other Classic Thought Experiments.* Oxford, UK: Blackwell.

Collins, Randall. 2004. "Rituals of Solidarity and Security in the Wake of Terrorist Attack." *Sociological Theory* 22: 53–87.

Columbia Encyclopedia. 1993. "Columbus, Christopher." New York: Columbia University Press.

Columbia Encyclopedia. 2000a. "Columbus, Christopher." New York: Columbia University Press.

Columbia Encyclopedia. 1975. "Jefferson, Thomas." New York: Columbia University Press.

Columbia Encyclopedia. 2000b. "Jefferson, Thomas." New York: Columbia University Press.

Columbia Encyclopedia. 2009. "Jefferson, Thomas." New York: Columbia University Press.

Columbia Encyclopedia. 2000c. "World's Columbian Exposition." New York: Columbia University Press.

Confino, Alon. 1997. "Collective Memory and Cultural History: Problems of Method." *American Historical Review* 102: 1386–1403.

Converse, Philip. E. 1964. "The Nature of Belief Systems in the Mass Public." Pp. 206–261 in *Ideology and Discontent*, edited by David E. Apter. New York: Free Press.

Converse, Philip E. 1987. "The Enduring Impact of the Vietnam War on American Public Opinion." Pp. 53–57 in *After the Storm: American Society A Decade after the Vietnam War.* Taipei: Academia Sinica.

Conway Martin A., and Helen L. Williams. 2008. "Autobiographical Memory." Pp. 893–909 in *Learning and Memory: A Comprehensive Reference*, vol. 2, *The Cognitive Psychology of Memory*, edited by Henry L. Roediger. New York: Elsevier.

Coolidge, Ellen Randolph. [1858] 1997. "Letter to Joseph Coolidge." Reprinted, pp. 258–260, in Annette Gordon-Reed, *Thomas Jefferson and Sally Hemings: An American Controversy.* Charlottesville: University Press of Virginia.

Corning, Amy D. 2010. "Emigration, Generation, and Collective Memories: The Presence of the Past for Emigrants from the Former Soviet Union." *Social Psychology Quarterly* 73: 223–44.

Corning, Amy, Vladas Gaidys, and Howard Schuman. 2013. "Transformative Events and Generational Memory: A Case Study over Time in Lithuania. *Sociological Forum* 28: 373–394.

Corning, Amy, and Howard Schuman. 2013. "Commemoration Matters: The Anniversaries of 9/11 and Woodstock." *Public Opinion Quarterly* 77: 433–454.

Coser, Lewis A. 1992. "Introduction: Maurice Halbwachs 1877–1945." Pp. 1–34 in *On Collective Memory*, edited and translated by Lewis A. Coser. Chicago: University of Chicago Press.

Crovitz, H. F., and H. Schiffman. 1974. "Frequency of Episodic Memories as a Function of Their Age." *Bulletin of the Psychonomic Society* 4: 517–518.

Cropper, William H. 2001. *Great Physicists: The Life and Times of Leading Physicists from Galileo to Hawking.* New York: Oxford University Press.

Crosby, Alfred W., Jr. 1973. *The Columbian Exchange: Biological and Cultural Consequences of 1492.* Westport, CT: Greenwood Press.

Crystal, David. 2005. *The Stories of English.* New York: Overlook.

Cumming, Geoff. 2012. *Understanding the New Statistics: Effect Sizes, Confidence Intervals, and Meta-Analysis.* New York: Routledge.

Curtin, Richard, Stanley Presser, and Eleanor Singer. 2000. "The Effects of Response Rate Changes on the Index of Consumer Sentiment." *Public Opinion Quarterly* 64: 413–428.

Davis, David Brion. 1975. *The Problem of Slavery in the Age of Revolution 1770–1823.* Ithaca, NY: Cornell University Press.

de Certeau, Michel. 1984. *The Practice of Everyday Life.* Berkeley: University of California Press.

de la Garza, Rudolfo O., Angelo Falcon, and F. Chris Garcia. 1996. "Will the Real American Please Stand Up: Anglo and Mexican-American Support of Core American Values." *American Journal of Political Science* 40: 335–351.

de Lancey, E. 1893. "Columbian Celebration of 1792: The First in the United States." *Magazine of American History* 39: 1–18.

de las Casas, Bartolomé. [1965] 1974. *The Devastation of the Indies: A Brief Account.* New York: The Seabury Press.

de las Casas, Bartolomé. 1992. *Witness: Writings of Bartolomé.* Edited by George Sanderlin. Maryknoll, NY: Orbis Books.

Delli Carpini, Michael X., and Scott Keeter. 1996. *What Americans Know about Politics and Why It Matters.* New Haven, CT: Yale University Press.

Deloria, Vine, Jr. 1969. *Custer Died for Your Sins: An Indian Manifesto.* New York: Macmillan.

Dickson, Ryan A., David B. Pillemer, and Elizabeth C. Bruehl. 2011. "The Reminiscence Bump for Salient Personal Memories: Is a Cultural Life Script Required?" *Memory and Cognition* 39: 977–991.

DiMaggio, Paul. 1997. "Culture and Cognition." *Annual Review of Sociology* 23: 263–287.

Druckman, James N., and Cindy D. Kam. 2011. "Students as Experimental Participants: A Defense of the 'Narrow Data Base.'" Pp. 41–57 in *Cambridge Handbook of Experimental Political Science*, edited by James N. Druckman, Donald P. Green, James H. Kuklinski, and Arthur Lupia. New York: Cambridge University Press.

Donald, David H. 1995. *Lincoln*. New York: Simon and Schuster.

Dubin, Steven C. 1999. *Displays of Power: Memory and Amnesia in the American Museum*. New York: New York University Press.

Durkheim, Emile. [1915] 1968. *The Elementary Forms of Religious Life*. New York: The Free Press.

Ebbinghaus, Hermann. 1885. *On Memory*. New York: Dover.

Edgerton, Gary R. 2007. *The Columbia History of American Television*. New York: Columbia University Press.

Eliot, T. S. 1952. "Fragment of an Agon." Pp. 79–85 in *The Complete Poems and Plays*. New York: Harcourt, Brace, and Company.

Ellis, Joseph J. 1996. *American Sphinx: The Character of Thomas Jefferson*. New York: Knopf.

Encyclopaedia Britannica. 1985. "Jefferson, Thomas." Chicago: University of Chicago Press.

Encyclopaedia Britannica. 2004. "Columbus, Christopher." Retrieved July 27, 2004 (http://www.britannica.com/EBchecked/topic/127070/Christopher -Columbus).

Encyclopaedia Britannica. 2009. "Jefferson, Thomas." Retrieved 2009 (http://www .britannica.com/EBchecked/topic/302264/Thomas-Jefferson).

Feros, Antonio. 2004. "Civil War Still Haunts Spanish Politics." *New York Times*, March 20: B9.

Figes, Orlando. 2002. "Who Lost the Soviet Union?" *New York Times Book Review*, January 20: 11.

Fine, Gary. 2001. *Difficult Reputations: Collective Memories of the Evil, Inept, and Controversial*. Chicago: University of Chicago Press.

Fineman, Mia. 2005. "The Most Famous Farm Couple in the World: Why American Gothic Still Fascinates. *Slate*, June 8. Retrieved 22 September 2014 (http:// www.slate.com/articles/arts/art/2005/06/the_most_famous_farm_couple _in_the_world.html).

Finkelman, Paul. 1996. *Slavery and the Founders: Race and Liberty in the Age of Jefferson*. Armonk, NY: M. E. Sharpe.

FitzGerald, Frances. 1979. *America Revised: History Schoolbooks in the Twentieth Century*. Boston: Little, Brown.

Foner, Eric. 1988. *Reconstruction: America's Unfinished Revolution 1863–1877*. New York: Harper and Row.

Foner, Eric. 2010. *The Fiery Trial: Abraham Lincoln and American Slavery*. New York: W.W. Norton.

Foster, Eugene A., M. A. Jobling, P. G. Taylor, P. Donnelly, P. de Knijff, R. Mieremet, T. Zerjal, and C. Tyler-Smith. 1998. "Jefferson Fathered Slave's Last Child." *Nature* 196 (November 5): 28–29.

Foucault, Michel. 1977. *Language, Counter-Memory, Practice: Selected Essays and Interviews*. Translated by D. F. Bouchard and S. Simon. Ithaca, NY: Cornell University Press.

Fox-Genovese, Elizabeth, and Elisabeth Lasch-Quinn, eds. 1999. *Reconstructing History: The Emergence of a New Historical Society*. New York: Routledge.

Fredrickson, George M. 2002. *Racism: A Short History*. Princeton, NJ: Princeton University Press.

French, Scot A., and Edward L. Ayers. 1993. "The Strange Career of Thomas Jefferson: Race and Slavery in American Memory, 1943–1993." Pp. 418–456 in *Jeffersonian Legacies*, edited by Peter S. Onuf. Charlottesville: University of Virginia Press.

Frisch, Michael. 1989. "American History and the Structures of Collective Memory: A Modest Exercise in Empirical Iconography." *Journal of American History* 75: 1130–1155.

Furstenberg, Frank F. 2000. "The Sociology of Adolescence and Youth in the 1990s: A Critical Commentary." *Journal of Marriage and the Family* 62: 896–910.

The Gallup Poll Monthly. 1991. February (No. 305).

Garfinkel, Harold. 1956. "Conditions of Successful Degradation Ceremonies." *American Journal of Sociology* 61: 420–424.

Gates, Henry Louis, Jr. 2008. "Personal History: Family Matters." *New Yorker*, December 1: 34–38.

Gillis, John R., ed. 1994. *Commemorations: The Politics of National Identity*. Princeton, NJ: Princeton University Press.

Glück, Judith, and Susan Bluck. 2007. "Looking Back Across the Life Span: A Life Story Account of the Reminiscence Bump." *Memory and Cognition* 35: 1928–1939.

Goffman, Erving. 1974. *Frame Analysis: An Essay on the Organization of Experience*. London: Harper and Row.

Gordon-Reed, Annette. 1997. *Thomas Jefferson and Sally Hemings: An American Controversy*. Charlottesville: University Press of Virginia.

Gordon-Reed, Annette. 1999. "The Memories of a Few Negroes." Pp. 236–252 in *Sally Hemings and Thomas Jefferson: History, Memory, and Civic Culture*, edited by Jan Ellen Lewis and Peter S. Onuf. Charlottesville: University of Virginia.

Gordon-Reed, Annette. 2008. *The Hemingses of Monticello: An American Family*. New York: W. W. Norton.

Gordon-Reed, Annette. 2012. "Thomas Jefferson Was Not a Monster: Debunking a Major New Biography of Our Third President." *Slate*, October 12 (http://

www.slate.com/articles/arts/culturebox/2012/10/henry_wiencek_s_the_master
_of_the_mountain_thomas_jefferson_biography_debunked.html).

Gray, Thomas. [1750] 1944. "Elegy Written in a Country Church-yard." Pp. 42–46
in *A Treasury of the Familiar*, edited by Ralph L. Woods. New York: Macmillan.

Griswold, Wendy, and Nathan Wright. 2004. "Cowbirds, Locals, and the Dynamic
Endurance of Regionalism." *American Journal of Sociology* 109: 1411–1451.

Groseclose, Barbara. 1992 "Monuments and Memorials." Pp. 475–485 in *The Christopher Columbus Encyclopedia*, edited by Silvio A. Bedino. New York: Simon
and Schuster.

Groves, Robert M., and Emilia Peytcheva. 2008. "The Impact of Nonresponse Rates
on Nonresponse Bias: A Meta-analysis." *Public Opinion Quarterly* 72: 167–189.

Guidebook to Monticello. 2011. Charlottesville: University of Virginia Press.

Haid, Charles, dir. 2000. *Sally Hemings: An American Scandal*. TV movie.

Halbwachs, Maurice. [1925] 1992a. *The Social Frameworks of Memory*. Pp. 37–189
in *On Collective Memory*, edited and translated by Lewis A. Coser. Chicago:
University of Chicago Press.

Halbwachs, Maurice. [1941] 1992b. "The Legendary Topography of the Gospels in
the Holy Land." Pp. 193–235 in *On Collective Memory*, edited and translated
by Lewis A. Coser. Chicago: University of Chicago Press.

Halbwachs, Maurice. [1950] 1980. *The Collective Memory*. Edited by Mary Douglas.
Translated by Francis J. Ditter and Vida Yazdi Ditter. New York: Harper and
Row.

Hampson, Rick, and Martha T. Moore. 2011. "How 9/11 Changed Us: Person by
Person." *USA Today*, September 7. Retrieved October 20, 2014 (http://usa
today30.usatoday.com/news/nation/story/2011-09-02/How-911-changed-us
-Person-by-person/50246434/1).

Hart, Avery. 2001. *Who Really Discovered America: Unraveling the Mystery and Solving
the Puzzle*. Charlotte, VT: Williamson Publishing Company.

Hayne, Harlene, and Fiona Jack. 2011. "Childhood Amnesia." *Cognitive Science*.
2: 136–145.

Hemings, Madison. [1873] 1997. "Memoirs." Originally published as "Life among
the Lowly No. 1," in the *Pike County (Ohio) Republican*, March 13. Reprinted,
pp. 245–248, in Annette Gordon-Reed, *Thomas Jefferson and Sally Hemings: An
American Controversy*. Charlottesville: University Press of Virginia.

Hetherington, Marc J. 1998. "The Political Relevance of Political Trust." *American
Political Science Review* 92: 791–808.

Himmelfarb, Gertrude. 1987. *The New History and the Old: Critical Essays and Reap-
praisals*. Cambridge, MA: Harvard University Press.

Hobsbawm, Eric, and Terence Ranger. 1983. *The Invention of Tradition*. Cambridge:
Cambridge University Press.

Holbrook, Allyson L., Melanie C. Green, and Jon A. Krosnick. 2003. "Telephone
versus Face-to-Face Interviewing of National Probability Samples with Long
Questionnaires: Comparisons of Respondent Satisficing and Social Desirability Response Bias." *Public Opinion Quarterly* 67: 79–125.

Holmes, Alison, and Martin A. Conway. 1999. "Generation Identity and the Reminiscence Bump: Memory for Public and Private Events." *Journal of Adult Development* 6: 21–34.

Hume, David. 1795–1796. *The History of England from the Invasion of Julius Cæsar to the Revolution of 1688*. Vol. 5, Ch. LXII. Philadelphia: Robert Campbell.

Hutton, Patrick H. 1993. *History as an Art of Memory*. Hanover, VT: University Press of New England.

Hyland, William G. 2009. *In Defense of Thomas Jefferson: The Sally Hemings Sex Scandal*. New York: St. Martin's Press.

Hyman, Herbert H., and Paul B. Sheatsley. 1956. "Attitudes toward Desegregation." *Scientific American* 195: 35–39.

Ioannidis, John P.A. 2005. "Why Most Published Research Findings Are False." *PLoS Med* 2 (8): e124.

Irving, Washington [1828] 1981. *The Life and Voyages of Christopher Columbus* (*The Collected Works of Washington Irving*. Vol. XI, edited by John Harmon McElroy). Boston: Twayne Publishers.

Ivory, James, dir. 1995. *Jefferson in Paris*, written by Ruth Prawer Jhabvala, produced by Ismail Merchant. France: Merchant-Ivory Productions.

Jansari, Ashok, and Alan J. Parkin. 1996. "Things That Go Bump in Your Life: Explaining the Reminiscence Bump in Autobiographical Memory." *Psychology and Aging* 11: 85–91.

Janssen, Steve M., Antonio G. Chessa, and Jaap M. J. Murre. 2007. "Temporal Distribution of Favourite Books, Movies, and Records: Differential Encoding and Sampling." *Memory* 17: 755–767.

Janssen, Steve M., and Jaap M. J. Murre. 2008. "Reminiscence Bump in Autobiographical Memory: Unexplained by Novelty, Emotionality, Valence, or Importance of Personal Events." *Quarterly Journal of Experimental Psychology* 61: 1847–1860.

Janssen, Steve M., Jaap M. J. Murre, and Martijn Meeter. 2008. "Reminiscence Bump in Memory for Public Events." *European Journal of Cognitive Psychology* 20: 738–764.

Janssen, Steve M., David C. Rubin, and Martin A. Conway. 2012. "The Reminiscence Bump in the Temporal Distribution of the Best Football Players of All Time: Pelé, Cruijff or Maradona?" *Quarterly Journal of Experimental Psychology* 65: 165–178.

Janssen, Steve M., David C. Rubin, and P. L. St. Jacques. 2011. "The Temporal Distribution of Autobiographical Memory: Changes in Reliving and Vividness over the Life Span Do Not Explain the Reminiscence Bump." *Memory and Cognition* 39: 1–11.

Jefferson, Israel. [1873] 1997. "Memoirs." Originally published as "Life among the Lowly No. 3," in the *Pike County (Ohio) Republican*, December 25, 1873. Reprinted, pp. 249–253, in Annette Gordon-Reed, *Thomas Jefferson and Sally Hemings: An American Controversy*. Charlottesville: University Press of Virginia.

Jefferson, Thomas. 1787. *Notes on the State of Virginia / by Thomas Jefferson.* Edited with an introduction and notes by William Peden. Chapel Hill: University of North Carolina Press.

Jennings, Francis. 1975. *The Invasion of America: Indians, Colonialism, and the Cant of Conquest.* Chapel Hill: University of North Carolina Press.

Jennings, M. Kent, and Ning Zhang. 2005. "Generations, Political Status, and Collective Memories in the Chinese Countryside." *Journal of Politics* 67: 1164–1189.

Johnson, Rossiter, ed. 1897. *A History of the World's Columbian Exposition.* Vol. 1. New York: D. Appleton.

Jordan, Winthrop D. 1968. *White over Black: American Attitudes toward the Negro 1550–1812.* Baltimore, MD: Penguin Books.

Kansteiner, Wulf. 2002. "Finding Meaning in Memory: A Methodological Critique of Collective Memory Studies." *History and Theory* 41: 179–197.

Kansteiner, Wulf. 2004. "Nazis, Viewers and Statistics: Television History, Television Audience Research and Collective Memory in West Germany." *Journal of Contemporary History* 39: 575–598.

Karnow, Stanley. 1983. *Vietnam, A History.* New York: Viking Press.

Katz, Jack. 1975. "Essences as Moral Identities: Verifiability and Responsibility in Imputations of Deviance and Charisma." *American Journal of Sociology* 80: 1369–1390.

Keeter, Scott, C. M. Kennedy, M. Dimock, J. Best, and P. Craighill. 2006. "Gauging the Impact of Growing Nonresponse on Estimates from a National RDD Telephone Survey." *Public Opinion Quarterly* 70: 759–779.

Kennedy, John F. 1962. "Remarks at a Dinner Honoring Nobel Prize Winners of the Western Hemisphere." Reproduced in *The American Presidency Project*, John T. Woolley and Gerhard Peters. Retrieved November 4, 2013 (http://www.presidency.ucsb.edu/ws/?pid=8623#axzz2jnEaFzsJ).

Kessler, Ronald C., et al. 2004. "The US National Comorbidity Survey Replication (NCS-R): Design and Field Procedures." *International Journal of Methods in Psychiatric Research* 13: 69–92.

Khong, Yuen Foong. 1992. *Analogies at War: Korea, Munich, Dien Bien Phu, and the Vietnam Decisions of 1965.* Princeton, NJ: Princeton University Press.

Kissell, Rick. 2000. "Minis Hit Skids on Net Skeds." *Variety*, June 12–18: 44.

Klady, L. 1996. "Box Office Performance of Films in 1995." *Variety* 8–14 January: 38.

Kligler-Vilenchik, Neta, Yaniv Tsfati, and Oren Meyers. 2015. "Setting the Collective Memory Agenda: Examining Mainstream Media Influence on Individuals' Perceptions of the Past." *Memory Studies* 7: 484–499.

Koch, Cynthia M. 1996. "Teaching Patriotism: Private Virtue for the Public Good in the Early Republic." Pp. 19–52 in *Bonds of Affection: Americans Define Their Patriotism*, edited by John Bodnar. Princeton, NJ: Princeton University Press.

Kolbent, Elizabeth. 2014. *The Sixth Extinction.* New York: Henry Holt.

Koppel, Jonathan, and Dorthe Berntsen. 2014. "Does Everything Happen When You Are Young? Introducing the Youth Bias." *Quarterly Journal of Experimental Psychology* 67: 417–423.

Krensky, Stephen. 1987. *Who Really Discovered America?* New York: Hastings House.

Krensky, Stephen. 1991. *Christopher Columbus.* (Step into Reading, Step 2). New York: Random House.

Lander, Eric S., and Joseph J. Ellis. 1998. "Founding Father." *Nature* 196 (November 5): 13–14.

Le Goff, Jacques. 1985. "Mentalities: a History of Ambiguities." Pp. 166–180 in *Constructing the Past: Essays in Historical Methodology*, edited by Jacques Le Goff and Pierre Nora. Cambridge: Cambridge University Press.

Le Goff, Jacques. 1992 (English), 1972 (French). *History and Memory.* New York: Columbia University Press.

Lewis, Jan, and Peter S. Onuf. 1998. "American Synecdoche: Thomas Jefferson as Image, Icon, Character, and Self." *American Historical Review* 103: 125–136.

Lewis, Jan Ellen, and Peter S. Onuf, eds. 1999. *Sally Hemings and Thomas Jefferson: History, Memory, and Civic Culture.* Charlottesville: University Press of Virginia.

Lichter, Robert. 1992. "The Instant Replay War." Pp. 224–230 in *The Media and the Gulf War*, edited by Hedrick Smith. Baltimore, MD: Foreign Policy Institute of the School of Advanced International Studies, Johns Hopkins University.

Lipka, Michael. 2013. "5 Facts about Atheists." *Fact Tank: News in the Numbers.* Pew Research Center. October 23, 2013. Retrieved November 4, 2013 (http://www.pewresearch.org/fact-tank/2013/10/23/5-facts-about-atheists/).

Lockhart, Robert S. 2000. "Methods of Memory Research." Pp. 45–58 in *The Oxford Handbook of Memory*, edited by Endel Tulving and Fergus I. M. Craik. New York: Oxford University Press.

Loewen, James W. 1992. *The Truth about Columbus.* New York: The New Press.

Loewen, James W. 1995. *Lies My Teacher Told Me: Everything Your American History Textbook Got Wrong.* New York: Simon and Schuster.

Maier, Pauline. 1997. *American Scripture: Making the Declaration of Independence.* New York: Knopf.

Malone, Dumas. 1970. *Jefferson the President: First Term, 1801–1805.* Boston: Little, Brown.

Malone, Dumas. 1981. *The Sage of Monticello.* Boston: Little, Brown.

Mann, James. 2004. *Rise of the Vulcans: The History of Bush's War Cabinet.* New York: Penguin.

Mannheim, Karl. [1928] 1952. "The Problem of Generations." Pp. 276–322 in *Essays on the Sociology of Knowledge.* London: Routledge and Kegan Paul.

McCombs, Maxwell. 2004. *Setting the Agenda: The Mass Media and Public Opinion.* Malden, MA: Blackwell.

McCullough, David. Interview by Charlie Rose. *Charlie Rose*, PBS, March 21, 2008.

Meacham, Jon. 2012. *Thomas Jefferson: The Art of Power.* New York: Random House.

Meillet, Antoine. 1911. *Méthode dans les Sciences.* Paris: Alcan.

Merton, Robert K. [1949] 1968. "On the Sociological Theories of the Middle Range." Pp. 39–72 in *Social Theory and Social Structure.* New York: The Free Press.

Miller, John Chester. 1977. *The Wolf by the Ears: Thomas Jefferson and Slavery.* New York: The Free Press.

Misztal, Barbara Q. 2003. *Theories of Social Remembering*. Maidenhead, England: Open University Press.

Morawska, Ewa. 2004. "Exploring Diversity in Immigrant Assimilation and Transnationalism: Poles and Russian Jews in Philadelphia." *International Migration Review* 38: 1372–1412.

Morgan, Edmund S. 1975. *American Slavery, American Freedom: The Ordeal of Colonial Virginia*. New York: W. W. Norton.

Morison, Samuel Eliot. 1942. *Admiral of the Ocean Sea: A Life of Christopher Columbus*. Boston: Little, Brown.

Nagel, Joane. 1995. "American Indian Ethnic Renewal: Politics and the Resurgence of Identity." *American Sociological Review* 60: 947–965.

National Council of the Churches of Christ in the USA. 1990. *A Faithful Response to the 500th Anniversary of the Arrival of Christopher Columbus*. Resolution, as adopted by the Governing Board, May 17. 475 Riverside Drive, NY.

Neiman, Fraser D. 2000. "Coincidence or Causal Connection? The Relationship between Thomas Jefferson's Visits to Monticello and Sally Hemings' Conceptions." *William and Mary Quarterly* (Third Series) 57 (1): 198–210.

Nora, Pierre. 1989. "Between Memory and History: Les Lieux de Mémoire." *Representations* 26: 7–24.

Novick, Peter. 1999. *The Holocaust in American Life*. New York: Houghton Mifflin.

Newsweek. 1991. "When Worlds Collide: A Joint Project with the Smithsonian's Natural History Exhibit: 'Seeds of Change.'" Columbus Special Issue. Fall/Winter.

New York Times. 1998. "The New Immigrant Tide." July 19: A13.

Obama, Barack. 2011. "Remarks by the President at 'A Concert for Hope.'" September 11, 2011. Retrieved October 15, 2012 (http://www.whitehouse.gov/the-press-office/2011/09/11/remarks-president-concert-hope).

Obama, Barack. 2012. "Presidential Proclamation–Columbus Day, 2012." October 5, 2012. Retrieved September 22, 2014 (http://www.whitehouse.gov/the-press-office/2012/10/05/presidential-proclamation-columbus-day-2012).

O'Connor, Margaret G., Mary Alice Sieggreen, Kristie Bachna, Laird S. Cermak, and Bernard J. Ransil. 2000. "Long Term Retention of Transient News Events. *Journal of the International Neuropsychological Society* 6: 44–51.

Olick, Jeffrey K. 1999. "Collective Memory: The Two Cultures." *Sociological Theory* 17: 333–348.

Olick, Jeffrey K. 2007. *The Politics of Regret: On Collective Memory and Historical Responsibility*. New York: Routledge.

Olick, Jeffrey K., and Joyce Robbins. 1998. "Social Memory Studies: From Collective Memory to the Historical Sociology of Mnemonic Practices." *Annual Review of Sociology* 22: 105–140.

Osborne, Danny, David O. Sears, and Nicholas A. Valentino. 2011. "The End of the Solidly Democratic South: The Impressionable Years Hypothesis." *Political Psychology* 32: 81–108.

Paniotto, Volodymyr. 2014. "Euromaidan: Profile of a Rebellion." *Global Dialogue* 4 (2). Retrieved October 12, 2014 (http://isa-global-dialogue.net/euromaidan-profile-of-a-rebellion/).

Pelta, Kathy. 1991. *Discovering Christopher Columbus: How History Is Invented*. Minneapolis: Lerner Publications.

Pennebaker, James W., and Amy L. Gonzales. 2009. "Making History: Social and Psychological Processes Underlying Collective Memory." Pp. 171–193 in *Memory in Mind and Culture*, edited by Pascal Boyer and James V. Wertsch. New York: Cambridge University Press.

Peterson, Merrill D. 1960. *The Jefferson Image in the American Mind*. New York: Oxford University Press.

Peterson, Merrill D. 1994. *Lincoln in American Memory*. New York: Oxford University Press.

Pew Internet and American Life Project. 2002. "One Year Later: September 11 and the Internet." September 5. Retrieved October 18, 2014 (http://www.pewinternet.org/files/old-media//Files/Reports/2002/PIP_9-11_Report.pdf.pdf).

Pew Research Center for the People and the Press. 2011. "9/11 Commemorations Capture Public Attention." Retrieved September 18, 2012 (http://www.people-press.org/2011/09/13/911-commemorations-capture-public-attention/).

Pew Research Center for the People and the Press. 2012. "Assessing the Representativeness of Public Opinion Surveys." May 15. Retrieved November 3, 2014 (http://www.people-press.org/2012/05/15/assessing-the-representativeness-of-public-opinion-surveys/).

Phillips, William D., Jr., and Carla Rahn Phillips.1992. *The Worlds of Christopher Columbus*. New York: Cambridge University Press.

Pillemer, David B. 1998. *Momentous Events, Vivid Memories*. Cambridge, MA: Harvard University Press.

Pillemer, David B., Lynn R. Goldsmith, Abigail T. Panter, and Sheldon H. White. 1988. "Very Long-Term Memories of the First Year in College." *Journal of Experimental Psychology: Learning, Memory and Cognition*. 14: 709–715.

Pinker, Steven. 2011. *The Better Angels of Our Nature: Why Violence Has Declined*. New York: Viking.

Prescott, William F. 1874. *History of the Reign of Ferdinand and Isabella the Catholic*. Vol. III. Philadelphia, J. B. Lippincott.

Radway, Janice A. 1991. *Reading the Romance: Women, Patriarchy and Popular Literature*. Chapel Hill: University of North Carolina Press.

Rakove, Jack N. 1999. "Our Jefferson." Pp. 210–235 in *Sally Hemings and Thomas Jefferson: History, Memory, and Civic Culture*, edited by Jan Ellen Lewis and Peter S. Onuf. Charlottesville: University of Virginia.

Randall, H. S. [1868] 1997. "Letter to James Parton." Pp. 254–257 in *Thomas Jefferson and Sally Hemings: An American Controversy*, by Annette Gordon-Reed. Charlottesville: University of Virginia Press.

Rhea, Joseph T. 1997. *Race Pride and the American Identity*. Cambridge, MA: Harvard University Press.

Ricks, Thomas E. 2006. *Fiasco: The American Military Adventure in Iraq.* New York: The Penguin Press.

Roediger Henry L., Franklin Zaromb, and Andrew C. Butler. 2009. "The Role of Repeated Retrieval in Shaping Collective Memory." Pp. 29–58 in *Memory in Mind and Culture,* edited by Pascal Boyer and James V. Wertsch. Cambridge: Cambridge University Press.

Rosenzweig, Roy, and David Paul Thelen. 1998. *The Presence of the Past.* New York: Columbia University Press.

Rothman, Joshua D. 2003. *Notorious in the Neighborhood: Sex and Families across the Color Line in Virginia, 1787–1861.* Chapel Hill: University of North Carolina Press.

Royal, Robert. 1992. *1492 and All That: Political Manipulations of History.* Washington, D.C.: Ethics and Public Policy Center.

Rubin David C., and Dorthe Berntsen. 2003. "Life Scripts Help to Maintain Autobiographical Memories of Highly Positive, but Not Highly Negative, Events." *Memory and Cognition* 31: 1–14.

Rubin David C., Tamara A. Rahhal, and Leonard W. Poon. 1998. "Things Learned in Early Adulthood Are Remembered Best." *Memory and Cognition* 26: 3–19.

Rubin David C. and Matthew D. Schulkind. 1997. "Distribution of Important and Word-Cued Autobiographical Memories in 20-, 35-, and 70 Year-old Adults." *Psychology and Aging* 12: 524–535.

Rundus, Dewey. 1971. "Analysis of Rehearsal Processes in Free Recall." *Journal of Experimental Psychology* 89: 63–77.

Ryder, Norman B. 1965. "The Cohort as a Concept in the Study of Social Change." *American Sociological Review* 30: 843–861.

Sale, Kirkpatrick. 1990. *The Conquest of Paradise: Christopher Columbus and the Columbian Legacy.* New York: Alfred A. Knopf.

Sandburg, Carl. 1926. *Abraham Lincoln: The Prairie Years.* New York: Harcourt Brace.

Schlesinger, Arthur M., Jr. 1991. *The Disuniting of America: Reflections on a Multicultural Society.* New York: W. W. Norton.

Schudson, Michael. 1989a. "How Culture Works: Perspectives from Media Studies on the Efficacy of Symbols." *Theory and Society* 18: 153–180.

Schudson, Michael. 1989b. "The Present in the Past versus the Past in the Present" *Communication* 11: 105–113.

Schudson, Michael. 1992. *Watergate in American Memory.* New York: Basic Books.

Schuman, Howard. 1972. "Two Sources of Antiwar Sentiment in America." *American Journal of Sociology* 78: 513–536.

Schuman, Howard. 2008. *Method and Meaning in Polls and Surveys.* Cambridge, MA: Harvard University Press.

Schuman, Howard, Hiroko Akiyama, and Bärbel Knäuper. 1998. "Collective Memories of Germans and Japanese about the First Half Century." *Memory* 6: 427–454.

Schuman, Howard, Robert F. Belli, and Katherine Bischoping. 1997. "The Generational Basis of Historical Knowledge." Pp. 47–77 in *Collective Memories of*

Political Events: Social Psychological Perspectives, edited by James W. Pennebaker, Dario Paez, and Bernard Rimé. Mahwah, NJ: Erlbaum.

Schuman, Howard and Amy Corning. 2000. "Collective Knowledge of Public Events: The Soviet Era from the Great Purge to Glasnost." *American Journal of Sociology* 105: 913–956.

Schuman, Howard, and Amy Corning. 2006. "Comparing Iraq to Vietnam: Recognition, Recall, and the Nature of Cohort Effects." *Public Opinion Quarterly* 70: 78–87.

Schuman, Howard, and Amy Corning. 2011. "The Roots of Collective Memory: Public Knowledge of Sally Hemings and Thomas Jefferson." *Memory Studies* 4: 134–153.

Schuman, Howard, and Amy Corning. 2012. "Generational Memory and the Critical Period: Evidence for National and World Events." *Public Opinion Quarterly* 76: 1–31.

Schuman, Howard, and Amy Corning. 2014. "Autobiographical Memory and Collective Memory: Similar but Not the Same." *Memory Studies* 7: 146–160.

Schuman, Howard, Amy Corning, and Barry Schwartz. 2012. "Framing Variations and Collective Memory: 'Honest Abe' vs. 'The Great Emancipator.'" *Social Science History* 36: 451–472.

Schuman, Howard, and Stanley Presser. [1981] with revised preface 1996. *Questions and Answers in Attitude Surveys: Experiments on Question Form, Wording, and Context.* Thousand Oaks, CA: Sage.

Schuman, Howard, and Cheryl Rieger. 1992. "Historical Analogies, Generational Effects, and Attitudes toward War." *American Sociological Review* 57: 315–326.

Schuman, Howard, Cheryl Rieger, and Vladas Gaidys. 1994. "Generations and Collective Memories in Lithuania." Pp. 313–333 in *Autobiographical Memory and the Validity of Retrospective Reports*, edited by Norbert Schwarz and Seymour Sudman. New York: Springer-Verlag.

Schuman, Howard, and Willard Rodgers. 2004. "Cohorts, Chronology and Collective Memories." *Public Opinion Quarterly* 68: 217–254.

Schuman, Howard, Barry Schwartz, and Hannah d'Arcy. 2005. "Elite Revisionists and Popular Belief: Christopher Columbus, Hero or Villain?" *Public Opinion Quarterly* 69: 2–29.

Schuman, Howard, and Jacqueline Scott. 1987. "Problems in the Use of Survey Questions to Measure Public Opinion." *Science* 236: 957–959.

Schuman, Howard, and Jacqueline Scott. 1989. "Generations and Collective Memories." *American Sociological Review* 54: 359–381.

Schuman, Howard, Charlotte Steeh, Lawrence Bobo, and Maria Krysan. 1997. *Racial Attitudes in America: Trends and Interpretations.* Cambridge, MA: Harvard University Press.

Schuman, Howard, Vered Vinitzky-Seroussi, and Amiram Vinokur. 2003. "Keeping the Past Alive: Israeli Memories at the Turn of the Millennium." *Sociological Forum* 18: 103–136.

Schwartz, Barry. 1991. "Social Change and Collective Memory: The Democratization of George Washington." *American Sociological Review* 56: 221–236.

Schwartz, Barry. 1999. "Memory and the Practices of Commitment." Pp. 135–146 in *Qualitative Sociology as Everyday Life*, edited by Barry Glassner and Rosanna Hertz. Thousand Oaks, CA: Sage.

Schwartz, Barry. 2000. *Abraham Lincoln and the Forge of National Memory*. Chicago: University of Chicago Press.

Schwartz, Barry. 2001. "Commemorative Objects." Pp. 2267–2272 in the *International Encyclopedia of the Social and Behavioral Sciences*, vol. 2, edited by Neil J. Smelser and Paul B. Baltes. New York: Elsevier.

Schwartz, Barry. 2005. "Ann Rutledge in American Memory: Social Change and the Erosion of a Romantic Drama." *Journal of the Abraham Lincoln Association* 26 (http://hdl.handle.net/2027/spo.2629860.0026.103).

Schwartz, Barry. 2008. *Abraham Lincoln in the Post-Heroic Era: History and Memory in Late Twentieth-Century America*. Chicago: University of Chicago Press.

Schwartz, Barry. 2013. "Georg Simmel on *The Problems of the Philosophy of History*: Realism, History, and Memory." Unpublished paper.

Schwartz, Barry, and Howard Schuman. 2005. "History, Commemoration, and Belief: Abraham Lincoln in American Memory, 1945–2001." *American Sociological Review* 70: 183–203.

Sears, David O., and Sheri Levy. 2003. "Childhood and Adult Political Development." Pp. 60–109 in *Oxford Handbook of Political Development*, edited by David O. Sears, Leonie Huddy, and Robert Jervis. New York: Oxford University Press.

Settersten, Richard A., Frank F. Furstenberg, and Rubén G. Rumbaut. 2005. *On the Frontier of Adulthood: Theory, Research and Public Policy*. Chicago: University of Chicago Press.

Sewell, William H., Jr. 2005. *Logics of History: Social Theory and Social Transformation*. Chicago: University of Chicago Press.

Siebert, Charles. 2006. "An Elephant Crackup?" *New York Times Magazine*, October 8: E72.

Smith, Tom W. 1994. "Generational Differences in Musical Preferences." *Popular Music and Society* 18: 43–59.

Snow, Richard. 1991. "Breaking and Entering." *American Heritage* 42 (October): 7.

Sreenivasan, Hariharan. 2011. "In Memory of My Father K. Sreenivasan." Retrieved September 27, 2013 (http://ompower.com/sreeni).

Stanton, Lucia. 2000. "The Other End of the Telescope: Jefferson through the Eyes of His Slaves." *William and Mary Quarterly* (Third Series) 57 (1): 139–152.

Stanton, Lucia, and Dianne Swann-Wright. 1999. "Bonds of Memory: Identity and the Hemings Family." Pp. 161–183 in *Sally Hemings and Thomas Jefferson: History, Memory, and Civic Culture*, edited by Jan Ellen Lewis and Peter S. Onuf. Charlottesville: University of Virginia.

Stember, Charles Herbert. 1966. "Recent History of Public Attitudes." Pp. 31–234 in *Jews in the Mind of America*, edited by Charles Herbert Stember et al. New York: Basic Books.

Stolberg, Sheryl Gay. 2009. "A Somber Obama Calls for Renewal." *New York Times*, September 11.

Stouffer, Samuel A. 1955. *Communism, Conformity, and Civil Liberties*. Garden City, NY: Doubleday.

Sturken, Marita. 2007. *Tourists of History: Memory, Kitsch, and Consumerism from Oklahoma City to Ground Zero*. Durham, NC: Duke University Press.

Sudman, Seymour, Norman M. Bradburn, and Norbert Schwarz. 1996. *Thinking about Answers: The Application of Cognitive Processes to Survey Methodology*. San Francisco: Jossey-Bass.

Summerhill, Stephen J., and John Alexander Williams. 2000. *Sinking Columbus: Contested History, Cultural Politics, and Mythmaking during the Quincentenary*. Gainesville: University Press of Florida.

Swarns, Rachel L. 2012. *American Tapestry: The Story of the Black, White, and Multi-racial Ancestors of Michelle Obama*. New York: Amistad.

Swarns, Rachel L., and Jodi Kantor. 2009. "First Lady's Roots Reveal Slavery's Tangled Legacy." *New York Times*, October 8: A1.

Swidler, Ann, and Jorge Arditi. 1994. "The New Sociology of Knowledge." *Annual Review of Sociology* 20: 305–329.

Sztompka, Piotr. 2000. *Trust: A Sociological Theory*. Cambridge: Cambridge University Press.

Taylor, Charles. 1994. "The Politics of Recognition." Pp. 25–74 in *Multiculturalism and the Politics of Recognition*, edited by Amy Gutmann. Princeton, NJ: Princeton University Press.

Taylor, Paul. 2014. *The Next America: Boomers, Millenials, and the Looming Generational Showdown*. New York: PublicAffairs.

Taylor, Yuval, and Jake Austen. 2012. *Darkest America: Black Minstrelsy from Slavery to Hip-Hop*. New York: W.W. Norton.

Thomsen, Dorthe K., David B. Pillemer, and Zorana Ivcevic. 2011. "Life Story Chapters, Specific Memories and the Reminiscence Bump." *Memory* 19: 267–279.

Times Record. c. 2009. "CMP's Reliability Called into Question": 7.

Toner, Robin. 1991. "The Unfinished Politician." *New York Times Magazine*, April 14: 42–43, 51, 57, 66–69.

Tukey, John W. 1977. *Exploratory Data Analysis*. Reading, MA: Addison-Wesley.

Tulving, Endel. 1972. "Episodic and Semantic Memory." Pp. 381–402 in *Organization of Memory*, edited by Endel Tulving and W. Donaldson. New York: Academic Press.

Tulving, Endel. 2008. "On the Law of Primacy." Pp. 31–48 in *Memory and Mind: A Festschrift for Gordon H. Bower*, edited by Mark A. Gluck, John R. Anderson, and Stephen M. Kosslyn. New York: Lawrence Erlbaum Associates.

Tumarkin, Nina. 1994. *The Living and the Dead: The Rise and Fall of the Cult of World War II in Russia*. New York: Basic Books.

U.S. Postal Service. 2001. *The Postal Service Guide to U.S. Stamps*. New York: Harper-Collins.

VanDeMark, Brian. 1995. *Into the Quagmire: Lyndon Johnson and the Escalation of the Vietnam War*. New York: Oxford University Press.

Vega, Tanzina. 2012. "Small Gain in Daily Newspaper Circulation." *New York Times* May 2: B7.

Vromen, Suzanne. 1975. *The Sociology of Maurice Halbwachs*. Unpublished Ph.D. dissertation, New York University.

Wagner-Pacifici, Robin, and Barry Schwartz. 1991. "The Vietnam Veterans Memorial: Commemorating a Difficult Past." *American Journal of Sociology* 97: 376–420.

Wanner, Catherine. 1998. *Burden of Dreams: History and Identity in Post-Soviet Ukraine*. University Park: Pennsylvania State University Press.

Watts, Duncan J. 2014. "Common Sense and Sociological Explanation." *American Journal of Sociology* 120: 313–351.

Weiner, Jonathan. 1995. *The Beak of the Finch*. New York: Vintage.

Wertsch, James V. 1998. *Mind as Action*. New York: Oxford University Press.

Wertsch, James V. 2002. *Voices of Collective Remembering*. New York: Cambridge University Press.

West, Delno C., and August Kling. 1989. "Columbus and Columbia: A Brief Survey of the Early Creation of the Columbus Symbol in American History." *Studies in Popular Culture* 12: 45–60.

White, Geoffrey M. 2004. "National Subjects: September 11 and Pearl Harbor." *American Ethnologist* 31: 293–310.

Whitman, Walt. 1874. "Prayer of Columbus." Originally published in *Harper's Monthly Magazine* 48 (March): 524–525. Retrieved September 22, 2014 (http://www.whitmanarchive.org/published/periodical/poems/per.00013).

Wiencek, Henry. 2012. *Master of the Mountain: Thomas Jefferson and His Slaves*. New York: Farrar, Straus, and Giroux.

Wikipedia. 2013a. "Christopher Columbus." Retrieved November 4, 2013 (http://en.wikipedia.org/wiki/Christopher_Columbus).

Wikipedia. 2013b. "Monticello Association." Retrieved November 4, 2013 (http://en.wikipedia.org/wiki/Monticello_Association).

Wikipedia. 2014. "Washington Redskins Name Controversy." Retrieved September 23, 2014 (http://en.wikipedia.org/wiki/Washington_Redskins_name_controversy).

Wilford, John Noble. 1991. *The Mysterious History of Columbus: An Exploration of the Man, the Myth, the Legacy*. New York: Vintage Books.

Wills, Garry. 2006. *Lincoln at Gettysburg: The Words That Remade America*. New York: Simon and Schuster.

Wilson, Douglas L. 1992. "Thomas Jefferson and the Character Issue." *Atlantic Monthly* 270 (5): 57–74.

Winsor, Justin. 1891. *Christopher Columbus and How He Received and Imparted the Spirit of Discovery*. Boston: Houghton, Mifflin.

Wohl, Robert. 1979. *The Generation of 1914.* Cambridge, MA: Harvard University Press.

Wood, Gordon S. 2009. *Empire of Liberty: A History of the Early Republic, 1789–1915.* New York: Oxford University Press.

Yerushalmi, Yosef Hayim. 1982. *Zakhor: Jewish History and Jewish Memory.* Seattle: University of Washington Press.

Yoder, Edwin M., Jr. 2013. "Letter to the Editor," in response to Gordon S. Wood review "In Quest of Blood Lines." *New York Review of Books*, July 11.

Yolen, Jane. 1992. *Encounter.* Orlando, FL: Harcourt Brace.

Young, Alfred F. 1999. *The Shoemaker and the Tea Party: Memory and the American Revolution.* Boston: Beacon Press.

Young, James E. 1993. *The Texture of Memory: Holocaust Memorials and Meaning.* New Haven, CT: Yale University Press.

Zapruder, Alexandra. 2013. "The Zapruder Legacy." *Parade*, October 19. Retrieved September 22, 2014 (http://parade.condenast.com/214978/alexandrazapruder /the-zapruder-legacy/).

Zelizer, Barbie. 1992. *Covering the Body: The Kennedy Assassination, the Media, and the Shaping of Collective Memory.* Chicago: University of Chicago Press.

Zelizer, Barbie. 1995. "Reading the Past against the Grain: The Shape of Memory Studies." *Critical Studies in Mass Communications* 12: 214–239.

Zinn, Howard. 1980. *A People's History of the United States.* New York: Harper and Row.

Index

Page numbers in italics refer to figures and tables. In the case of frequently-used terms (such as "education," "recall"), only locations of direct importance to the main themes of the book are given.

9/11. *See* September 11, 2001, attack

ABC News/*Washington Post* Poll, 193, 205
Abe Lincoln in Illinois (film), 64, 67
Abraham, Katharine G., 221
Abu Ghraib, 155
acquiescence bias, 151
adolescence, 7, 32, 60, 78–79, 81, 135, 146, 161, 172–73, 175. *See also* critical years effect; youth
advertisements, 49, 59, 216
Afghanistan, 125, 132, 139, 210
African Americans, 3, 5, 13, 41, 47, 48, 52, 53, 63, 101, 187; and collective knowledge, 58–59, 201; and Columbus, *35*; and Hemings and Jefferson, 26, 51, 56, 58–59, 58–60, 62, 212; and September 11 commemoration, 198, 199, 208. *See also* race
age. *See* cohort
"aggregated" memories, 11. *See also* Olick, Jeffrey
Akiyama, Hiroko, 105n, 106
Alba, Richard, 137
Alwin, Duane F., 77
American Gothic, 5–6
American Heritage Dictionary, 15
American Indians: and Columbus, 34–35, 41; protests by, 27, 28,

39; public beliefs about, 29–30, 33, 43; in textbooks, 34–37, 41, 216; treatment of by whites, 24, 25–28, 37–39, 41
analogies, 150–54, 156–58
Anderson, Marian, 67
Anderson, Michael C., 191
anniversary. *See* Atta, Mohammed; Columbus, Christopher; commemoration; September 11, 2001, attack; Woodstock Festival
Appiah, Kwame Anthony, 58
Arditi, Jorge, 65
Armstrong, Neil, 97
Assmann, Aleida, 8–9, 191
Atta, Mohammed, *54*, 55, 58, 60, 200, 202, 203
attitudes, 15, 19, 24, 41, 47, 61, 63, 199, 214; critical years experience and, 18, 115, 133, 147–59, 218
Austen, Jake, 5
autobiographical memory, 18, 133, 160–76, 214. *See also* reminiscence bump
Axtell, James, 28
Ayers, Edward L., 50

baby boomer, 16, 17n, 76
Baddeley, Alan, 83, 191
Bahrick, Harry P., 90

Barger, Herbert, 53
Bartlett, Frederic C., 135, 184
Belarus, 119
Belli, Robert F., 172, 183n
Bennett, Lerone, Jr., 58
Berlin Wall, *85, 86,* 87, 97, 99, 102, *139,* 160, 166,
Berntsen, Dorthe, 174
Best, Jonathan, 221
birth cohort. *See* cohort
Bischoping, Katherine, 172, 183n
bivariate analysis, 219, 224
blacks. *See* African Americans; Hemings, Sally; race
Blight, David W., 12–13, 14
Bluck, Susan, 161
Bobo, Lawrence, 41
Bodnar, John, 12
Bourdieu, Pierre, 208
Bower, Gordon H., 82, 90, 153, 161
Boym, Svetlana, 144
Bradburn, Norman M., 175
Brezhnev, Leonid, *139,* 143
Brodie, Fawn M., 46, 47, 53, 61
Brodsky, Joseph, 136
Bromet, Evelyn, 120
Brown, Roger, 58, 111
Browne, Janet, 2, 3
Bruehl, Elizabeth C., 174
bump. *See* reminiscence bump
Burley, Nancy Tyler, 161n
Burlingame, Michael, 67
Burns, John F., 5
Buruma, Ian, 107
Bush, George H. W., 147, 148, 149, 150, 154
Bush, George W., 4–5, 147, 154, 155, 194
Butler, Andrew C., 191

Callender, James, 46
Calley, William, 203
Campbell, Angus, 151n
Cantril, Hadley, 82, 175
Cave, Damien, 199
Challenger disaster, 60, 181
Chase-Riboud, Barbara, 47, *49,* 57, 59
Chechnya, *125,* 138, 139
Chernobyl disaster, 119–21, *128,* 130, *139*
Chessa, Antonio G., 172
Chicago Metropolitan Area Study, 225
childhood amnesia, 81n, 164

children: and critical years effect, 81–82, 89, 94–96, 102–3, 119–20, 129–30, 161n, 165, 182, 212, 217–18; and learning about Columbus, 27, 39, 40, 42. *See also* adolescence; critical years effect; youth
China, 18, 79n, 104, 109–11, 115, *124, 125,* 216, 225
civil rights, 26, 67, 70–71, 72, 80, *86,* 101, 140, 157, 189, 201, 210
Clinton, Bill, *86,* 101, *139*
Coates, Eyler Robert, 52
Cohen, Martin, 78
cohort: and Ann Rutledge, 64; birth, 15–16, 19; and Columbus, 33, 37, 40, 44; and Hemings and Jefferson, 59; and Lincoln, 70, 71; as specifying generation, 17, 76, 77, 78. *See also* critical years effect; generation
cohort replacement, 74, 78
Coles, Edward, 63
"collected" memory, 9, 11–12, 14. *See also* Olick, Jeffrey
collective forgetting, 106–7
collective ignorance, 184–90. *See also* collective knowledge
collective knowledge, 18, 20, 53–65, 133, 177–90, 199, 207, 215
collective memory: Assmann on, 8–9; Blight on, 12–13; conceptualized as beliefs of individuals, 6–14, 15–16; conceptualized as public discourses or narratives, 24; vs. collective memories, 3n; Confino on, 13–14; Halbwachs on, 6–9; Kansteiner on, 13–14; Olick on, 9, 11, 14, 24; relation to generation, 15–16; Schwartz on, 9–11; variation in conceptualization, 1–6; Yerushalmi on, 34, 45, 109; Young on, 11–12
Collins, Randall, 208
Columbia Encyclopedia, 24, 27, 47, 51, 52
Columbus, Christopher, 17, 19, 21, 23–45, 73, 74, 176, 213, 215, 216, 217. *See also* American Indians
commemoration, 39, 191–209, 218; of Columbus, 23–25, 27–28, 39, 42, 73–74; individual participation in, 192, 204–7; in Israel, 108–9, *128,* 131; in U.S.S.R., 140, 143, *145,* 146
compound event, 79
computers, 101, 226

Confino, Alon, 13
Congressional Record, 38
consumption. *See* reception
content analysis, 19, 34–38, 53, 70–71, 192–
    96, 200, *201*, 216
Converse, Philip, 28, 151
Conway, Martin A., 163, 173, 174
Coolidge, Ellen Randolph, 50
Corning, Amy, 54, 68, 87, 88, 111, 136,
    156, 162, 182, 183, 192
Coser, Lewis A., 6n, 7, 137
Craighill, Peyton, 221
critical years effect: and attitudes, 147–54;
    confounding forces, 87–91; vs. emigra-
    tion effect, 135–46; exceptions to,
    94–96, 97–100; hypothesis and basis,
    17–18, 75, 78–79, 80–83; vs. lifetime ef-
    fect, 88–90, 91–92, 96, 99, 112–15, 116,
    123, 129, 157–59; vs. recency effect, 90–
    92, 96–97, *102*, *124–28*, 163–64, 166;
    shape of, 82, 92–93, 105, 108, 111, 119,
    166, 179, 197; summaries of evidence
    on, 101–3, 123–32; testing of, 91–93,
    96–97; in various countries, 104–29
Cropper, William H., 40
Crosby, Alfred W., Jr., 25
Crovitz, H. F., 160
Crystal, David, 4
cued recall, 83. *See also* word cues
Cultural Revolution, 110, 111, 115, *124*
Cumming, Geoff, 19
Curtin, Richard, 221

d'Arcy, Hannah, 29n
Darwin, Charles, 2
DAS 1991. *See* Detroit Area Study (DAS)
    1991
Davis, David Brion, 63
Dean, John, *179*, 181, 188
de Certeau, Michel, 14
de Gaulle, Charles, 94
de la Garza, Rudolfo O., 34
de Lancey, Edward F., 23
de las Casas, Bartolomé, 26
Delli Carpini, Michael X., 40
Deloria, Vine, Jr., 34
Detroit Area Study (DAS) 1991, 16, 175,
    178, 179, 180, 184, 185, 205, 206
Dickson, Ryan A., 174
DiMaggio, Paul, 54

Dimock, Michael, 221
DNA evidence, 50, 51, 52, 53, 59, 62
Donald, David H., 66
Druckman, James N., 105, 221
Durkheim, Emile, 198, 208, 218

East Germany, 105n
Ebbinghaus, Hermann, 90
Edgerton, Gary R., 97
education (as variable): and commemora-
    tion, 109, 131, 201–2, 208; and histori-
    cal figures, 32–33, 44–45, 57–58, 62; and
    knowledge, 180–81, 183; and memory,
    73, 88n, 100n, 144, 172. *See also* school
Eliot, T. S., 77
Ellis, Joseph J., 47, 50
emigration, 18, 133, 135–46, 191, 216
Encyclopaedia Britannica, 42, 51–52
ethnicity, 17, 79, 198; and Columbus, 24,
    26, 34–35, 41; and emigrants, 136, 137,
    143, 144; in Lithuania, 111n, *128*; in
    Russia, 143; in Ukraine, 116–17, 121.
    See also American Indians; African
    Americans; race
Euromaidan. *See* Maidan
European Community, 106, 107, 124
European Union, accession of Lithuania
    to, 112
Events question. *See* standard Events
    question
event: term and concept of, 20, 79–80. *See
    also* compound event; intermediate
    event; resurrected event; sub-event;
    transformative event; *and individual
    events*
experiment, 67–69, 151, 153, 163, 169, 175,
    192, 214–15, 221
Eysenck, Michael W., 191

factor analysis, 226
Falcon, Angelo, 34
famine. *See under* Ukraine
Feros, Antonio, 5
Figes, Orlando, 40
figures: graphic presentation of data in,
    19, 88n
films, 4, 38, 48–50, 55, 57, 58, 59, 61, 62,
    64, 67, 83, 161, 200, *206*, 216
financial crisis, *86*, 87, *88*, 100, 197. *See also*
    Great Depression

Fine, Gary, 26
Fineman, Mia, 6
Finkelman, Paul, 63
first experiences, 78, 81, 95, 96, 101, 115, 130, 131, 135, 146, 174, 176. *See also* critical years effect; "firstness"; primacy
"firstness," 42, 176. *See also* critical years effect; first experiences; primacy
FitzGerald, Frances, 21
flashbulb memories, 58, 111, 115
follow-up "Why" questions, 31, 94, 98–99, 114, 214
Foner, Eric, 3, 66, 72
Ford, John, 67
Foster, Eugene A., 50
Foucault, Michel, 25
Fox-Genovese, Elizabeth, 42
Fredrickson, George M., 41
French, Scot A., 50
Frisch, Michael, 36, 42
Furstenberg, Frank F., 79, 146

Gagarin, Yury, *139*, 143
Gaidys, Vladas, 111
Gallup, 70, 149, 150, 155
Gallup Poll Monthly, The, 150
Garcia, F. Chris, 34
Garfinkel, Harold, 68
Gates, Henry Louis, Jr., 3, 58
gender, 24, 79n, 179; as variable, 59, 62, 70, 73, 84n, 88n, 109, 172, 179, 182, 189, 205
General Social Survey (GSS), 84n, 178
generation, 1, 7, 8, 12, 29, 64, 74, 212; and attitudes, 133, 147–59; concept of, 14–17; generational consciousness, 75–76; relation to collective memory, 15–16; subjective generational identification, 16–17, 76; summaries of effects of, 101–3, 145–46; two forms of effects of, 112–13, 115, 131, 132. *See also* critical years effect
Germany, 18, 78, 79n, 104–7, *124–27*, *139*, 151, 212, 213, 216, 225
Gettysburg Address, 10, 67
Gillis, John R., 12
glasnost. *See* perestroika
Glück, Judith, 161
Goffman, Erving, 67
Gonzales, Amy L., 82

Gorbachev, Mikhail, 40, 16, 138, *139*, 141
Gordon-Reed, Annette, 48, 49, 50, 51
Gray, Thomas, 66
Great Depression, 84, *85*, *88*, 100, *102*, 213, 226
Great Patriotic War, 118, 122, *126*, 138, *139*, 141, *145*
Great Purges, 142
Great Recession. *See* financial crisis
Green, Melanie C., 87
Griswold, Wendy, 137
Groseclose, Barbara, 23
Groves, Robert M., 221
GSS. *See* General Social Survey (GSS)
Gulf War: and attitudes, 147–54, 155, 156n, 157, 158, 214; and memory, 78, *85*, 97, 99, *102*, 106, 115, *124*, *125*, 130, 140, 158, 169–70

Haid, Charles, 49
Halbwachs, Maurice, 6–8, 9, 13, 184, 197
Hart, Avery, 27
Harvey, William, 81, 82
Hayne, Harlene, 81n
Helms, Sara, 221
Hemings, Madison, 48, 51, 57
Hemings, Sally, 46–65, 73
Hetherington, Marc J., 72
Himmelfarb, Gertrude, 42
Hiroshima, 79, 80, 107
Hispanics, 48–49
Hobsbawm, Eric, 12
Holbrook, Allyson L., 87
Holmes, Alison, 174
Holocaust, 11, 107, 108, 109, *128*, 131, 141, 197, *206*
Hume, David, 81, 82
Hussein, Saddam, 148, 150, 151, 155
Hutton, Patrick H., 14
Hyland, William G., 52
Hyman, Herbert H., 41

immigrants, 109. *See also* emigration
Imperial System, 106, *125*
importance of events, 80, 87, 99
impressionable years, 157, 161n. *See also* critical years effect
independence: of Israel, 108; of Lithuania, 80, 111, 112–14, 116, 123, 127, 130,

131, 132, 144, 157, 158, 214, 216; of
Ukraine, 122, *128*
Independence Square (Ukraine), 116. *See
also* Maidan
Indians. *See* American Indians
infantile amnesia. *See* childhood amnesia
intermediate event, 82, 91–92, 96, 106, 111,
119, 166, 169–70
inversions. *See* collective ignorance
Ioannidis, John P. A., 19
Iraq War, 5, *86*, 115, 130, 147, 155–57, 214
Irving, Washington, 23
Israel, 18, 104, 108–9, 122, 123, *124–28*,
131, 138, *139*, 144, 197, 198, 216
Ivcevic, Zorana, 174
Ivory, James, 48, 50

Jack, Fiona, 81
Jansari, Ashok, 164, 172
Janssen, Steve M., 164, 172, 173, 181
Japan, 18, 104–7, 121, 124–26, 128, 213,
216, 225
Jefferson, Israel, 48
Jefferson, Randolph, 51
Jefferson, Thomas, 15, 17, 21, 46–64, 73,
213. *See also* Hemings, Sally
Jefferson in Paris (film), 48, 49, 50, 59
Jefferson Memorial, 47
Jennings, Francis, 25
Jennings, M. Kent, 110, *128*
Jews, 8, 33, 41, 107, 108, 109, 136, *139*,
141–42, 143, 144
Jhabvala, Ruth Prawer, 50
Johnson, Lyndon B., 92, 154
Johnson, Rossiter, 24
Jordan, Winthrop D., 47, 51

Kam, Cindy D., 105, 221
Kansteiner, Wulf, 13, 14. *See also* reception
Kantor, Jodi, 53
Karnow, Stanley, 92
Katz, Jack, 68
Keeter, Scott, 40, 221
Kennedy, Courtney M., 221
Kennedy, John F., 47, 53; assassination,
4, 75, 80, 82, *85*, 91–96, 98, *102*, 106,
120, 130, 132, 140, 165, 166, 197, 214,
217, 225
Kerrey, Bob, 150
Kessler, Ronald C., 84n

Khong, Yuen Foong, 154
Khrushchev, Nikita, 142
Kiev International Institute of Sociology
(KIIS), 117
King, Martin Luther, 67, *95*, 171
Kissell, Rick, 50
Klady, L., 50
Kligler-Vilenchik, Neta, 198
Kling, August, 24
Knäuper, Bärbel, 105n, 106
KnowledgePanel, 162n
Koch, Cynthia M., 23
Kolbert, Elizabeth, 217
Koppel, Jonathan, 174
Krensky, Stephen, 27, 39
Krosnick, Jon A., 87
Krysan, Maria, 41
Kulik, James, 58, 111

Laika, 143, *182*, 183
Lander, Eric S., 50
Lasch-Quinn, Elisabeth, 42
"law of primacy," 82, 176. *See also* Tulving,
Endel
Lee, Ang, 200
Le Goff, Jacques, 40, 80
Levy, Sheri, 161
Lewis, Jan Ellen, 50, 51, 53
Lichter, Robert, 150
life scripts, 174
lifetime effect: and attitudes, 153, 157–59;
concept of, 88–90, 115; confounding
with critical years effect, 96, 99, 133,
166; distinguishing from critical years
effect, 91–92, 96, *102*, 129, 130–31, 132;
and transformative events, 89, 112–15,
116, 123, *125–28*, 130, 144–46, 214, 216
Lincoln (film), 67
Lincoln, Abraham, 10–11, 17, 21, 56, 64,
66–73, 175, 213, 214, 215
Lincoln Portrait (score), 67
Lipka, Michael, 33
Lithuania, 18, 80, 104, 111–15, 116, 123,
124–28, 129–31, 132, 144, 157, 158, 212,
214, 216, 225
Live Aid, 170, *171*
Lockhart, Robert S., 83
Loewen, James W., 26
"losings," 177, 181–83, 189–90
Lycheva, Katya, 182, 183

MacArthur, Douglas, 187
Maidan, 116, 117–18, 121n, 122, 125
Maier, Pauline, 63
Malone, Dumas, 48, 49
Mann, James, 5
Mannheim, Karl: on emigration, 135; on
    generations, 16, 32, 75, 77–79, 80, 81,
    96, 212; on knowledge, 177
McAuliffe, Christa, 54, 60, 179, 181
McCammon, Ryan J., 77
McCarthy, Joe, 28, 54, 184–89, 190, 214
McCombs, Maxwell, 193
McCullough, David, 81, 82
Meacham, Jon, 51, 61
Meeter, Martijn, 181
Meillet, Antoine, 78
Merchant, Ismael, 50
Merton, Robert, 18
methods. See content analysis; Pew experi-
    ments; qualitative evidence; replication;
    statistical testing
Mexican Americans. See Hispanics
Meyers, Oren, 198
middle range hypothesis, 17–18
Miller, John Chester, 50
Miller, Warren E., 151
Misztal, Barbara Q., 14n
mode of survey, 87n
Mohammed, Khalid Shaikh, 60
Monticello, 46, 48, 49, 50, 51, 52, 62, 63
moon landing, 80, 85, 86, 97–99, 102, 103,
    131, 140, 143, 210, 214
Moore, Martha T., 194
Morawska, Ewa, 136, 137
Morgan, Edmund S., 47
Morison, Samuel Eliot, 26
Mount Rushmore, 63
Murre, Jaap M. J., 172, 181
My Lai massacre, 54, 179–80, 203

Nagel, Joane, 26, 41
National Comorbidity Survey (NCS), 84n,
    94–95
National Council of the Churches of Christ
    in the USA, 27
National Day of Participation, 98
national unification in China, 110
Native Americans. See American Indians
NCS. See National Comorbidity Survey
    (NCS)
Nee, Victor, 137

Neiman, Fraser D., 51
newspapers, 2, 10, 188, 206, 216; and
    Columbus, 27, 37, 40; and Hemings and
    Jefferson, 46, 48, 50, 52–53, 55, 57, 64;
    and Lincoln, 70–71; and September 11,
    192–95, 203; and Woodstock, 200
Nixon, Richard M., 98, 179, 181
nonresponse, 163n, 221
Nora, Pierre, 10
NORC, 84n
Novick, Peter, 2, 141

Obama, Barack, 38, 86, 194, 198, 208, 212
Obama, Michelle, 53
O'Connor, Margaret G., 90
oil shock, 106, 107
Olick, Jeffrey, K., 9, 11, 14, 24
Onuf, Peter S., 50, 51, 53
open-ended questions, 19, 28, 31, 83, 84,
    94, 98–99, 145, 177, 192, 213–14, 226.
    See also follow-up "Why" questions;
    standard Events question
Orange Revolution, 116, 117, 118, 125
order effects, 82, 151, 163
Osborne, Danny, 157

Pakistan, 18, 104, 122–23, 128
Parkin, Alan J., 164, 172
Parks, Rosa, 54, 55, 58–59, 187, 199, 201
party identification: as variable, 10, 157,
    156n
Pelta, Kathy, 27
Pennebaker, James W., 82
People's Republic of China: founding of,
    111. See also China
perestroika, 116, 124, 127, 138, 139, 141,
    142, 144, 145
period effect. See lifetime effect
Peterson, Merrill D., 11, 48
Pew experiments, 221
Pew Internet and American Life Project, 193
Pew Research Center for the People and the
    Press, 193, 221
Peytcheva, Emilia, 221
Phillips, Carla Rahn, 28
Phillips, William D., 28
Pillemer, David B., 135, 174
Pinker, Steven, 24
political socialization, 161n
Poon, Leonard W., 160, 161, 162
Prescott, William, 24

Presser, Stanley, 175, 221
primacy, 81, 82, 90, 146, 175–76. *See also*
    first experiences; "firstness"
probability sample, 87n, 162, 163
"Problem of Generations, The," 16, 32,
    75, 77, 78, 80, 135, 177, 212. *See also*
    Mannheim, Karl
p-values, 219

qualified responses, 55, 60
qualitative evidence, 19, 36, 94–95, 98–99,
    114, 184–89, 214, 216, 217
Quincentenary, 25, 26, 27, 28–29, 32, 34,
    37, 38, 40, 42, 43, 215

Rabin, Yitzhak, 108, *125*
race, 12, 13, 17n, 34–35, 47, 48, 50, 51,
    63, 64, 73, 198; as variable, 10, 17n,
    35, 58–59, 70, 73, 84n, 88n, 101, 172,
    198, 199, 200, 201, 208. *See also* African
    Americans; American Indians
Radway, Janice A., 59
Rahhal, Tamara A., 160, 161, 162
Rakove, Jack N., 63
Randall, Henry S., 50
Ranger, Terence, 12
recall: cued, 83–84; influence of recency
    on, 90–91, 161; vs. judgment, 203–4; of
    music and sports, 172–73; of national
    and world events, 80–81, 84; of personal
    events, 160. *See also specific events
    recalled*
recency, 99, 153, 163; distinguishing critical
    years effect from, 90–92, 96–97, *102*,
    124–28, 166
reception, 13–14, 65
region: as variable in Ukraine, 117, 120,
    121–22; as variable in U.S., 10
rehearsal, 74, 82, 175, 176, 197, 218
reliability, 19, 105n, *128*, 162
religion: as variable, 33, 109
reminiscence bump: comparison to critical
    years effect, 167–76; concept, 160–62;
    for personal memories, 163–65, 166,
    167, 173–74. *See also* critical years effect
replication, 18, 43n, 45, 68, 70, 72, 101,
    104–32, 162, 163, 167–72, 178–83,
    189–90, 197; importance of, 19–20, 110,
    214–17, 219
reputation, 24, 26, 32, 35, 37, 39, 40,
    42, 45, 47, 48, 53, 61, 73. *See also*

Columbus, Christopher; Jefferson,
    Thomas; Lincoln, Abraham
response rate, 29n, 43n, 54n, 68n, 87n, 117,
    163n, 221
resurrected event, 99–100
reunification of Germany, 105–6
Rhea, Joseph T., 26
Ricks, Thomas E., 155
Ride, Sally, 57
Rieger, Cheryl, 111n, 151n, 154n
Robbins, Joyce, 14n
Rodgers, Willard, 88n, 100n, 223, 224
Roediger, Henry L., 191
Rosenzweig, Roy, 34
Ross, Betsy, 42
Rothman, Joshua D., 62
Royal, Robert, 26
Rubin, David C., 160, 161, 162, 164, 172,
    173, 174, 176
Rumbaut, Rubén G., 136, 146
Rundus, Dewey, 176
Russia, 18, 104, 117, 119, 121, 122, 216,
    225; collective knowledge in, 182–83,
    190; collective memory in, 112, *113*,
    115–16, 123, *125–28*, 130, 136, 138,
    139, 142, 143, 144, 158, 216. *See also*
    emigration; U.S.S.R.
Rutledge, Ann, 64, 73, 178, 199
Ryder, Norman B., 77, 79, 90

Sale, Kirkpatrick, 26
Sally Hemings: An American Scandal (TV
    miniseries), 49, 50
Sally Hemings: A Novel, 47–48, 49, 57, 59
sampling, 68n, 104, 105n, 115, 117, 151n,
    162, 163n, 221
Sandburg, Carl, 64, 67
Schiffman, H., 160
Schlesinger, Arthur M., Jr., 42
school: and collective knowledge about
    Jefferson and Hemings, 57, 62; and
    commemoration, *206*; and learning
    about events, 83, 94, *95*, 103, 130, 131,
    140, 143; as source of personal memo-
    ries, 174; and views of Columbus, 29,
    34, 36–37, 39, 40, 42, 45, 74, 215. *See
    also* education
Schudson, Michael, 12, 39
Schulkind, Matthew D., 161, 164, 172, 176,
Schuman, Howard: on beliefs about
    Vietnam, 28, 149; on collective and

Schuman, Howard (*cont.*)
autobiographical memory, 160, 162n;
on collective knowledge, 172, 182,
183n; on collective memory and
attitudes, 151n, 154n, 156n; on collective memory in Germany and Japan,
105n, 106; on collective memory in
Israel, 109n; on collective memory in
Lithuania, 111; on collective memory
in the U.S., 54n, 70, 83, 87n, 88n,
98, 100n, 192n, 223–24; on question
wording, 175; on racial attitudes, 41; on
robustness of events question, 225–26;
on views of Columbus, 29n; on views of
Lincoln, 68n, 70
Schwartz, Barry: on collective memory, 2,
8, 9–11, 13, 14, 15, 29n, 146, 197; on
commemoration, 198; on erosion of
reputations, 32, 41; on interest in slavery, 53; on Lincoln, 66, 67, 68n, 70; on
politics of memory, 12; on Rutledge, 64;
on Vietnam Memorial, 149, 208
Schwarz, Norbert, 175
Schwarzkopf, Norman, *54*, 148
Scott, Jacqueline, 83, 98, 100n, 160, 225
Sears, David O., 157, 161n
semantic memory, 184
September 11, 2001, attack: 2, 60, 79,
80, 82, 84n, *86*, 128, 132; collective
memory of in U.S., 87, 90–91, 92, *102*,
108, 111, 112, 130, 160, 166, 170, 176,
217–18; commemoration and memory
of, 191, 192–99, 200, 202, 207–8, 214,
216; judgments of importance of, 202–3
Settersten, Richard A., 146
Sewell, William H., Jr., 79, 114
sex, 46, 47, 48, 50, 51, 56, 59, 61, 62, 199
Sheatsley, Paul B., 41
Sherwood, Robert, 67
Siebert, Charles, 6
Singer, Eleanor, 221
sixties generation, 16
Smith, Samantha, 183
Smith, Tom W., 172
Snow, Richard, 26
Sopranos, The, 27
Soviet Union. *See* U.S.S.R.
space exploration, 57, *86*, 98–99, 225; in
U.S.S.R., 127, 139, 140, 143, *145*, 146,
182. *See also* McAuliffe, Christa; moon
landing

Spanish Civil War, 5
Spielberg, Steven, 67
split sample design, 68, 225
Sputnik, 143
SRC monthly survey. *See* Survey Research
Center (SRC) monthly survey
Sreenivasan, Hariharan, 4
Stalin, 118, *139*, 140, 142–43, 144, *145*
standard Events question, 104, 107, 136,
162, 165, 177, 192, 199, 203, 205;
first versus second response to, 204,
226; logic and wording of, 83–84;
modification of, 110; robustness and
validity of, 84, 225–26
Stanton, Lucia, 50, 58
statistical significance. *See* statistical testing
statistical testing, 19, 82n, 219, 223
Steeh, Charlotte, 41
Stember, Charles Herbert, 41
St. Jacques, P. L., 164
Stokes, Donald E., 151n
Stolberg, Sheryl Gay, 198
Stouffer, Samuel A., 28
Sturken, Marita, 193
sub-event, 79, 80, *86*
Sudman, Seymour, 175
Summerhill, Stephen J., 27, 28, 40
Survey Research Center (SRC) monthly
survey, 29n, 43n, 54n, 68n, 84n, 98,
178, 192n, 221
Swann-Wright, Dianne, 58
Swarns, Rachel L., 53
Swidler, Ann, 65
Sztompka, Piotr, 72

Taiwan, 110
Taking Woodstock (film), 200
Taylor, Paul, 17n
Taylor, Yuval, 5
television: and collective memory, 8, 9, 14,
79, 130, 188; and Columbus, 27, 32,
38; and commemoration, 192–95, 200,
206; content analysis of, 38, 192–95;
and Gulf War, 150; and Hemings, 49–
50, 52, 55; and Kennedy assassination,
92, 94, *95*, 132; and moon landing, 97–
98, 99, 103, 132; and September 11, 90,
216, 217, 218; and Vietnam, 92; and
Woodstock, 200, 216
temporal displacements. *See* collective
ignorance

Tet Offensive, *54*, 92, 93, 178–79, 180, 187, 188, 189
textbooks, 8, 21, 29, 34–37, 39, 41, 42, 62, 74, 212, 216
Thelen, David Paul, 34
Thomas Jefferson Foundation, 51
Thomsen, Dorthe K., 174
Tiananmen Square, 110, *124*
Toner, Robin, 150
transformative event, 79, 80, 114, 115, 130, 144, 212. *See also* lifetime effect
transitional period, 18, 79, 133, 135, 137, 141, 146, 174
Tsfati, Yaniv, 198
Tukey, John W., 19
Tulving, Endel, 82, 146, 176, 184. *See also* primacy
Tumarkin, Nina, 141

Ukraine, 18, 104, 116–22, 123, *125*, *127*, 212, 225; Chernobyl, 119–21, *128*, 130, *139*; famine, 118–19, 121, 122, *127*, *139*; Maidan and related events, 116–18, 121, 122, *125*; regions, 117, 120, 121–22, 213
U.S. Postal Service, 38
U.S.S.R., 28; collapse of, 87, 112, *113*, 119, 122, 123, *127*, 130, 158, 216; and collective knowledge, 182–83; emigrants from, 136–46, 216; and Lithuania, 111–15, 129, 130, 132, 157; and Ukraine, 118, 121, 122; and World War II, 116, 118, 216. *See also* Lithuania; Russia; Ukraine; *and specific events*

Valentino, Nicholas A., 157
VanDeMark, Brian, 150
Vanderlyn, John, 23
Vega, Tanzina, 193
Vietnam Memorial, 149, *206*, 208
Vietnam War, 28, 32, 210; as analogy to later wars, 147–54, 156–58, 214; and collective knowledge, 178–80, 187, 203; collective memory of, 78, 80, *85*, 91–94, 96, 97, *102*, 106, 115, 166, 169–70, 196, 197, 203, 225, 226; commemoration of, 205–6, 208. *See also* My Lai massacre; Tet Offensive
Vilnius TV tower attack, 111–12, *113*, 114, *124*, 129, 131
Vinitzky-Seroussi, Vered, 109n

Vinokur, Amiram, 109n
Vromen, Suzanne, 8

Wagner-Pacifici, Robin, 149, 208
Wanner, Catherine, 122
Warren Commission, 132
Washington, George, 10, 15, 63
Watergate, 32, *179*, 181
Watts, Duncan J., 217
Weiner, Jonathan, 217
Wertsch, James V., 14, 140
West, Delno C., 24
West Germany, 105n
White, Geoffrey M., 193
Whitman, Walt, 24
Wiencek, Henry, 51
Wikipedia, 39, 42, 52
Wilford, John Noble, 23, 24
Williams, Helen L., 164
Williams, John Alexander, 27, 28, 40
Wills, Garry, 10–11
Wilson, Douglas L., 63
Winsor, Justin, 26
Wohl, Robert, 75–76, 78
Wood, Gordon S., 51
Woodstock Festival: collective knowledge of, *54*, 55, 178–80, 192; commemoration and, 199–202, 203, 208, 214, 216
word cues, 160–72, 174, 176. *See also* cued recall
Work Projects Administration. *See* WPA
Works Progress Administration. *See* WPA
World War II: 7, 16, 27, 41, 59, 67, 76, 79, 80, 81n, 184, 187, 189; as analogy to later wars, 147–59; collective memory of in other countries, 105–7, 108, 111, 114–16, 118, *119*, 122, 123, *125–27*, 132, 212, 213, 214, 216; collective memory of in U.S., 84, *85*, *86*, 87, 88–89, 96, 97, *102*, 160, 166, 196, 223–24, 225, 226; commemoration of, 197, 205–6; emigrants' collective memory of, 138–39, 140, 141–43, 144–45
women. *See* gender
World's Columbian Exposition, 24
WPA, 54, 179, 180–81, 189, 199
Wright, Nathan, 137

Yanukovych, Viktor, 117
Yerushalmi, Yosef Hayim, 34, 45, 109
Yoder, Edwin M., Jr., 52

Yokohama, 105n
Yolen, Jane, 27
Young, Alfred F., 83
Young, James E., 11–12, 13, 15
Young Mr. Lincoln (film), 64, 67
youth, 174; and attitudes toward new
    issues, 148, 152–54, 156–57, 177, 197;
    and autobiographical memory, 160–65,
    167–69, 171–72, 172–76; and collective
    knowledge, 180–83, 185, 187; and col-
    lective memory, 78–103, 104–32, 125–
    46, 165–67, 169–76, 197, 212, 214; and
    generational formation, 71, 75, 78, 79;
and recency, 90; and views of historical
    figures, 32–33, 37, 40–41, 43–44, 59–60,
    62, 64, 70, 215–16. *See also* adolescence;
    children; critical years effect; first expe-
    riences; reminiscence bump
"youth bias," 174

Zapruder, Alexandra, 4
Zapruder film, 4
Zaromb, Franklin, 191
Zelizer, Barbie, 9
Zhang, Ning, 110, *128*
Zinn, Howard, 25